DIARY OF A DIRTY LITTLE WAR

THE SPANISH-AMERICAN WAR of 1898

HARVEY ROSENFELD

Westport, Connecticut
London

Library of Congress Cataloging-in-Publication Data

Rosenfeld, Harvey.
    Diary of a dirty little war : the Spanish-American War of 1898 /
Harvey Rosenfeld.
      p.   cm.
    Includes bibliographical references and index.
    ISBN 0–275–96673–9 (alk. paper)
    1. Spanish-American War, 1898.   2. Spanish-American War, 1898—
Social aspects—United States.   I. Title.
    E715.R75   2000
    973.8′9—dc21   99–27610

British Library Cataloguing in Publication Data is available.

Library of Congress Catalog Card Number: 99–27610
ISBN: 0–275–96673–9

First published in 2000

Praeger Publishers, 88 Post Road West, Westport, CT 06881
An imprint of Greenwood Publishing Group, Inc.
www.praeger.com

Printed in the United States of America

The paper used in this book complies with the
Permanent Paper Standard issued by the National
Information Standards Organization (Z39.48–1984).

10 9 8 7 6 5 4 3 2 1

Copyright Acknowledgments

Every reasonable effort has been made to trace the owners of copyright materials in this book, but in
some instances this has proven impossible. The author and publisher will be glad to receive information
leading to more complete acknowledgments in subsequent printings of the book and in the meantime extend their apologies for any omissions.

CONTENTS

Photo essay follows page 105

PREFACE AND ACKNOWLEDGMENTS

Diary of a Dirty Little War is the recording of the Spanish-American War. Most of the presentation is based on the filtering of developments as presented in the newspapers and journals of the period, as well as commentaries in books. Except where otherwise specified, the news and commentary for each entry are based on reports in the *New York Times* of that day.

I would like to express my gratitude to the Pace University Library and its staff for their gracious help with this project. I would also like to thank Heather Ruland Staines, Ph.D., and her staff at Greenwood Publishing Group, Inc., and Peri Hoffman of P. Hoffman & Associates/PERIodicals, for their editorial expertise and professional advice. Most of all, I thank my wife, Pearl, and son, Robbie, for their continual support and assistance.

INTRODUCTION

A GLORIOUS WAR

American diplomat John Hay, later Secretary of State, called the Spanish-American War "a splendid little war"; and why not? Its proceedings made it America's most popular war since nationhood.

Aside from the fratricidal Civil War, America had taken up arms in two wars. The issues in the War of 1812 were national pride, a hunger for new territory, Indian troubles, and the fur trade; the war divided America and the end satisfied few with no new territory added and none of the issues, such as impressment of American seamen or neutral rights at sea, resolved. The Mexican War, an expansionist war consistent with President James Polk's aim of acquiring territory from Texas to the Pacific Ocean, began with the annexation of Texas and achieved Manifest Destiny by the cessation of hostilities (two-fifths of Mexican land had been ceded to the United States), yet despite this "euphoria," it has long been regarded as an aggressive war on the part of America.

The same cannot be said for the Spanish-American War. From the start, as popular thinking went, America was acting from humane causes, seeking to end the oppression and brutality that Spain had wreaked upon the innocent Cubans. To support the war was the highest form of patriotism. Those who fought were stirred by the song "Stars and Stripes Forever." There were glorious heroes: Legends such as Commodore George Dewey and Theodore Roosevelt and the Rough Riders; other colorful figures like Admiral William T. Sampson and the 300-pound Civil War hero General William R. Shafter; and Naval Constructor Richmond Pearson Hobson, who emerged from obscurity to dazzle and win—first, the admiration of Spain, and later that of his fellow countrymen.

Fewer than 40 years before, the Union had nearly been destroyed as North fought South. Now, they fought alongside each other, with Northern President William McKinley offering Major General of Volunteers posts to three Southerners: Generals

Fitzhugh Lee, Joseph Wheeler, and M. C. Butler.

Major General Shafter spoke of this spirit at a special service in December 1898 at the Tabernacle Baptist Church in Brooklyn: "The Spaniards learned a lesson they will remember for a long time, and for the first time in the history of this Nation, every person in it was in hearty accord. The scars and bitterness left after the War of the Rebellion were all wiped out, and in thinking of this war we have forgotten the other."

A stunning victory at Manila Bay, glorious heroism at San Juan Hill in Cuba, and total surrender at Puerto Rico—all this and more in three-plus months—were portrayed magnificently by an army of writers such as Stephen Crane and Richard Harding Davis and artists like Frederic Remington. No previous war had attracted such media coverage.

When a peace treaty was signed in the fall of 1898, Spain relinquished all claims to Cuba and turned over to the United States Puerto Rico, Guam, and the Philippines. All this was gained at minimal "cost": fewer than 3,000 lives and expenditures of only $250 million. America had become a majestic world power. Yes, a splendid little war.

GLORIOUS OR DIRTY?

Once the glow of victory had disappeared and after decades of analysis, the Spanish-American War might better be described as a dirty little war; altruism, selflessness—discard all that. Partisan politics and economic interests dictated the need to end the presence and influence of Spain in Cuba.

While disclaiming expansionist interests, America did not intend to lose Puerto Rico. Interest in Hawaii had been intense for decades, but annexation had split Congress. The Spanish-American War, however, gave annexationists the votes to dispatch the question. By design or "accident" the United States had joined the European powers in pursuit of an empire, scattered over the Caribbean Sea and the Pacific Ocean.

While the popular, jingoist press successfully conveyed the impression that every-one stood behind the war, dissent was not absent. While Americans gloried at the exploits of military heroes, the army was poorly equipped and miserably fed. Nearly 75 percent of American soldiers' lives were lost because America coped horribly with yellow fever and other diseases. Medical treatment and hospital accommodations were often a national disgrace.

No group was more disgraced by America than its black soldiers, the "smoked Yankees." Their heroism—only grudgingly admitted—perhaps saved Roosevelt and his Rough Riders from annihilation after ambush by the Spaniards. America, however, did nothing to protect these soldiers from open discrimination in Southern camps. In Lakeland, Florida, for example, a white barber used guns to prevent their being served in an adjoining drug store. No wonder a white chaplain asked in anger: "Is America any better than Spain?" (Gatewood 27).

THE ORIGINS OF THE WAR

The expressed reasons for American intervention in Cuba concerned Spanish mistreatment of the Cubans and the island's struggle for independence. This struck sympathetic chords, according to Professor Booker T. Washington, with "all that is chivalric and noble in the American character" (Washington 15).

These struggles, first known as the Ten Years' War, began in 1868; the last of the series of wars began in 1895. Despite its humanitarian leanings, Americans exacerbated the situation by its tariff law of 1894, which placed a duty on raw sugar. This worsened economic conditions on the island.

When Spain acted against the Cubans, the latter destroyed the canefields, sugar mills, and other properties. In response, Spain initiated a policy of "reconcentration." Conducted by Spanish commander General Valeriano Weyler, this policy—a forerunner of Nazi policy during the Third Reich—herded men, women, and children from large areas of Cuba into prisons or concentration camps. They were watched by armed guards, restrained by barbed wire, and victimized by famine or disease. By 1898 some 200,000 Cubans, or one-eighth of the population, had been wiped out.

What had all this to do with the United States, which had adopted a policy of neutrality, since Spain was a sovereign and independent country? Economics! America had more than $50 million invested in Cuban plantations, transportation, and other business enterprises and the series of wars between Spain and Cuba had devastated trade between America and the island. Why not recognize the government established by Cuban revolutionaries? America still wanted Spain to protect its $50 million investment as well as the lives of American nationals, so its approach was to nudge Spain to grant Cuba enough autonomy to satisfy the revolutionaries.

That plan would not work. Already having witnessed the crumbling of its 400-year-old empire, Spain could not elect a government that would give away Cuba, Puerto Rico, Guam, and the Philippines.

The policies of "Butcher" Weyler worsened matters. The jingoist press of William Randolph Hearst's *New York Journal* and Joseph Pulitzer's *New York World* sensationalized the barbarities of the Spaniards while minimizing the actions of the Cuban revolutionaries, including burning U.S. property. They were joined by down-right imperialists such as Captain Alfred Mahan, Assistant Secretary of the Navy Theodore Roosevelt, and U.S. Senator Henry Cabot Lodge. The jingoists thirsted for expansion and military grandeur and were embraced by Populists, Progressives, and aggressive labor leaders. No wonder America was whipped into a frenzy for war.

However, McKinley was not convinced. While it was not good politics to eschew war, it would be economically disastrous to recognize the revolutionary Cubans and plunge America into war. Businessmen and conservative politicos told the President that a war could only be financed by coining more silver, which would devalue the dollar and destroy American credit abroad. Annexation of Spanish possessions would create Constitutional problems. For this reason, McKinley endeavored to enact reforms. Acting to avoid a crisis, Spain recalled "Butcher" Weyler. But the march to war had advanced too far.

McKinley would avert war if at all possible. At the end of February 1898, that possibility had all but vanished. On February 9, American newspapers headlined a letter from Spain's Minister in Washington, Enrique Dupuy de Lohm. That stolen letter, written to a friend in Havana, characterized McKinley as a "would-be politician . . . weak and a bidder for the admiration of the crowd." Americans concluded that this revulsive insult reflected the common attitude of Spaniards.

Hardly had this story been digested by Americans when on February 15, the American battleship *Maine*, sailing into Havana on a mission of peace, was blown up by torpedo mines, with 266 American Navy officers and enlisted men losing their lives.

Havana responded by flying flags at half-mast, closing theaters and places of business, and forwarding messages of sympathy and condolence to Washington. Madrid proposed a joint investigation. But yellow journalists and jingoist politicians shouted "war," and Americans needed little convincing. Professor Washington wrote: "A wave of horror and indignation swept over the country. The belief was instinctive that the act was the product of treachery" (Washington 18).

The President argued that the country was not ready for war militarily and would suffer economically. Stalling for time, he set up an investigation. In its report, the board of inquiry returned an indictment of Spain: "The loss of the *Maine* was not in any respect due to fault or negligence on the part of any of the officers or members of her crew. . . . The ship was destroyed by an explosion of a submarine mine, which caused the partial explosion of two or more of her forward magazines. . . . No evidence has been obtained fixing the responsibility for the destruction of the *Maine* upon any person or persons." A thorough investigation in 1976 concluded that the tragedy was not caused by Spain or its agents; the blame was placed on an internal explosion, perhaps in the boiler room.

But for Americans in 1898, Spain was judged guilty and the cry was raised, "Remember the *Maine!*" Even before the inquiry was completed, Congress unanimously appropriated $50 million for national defense.

If McKinley needed another issue to convince himself to send America to war it was the continuing crisis in the Far East. Following its victory over China in 1894–95, Japan had its eyes on additional foreign policy spoils. By 1897 it was sending warships to Hawaii. The Philippines, which had begun to rebel against Spanish dominion, would be an ideal base from which to protect Hawaii from becoming a Japanese colony.

Big business urged McKinley to lead America into war. American properties were quickly being destroyed in Cuba, and businessmen were now convinced America could meet costs without coining silver.

McKinley was still willing to give Spain the opportunity of forestalling war. He issued a series of demands to Madrid beginning March 20: indemnity for the *Maine*; abandonment of Weyler's *reconcentrado* policy, which forced the population into central locations under Spanish military jurisdiction; cessation of all fighting in Cuba; and negotiation for Cuban independence through American mediation. All were acceptable except the last. No Spanish government could continue to rule while giving Cuba its independence.

In actuality, Madrid did not flatly say no to the last point; it would be fair to say it hedged. That led the American Minister in Madrid to conclude that something could be worked out during an armistice. He cabled the President, "I hope that nothing will now be done to humiliate Spain."

McKinley was not convinced. Long reluctant, McKinley was now ready to bring America into war, which would, he reasoned, protect American property in Cuba; put a brake on the Cuban revolution before it became ensconced on the left; solidify Republican rule and ward off accusations of cowardice from Democrats; and challenge Japanese expansion in the Far East.

Lincoln's celebrated biographer Carl Sandburg enlisted with his local company from Galesburg, Illinois, and experienced the war in Cuba and Puerto Rico firsthand. In his recollections, *Always the Young Strangers*, he responded to journalist Richard Harding Davis, who called the service of General Nelson Miles and his troops in Puerto Rico a "picnic." Perhaps Davis was speaking, Sandburg writes, of "the dry corners he slept in, the roads where he never walked carrying 50 pounds in a baking sun, the mosquitoes that never bled him nor closed an eye for him, the graybacks he never picked from an inhabited shirt, the rains he never stood in waiting for the rain to let down . . . as picnics go, the war in Puerto Rico, while not bloody, was a dirty and lousy affair while it lasted" (Sandburg 417–18).

1

TEN DAYS OF INDECISION

SUNDAY, APRIL 10: Sunday was usually enough reason to rest from the usual government business, Easter Sunday even more so. However, on Easter Sunday, 1898, cabinet meetings were held at the White House, the first time such Sunday gatherings were held—at least in the memory of participants.

The morning session ran from 11 to 2; the night session, from 9 until past 11. Secretary of State John Sherman was the only official missing, but he was represented by Judge William Day who was closeted with President William McKinley from 7:30 until after midnight. The agenda was negotiations with Spain and the message to be sent to Congress. The tone was said to be clear and forceful. Nothing had changed since the President's position of April 2: armed intervention and recognition of Cuba's independence. Rejected was Spain's call for a unconditional armistice in Cuba since there was no provision for Cuban freedom.

Meanwhile in Key West the U.S. Consul General Fitzhugh Lee and his staff arrived from Havana on the *Fern*. It was assumed that he would testify before the Senate Committee on Foreign Relations concerning Spain's responsibility for destroying the *Maine*. The Consul went to greet the crowded decks of the *Olivette*. The ship had arrived at 2 a.m. with 249 refugees from Havana.

War preparations proceeded on Easter Sunday. Commodore Winfield Scott Schley announced at Fort Monroe, Virginia, that the flying squadron could be at sea within three hours after receiving sailing orders. On the *Columbia* and the *Minneapolis*, new recruits were drilled at the guns; on the *Brooklyn*, men took on ammunition. The Commodore outlined plans of action at a meeting with the Captains of the three vessels.

The highest level of readiness was visible at the Brooklyn Navy Yard. More signs of an impending war could be seen than on any other previous day. More than 4,000 men and all officers were at work on Easter Sunday. Orders came from Washington that no more reports would be issued on the work being done at the Yard. For the first time since the Civil War, no one could visit the Yard without a pass signed by the Captain of the Yard.

The mood was patriotic in Lakewood, New Jersey, where the playing of "The Star-Spangled Banner" at a Lakewood House concert "aroused great enthusiasm," according to the *New York Times*. The 300 guests, from all over the country, "each tried to outdo the other in voice. While the effect was not exactly perfect harmony, it was entirely satisfying to the patriotic spirit of the singers."

The mood was somber at the Marine Hospital on Flushing Avenue, Brooklyn, as George Schwartz entered the facility. He had been ship cook on the *Maine* and was thought to be one of the few untouched by the explosion in Havana harbor. After arriving from Key West about three weeks before, Schwartz said that he was fine. However, he began to complain of not being able to sleep. One of the four other survivors said of Schwartz, "Yes, sir, Schwartz is gone, and he knows it. I don't know what's the matter with him and he don't know. But he's hoisted his Blue Peter and is paying out his line." After his removal from the gunboat *Mayflower* to Marine Hospital, however, doctors said Schwartz's nervous system had been completely damaged when he was blown from the deck of the *Maine*.

Another survivor, John H. Load, Master of Arms third class, was angered that instead of leaving for the *Iowa* and possible battle, he was placed on the *Saturn*, which would be used as a collier. Some 2,800 tons of coal would be carried to the Cape Verde Islands, the present rendezvous of the Spanish flotilla.

He was clearly disappointed about his status as noncombatant: "I guess the collier will have to be in the thick of it anyhow, serving the torpedo boats, and that's where I want to be. That's where I ought to be."

Secretary John Long was said to have decided to divide the surviving members of the *Maine*'s crew among as many ships as possible as a means of inspiring the other shipmen in case America went to war. This was leading, however, to unhappiness among survivors such as Load, who eagerly thirsted to be on a fighting vessel.

MONDAY, APRIL 11: What would President McKinley say? The international community waited and wondered. Nowhere was the anxiety greater than in Madrid, where American Minister General Stewart Woodford remained confident: "I have no expectation that my Government will direct me to apply for my passports, or that the Spanish Government will present them to me."

His Cuban counterpart, General Juan Melquizo, was certain that "the true public opinion of the United States is opposed to war, and only the jingoes, the Cuban filibustering element, and speculating politicians, aided by the sensational press, keep up the war note."

When the doors of the Capitol swung open, a massive crowd competed for admission to the House and Senate. However, only those with tickets were guaranteed seating in the galleries. Many in the audience were women decked out in their spring finery, including bonnets. The roster of VIPs included the British Ambassador, the Austrian Minister, the Minister of Denmark, Chancellor of the French Legation, Secretary of the Legation of Guatemala, the Swiss Minister, and three Attachés of the Chinese Legation.

President McKinley was determined that his message be read before any other business was taken up. White House Secretary Oscar Pruden arrived after the chaplain finished his prayer and announced: "Mr. Speaker, a message from the President of the United States."

The clerk began reading at 12:12. The galleries followed every word, eagerly awaiting the magic word "war." It did not come. The closest pronouncement, that "the war in Cuba must stop," drew the only applause during the reading.

When the reading ended, the galleries were silent; the Democrats groaned; the Republicans halfheartedly applauded. The Speaker announced unemotionally that the message "will be referred to the Committee on Foreign Affairs."

According to the *New York Times*, "The galleries had been apathetic from beginning to end. The reception of the message ... essentially cold. The members ... betrayed no enthusiasm, and the occupants of the galleries dispersed quickly, commenting on the small prospect for war held out by the President." The House was emptied by 1 p.m.

Congress was clearly not fully supportive of the President. The Senate Foreign Relations Committee had hope there would be no debate on the message; however, Nevada's Populist Senator William Stewart quickly took the floor and said, "Just see what we are asked to do. The President proposes that the United States shall intervene in Cuba, shall drive Spain out, and then shall see to it that the island has a stable form of government, without calling upon the existing republic to go on and make stable the government they have established there."

The theme of the President was diplomacy and deliberation but, "What this country wanted was action and not talk," observed one Senator. One Republican member of the House Committee on Foreign Affairs said, "I am now firmly convinced that if Feb. 16, the morning after the *Maine* was blown up by a Spanish mine, our fleet had been ordered over from Key West to batter Havana for a day or two, and we had waited until Spain put up a white flag before ceasing the work of the reprisal, we should have got better terms diplomatically."

How would the general public react? One dovish Senator revealed a dispatch from a constituent: "Dynamite the McKinley-Hanna Administration and come home."

Although few public responses were as volatile, the public was without doubt confused and unhappy. The United States was seen as playing into the hands of Madrid, who was just stalling for time.

The happiest man in Washington was the President. He spent a "pleasant evening" at the White House with friends. Ever since the *Maine* disaster, he had endured a heavy, nervous, and physical strain. The delivery of the message was the perfect prescription. McKinley entered the telegraph office in the White House and formally inaugurated the Masonic fair in Washington.

The President retired to the Blue Room, where he received personal friends, among them Supreme Court Justice Joseph McKenna, former Republican National Committee chairman James Clarkson, and Samuel Fessenden of Connecticut.

TUESDAY, APRIL 12: Many Congressmen arose, prepared for a day of legislative work, in a very nasty mood. Congressmen and Senators alike were severely disappointed that McKinley's message did not demand that Cuba be independent and did not reveal that the United States had ever demanded that the island be freed from Madrid's rule. The thinking on Capitol Hill was that Congress would declare for immediate armed intervention and Cuban independence.

Congress was generally angry about talks of delay or of negotiating with Spain. Reports of the Foreign Committees of the House and Senate were nearly complete and were expected to pass nearly unanimously in both chambers the following day. The resolutions of Ohio's Republican Senator Joseph Foraker called for recognition of Cuba before intervention. Said one irate Republican Senator, "The President gave us history and philosophy and talked about peace and stable government. But he did not ask us to get rid of Spain's control of Cuba or ... to use force to accomplish the things he pointed out as desirable."

The Senate Committee met at noon. The House Committee had met earlier in the morning, with the Republican members favoring Republican Foraker's resolutions. The Democratic members planned to offer a substitute for the majority report. A key question was recognition of Cuba as part of the call for intervention.

The war spirit in Washington was fanned by the appearance in Washington of General Fitzhugh Lee, nephew of Robert E. Lee. It was surprising that the General and the other Consuls were called home and Americans were advised to leave Cuba. The situation had not worsened, it seemed, for Americans.

Lee traveled from Tampa to Washington in 24 hours, the fastest long-distance run ever made by a train in America—1,063 miles at about 45 miles an hour. The Cuban Consul made his first stop in Richmond. An estimated 10,000 admirers were present, including the Governor and the Richmond Light Infantry Blues.

"The time for talk is over; now we must back up our words in war," he said to the delight of the crowd, concluding, "I cannot talk to you now. In fact, this is not the time for talk, but the time for action."

He was greeted at Washington's Pennsylvania Station by a wild, cheering crowd of admirers. As soon as he was recognized, women waved their handkerchiefs and blew kisses while men waved their hats. The crowd was so dense that it was difficult for him to reach the platform, even with police assistance.

Lee was hurried to the State Department for meetings where, again, he was met by a huge crowd, a scene said to be unprecedented in State Department corridors. Staffers popped out from every room to lend their applause.

Meanwhile thousands gathered at the Shoreham Hotel, waiting hours to get a look at their hero. Some 10,000 were outside the hotel as he was serenaded by the 71st Regiment Band. He finally came out on a hotel balcony at 9:00, accompanied by a committee of the Veterans' Legion and the Confederate Veterans Association, joint sponsors of the concert. The crowd roared as the band struck up the "The Star-Spangled Banner," followed by fireworks.

"Speech, speech," the throng demanded. "After all the speeches I have been forced to make in the past two days," Lee responded, "I can only assure you that such a great demonstration seems to me out of all proportion to the simple fact of my humble presence here, and I am frank to say that I don't deserve it, having only tried to do my duty as an American."

He continued: "I have not come to talk of war, but if war comes in a few days or a few weeks, the present crisis has proved that it will find us a united people, and the only contest will be as to who can carry the flag farthest and fastest."

A zealot in the crowd shouted, "You can act pretty quick." Another joined in, "War! Fight!" The cheering drowned out all other responses.

A *New York Times* editorial indicated that when such a humanitarian as Fitzhugh Lee—who attended the funeral of President Ulysses Grant—condemned Spain, he had to be listened to: "When a man as kindly as Gen. Lee shows a deep hostility to the Spanish Government in Cuba, in spite of the pleasant relations he has sustained with the Spanish Governor, the presumption that it deserves his hostility is overwhelming. . . . When such a man says that the time for action has come, his countrymen . . . believe him. When he says . . . he was ready to 'turn back to Havana,' there is no doubt he could find enough eager volunteers to follow him. The President could make no wiser use of the powers of Commander in Chief than to offer a General's commission to Fitzhugh Lee."

While Americans were thought to be safe in Cuba, the same could not be said of Matanzas Consul Alexander C. Brice, his staff, and their families, who arrived at the Amity Street pier in Brooklyn on the Norwegian steamer *Herman Wedel Jarlsberg*. They had been warned by Gen. Lee to leave quickly, but not via Havana.

Brice revealed that 50,000 Cubans were starving in the provinces and that guerrillas had been snatching peasants, the reconcentrados, and using them as human targets. "Then they would bring their bullet-ridden bodies into the city slung across their horses," he said, "and make a show of their tortured victims."

What did Brice think of McKinley's message? "I wanted a little more vigorous policy," he said, "for I have been in Cuba, seen the devastation and misery, and I know what should be done. Anyone who has seen what I have, who has lived among the hordes of starving, miserable people, could not help but wish for a speedy end to their sufferings, which can only be realized through the expulsion of the Spaniards from the island."

WEDNESDAY, APRIL 13: Intense activity marked the day in both houses of Congress. The Senate supported the President in giving Spain "another chance" at resolving the crisis and in not recognizing the revolutionary government of Cuba. Sen. Foraker was the only Republican to call for immediate recognition. The Senate considered the advice of Gen. Lee, who counseled against recognition since Cuba did not yet have a stable government.

In support of the resolutions, the Senate Foreign Relations Committee reported that America must "consider all our relations with Spain for the last three years, including the destruction of the *Maine*, as one of the incidents . . . of the war which . . . has devastated the Island of Cuba." While the resolutions of the Senate Foreign Relations Committee were passed amicably, the work of the House Committee on Foreign Affairs was partisan and acrimonious.

Meeting late in the afternoon, the House of Representatives concluded its business, according to the *New York Times*, "after a session marked by scenes of tumult and disorder as rarely have been known in the history of the American Congress." By a vote of 332–19, the House called for intervention: "Resolved, That the President is hereby authorized and directed to intervene at once to stop the war in Cuba . . . with the purpose of securing permanent peace and order there and establishing by the free action of the people thereof a stable and independent Government of their own . . . and the President is hereby authorized and empowered to use the land and naval forces in the United States to execute the purpose of this resolution."

Although the vote was near unanimous, the partisan combativeness was apparent throughout the debate. A fist fight was barely avoided when Democratic Congressman Charles Brumm of Pennsylvania assailed a comment of Republican Charles Bartlett of Georgia as a lie. In response, the Georgian flung a book at the Democrat and hurried down the aisle ready for fisticuffs. Bartlett was restrained by fellow legislators as Speaker Thomas Reed of Maine pounded the mace to restore order.

Spain was closely monitoring developments in Congress. President McKinley was repudiated at a cabinet meeting that declared that his recommendations were incompatible with the sovereignty and rights of Spain "and are an interference in the internal affairs of this country." But Madrid would not have more to say "so long as the resolutions of Congress or the initiative of President McKinley do not lead to concrete acts."

Comments in the Madrid press united to denounce the McKinley message and called on the government to stand firm. The Conservative *El Epoca* took note of Congress: "The Congressional debates prove President McKinley's tight position, and it is still doubtful whether he will succeed in controlling the warlike elements in America."

In the Vatican, Pope Leo XIII pleaded with Austrian Emperor Francis Joseph I to exercise his influence to bring an accord between Spain and America. He prayed in the Sistine Chapel, a prayer the *New York Times* called "pathetic words." The Rome correspondent of the *London Daily News* quoted the Pontiff, "I have prayed to God with the whole force of my being and . . . deepest fervor to avert this sad war and not . . . allow my Pontificate to end in the smoke of battle. Otherwise I have implored the Almighty to take me to Himself that I might not behold such a sight."

In the United States, military preparations were underway. Meetings and conferences were convened by the Naval Strategy Board, the joint War and Naval Board, and other government and military officials. The consensus was that there needed to be a joint movement of American land and naval forces against the Spaniards in Cuba.

The question: should Capt. Sampson's fleet wait until the army was ready? The navy could advance on Havana an hour after war's declaration while the army would require 48 hours. The troops could then land in Pinar del Rio and join the armies of Máximo Gómez and Calixto García.

Arrangements were made for the immediate mobilization of the nearly total military force at Chickamauga National Park. The first call would be for some 40,000 troops, ideally from the National Guard. If a Cuban invasion were called for, this would rise to 100,000, from regular troops and volunteers. Maj. Gen. Nelson A. Miles planned to mobilize 17 of the 25 infantry regiments and 5 of 10 cavalry at Chickamauga as soon as possible.

The officers and men were becoming antsy, so Commodore Winfield Scott Schley moved the Flying Squadron to sea from Hampton Roads. The Navy Department was quick to announce it was not going for war, but merely for a practice cruise of 48 hours.

THURSDAY, APRIL 14: Congress was clearly split on the form that would direct the United States to intervene in Cuba and that would lead to Cuba's freedom. It seemed likely that the Senate's final resolution would be intervention and recognition of Cuba. Although the House resolution basically called for the same ends, critics complained that the House wording was "wordy, loose, and ill-framed" and that "hairsplitting" was effected by seeking "to create a distinction between intervening and using the land and naval forces." Simply put: intervention equaled war, period.

Massachusetts Republican Senator George F. Hoar was aged and conservative. He defended the President and counseled against recognizing Cuba; however, he still felt strongly about the duty of intervention and the resultant war. "It will be the most honorable war in history," he asserted.

Would the House go along with the recognition of Cuba? The 19 Congressmen who voted against the resolution explained their views. Some wanted directed, immediate armed intervention and recognition of the Cuban Republic. Eight Georgia Democrats voted against the resolution because it was "wrong in principle . . . violated the Monroe Doctrine by interfering in the affairs of another nation, and . . . delegated to the President the right to make war at his discretion, which we believe to be unconstitutional."

Others, like California Representative Eugene Loud, were convinced that at this point there was no necessity for war: "I would never take such steps as would lead to war until every reasonable means had been exhausted to preserve peace. While conditions . . . in Cuba have . . . horrified my sensibilities . . . I could not consent to the sacrifice of lives of American citizens to stop an inhuman war in another country."

Public discussions became more intense after public release of the testimony on Spanish-American relations given before the Senate Committee on Foreign Relations. Especially damning in the 650-page document was the testimony given by Consul General Fitzhugh Lee. Within the last two months, Spain had placed two rows of torpedoes at the mouth of the Havana harbor. Moreover, Lee had strong reasons to believe that the harbor was mined before the blowing up of the *Maine*. Citing an incriminating letter and telegram, Lee placed the fault at the feet of Cuban General Valeriano Weyler.

It is the *Maine*, as editorialized in the *New York Times*, that must bring armed intervention against a "nation which had rendered itself responsible for such a crime . . . an act of treachery and cruelty unprecedented in the history of any civilized nation."

In another editorial, the *Times* pleaded with the "extreme opponents of forcible intervention" to understand the motives of those who call for intervention, namely to rescue "the hapless victims of Spanish cruelty and impotence and greed." They "have determined that the duty of our Government, in the light of reason and humanity, for the promotion of civilization and lasting peace, is intervention with such force as shall make the end sure. That is the true war feeling of . . . the United States. We have not hesitated to recognize, and . . . to guide it."

Not all citizens shared this view. Entrepreneur John Wanamaker, former Postmaster General, wired the Secretary of War that he was "opposed to war unless honorably unavoidable." But if war should come, he was ready to raise a regiment of Pennsylvanians and join them in service. After wiring that cable, he posted notices indicating that he would grant concessions to employees who served in the war.

More immediate operations were already underway. Two companies of the 25th Infantry arrived at Key West. They had been expected to arrive at Chickamauga, Tennessee, but plans were changed at the last moment without explanation.

More thought out was the set of hygienic instructions for war in a "tropical climate," issued by the Board of Officers of the War Department. The National Guardsmen would be serving in Cuba, and Col. Greene, commander of New York's 71st Regiment, asked the War Department to help prepare them for the ordeal. The "Medical Directives for Tropical Climate" warned: "Do not drink water unless it has been boiled; do not bathe in water unless it has been boiled; cook food thoroughly; avoid the use of alcohol internally; avoid being out in the night air or dew, if this cannot be avoided, wrap up carefully covering the face well; avoid dampness at all times, changing your clothes the moment they are wet or damp when practicable; be moderate in eating and do not eat heartily when tired or overheated; at the end of a march, bathe the feet in boiled water. Dry well and powder them with compound talcum powder or some foot powder; never put on stockings that are damp, or stockings at any time when the feet are not thoroughly dry.

"Do not eat fruit of any kind unless perfectly ripe and do not eat it at all in the summer; before going out in the morning, take three or five grains of quinine and a cup of hot coffee—this is imperative; always wear a flannel band over the abdomen; change all your clothes every day when practicable, especially stockings and drawers; avoid excesses of all kinds; avoid exposure to the sun when possible and if exposed much keep a wet handkerchief in your hat all the while so exposed; be vaccinated; [and eat a] piece of chocolate."

FRIDAY, APRIL 15: Having passed its resolution by an overwhelming margin, the House awaited the final resolution from the Senate. It was near certain that a majority of Congressmen would not adopt any clause recognizing an independent Cuba, necessitating a conference on the disagreement between House and Senate.

Fear was voiced that Vice President Garrett Hobart would select Senate conferees who would be more amenable to House sentiment. A greater fear was that McKinley would veto any resolution calling for recognition. However, the President was satisfied with the patriotic tone of the Senate debate and unequivocally told the *New York Times* he would not oppose any decision reached by Congress.

The Senate met for more than 12 hours but did not finish its business. It announced it hoped to vote by 7 p.m. Saturday but, if necessary, would continue until Sunday. "This will pass as one of the great days of the Senate," reported the *New York Times*. "Thronged galleries looked down upon the half-circular chamber." Every Senator was present except the ailing Democratic Senator Edward Walthall of Mississippi. Among the 100-plus VIPs were Congressmen, Supreme Court justices, members of the President's Cabinet, and other distinguished figures in American public life. Throughout the proceedings, the audience stayed "as if held under some spell."

While no vote was taken, activity throughout America indicated that the country was one day closer to war. "We'll show 'em some Indian fighting," said a sergeant from a colored company of the 25th infantry passing through Jacksonville, Florida. The companies, under Captain John Daggett, were greeted by 2,000 people and two brass bands. The sergeant told the cheering crowd, "We can give the insurgents some pointers, and I guess we'll have a chance soon, too, to do it." The mood was festive. The troops left for Key West and the Tortugas to cheers and the singing of "The Star-Spangled Banner" and "Rally Round the Flag, Boys."

The tone was more official at Hoboken, New Jersey, where the second squad of the New Jersey Naval Militia Battalion of the East detailed to go to League Island to aid in preparing the monitor *Montauk* for her trip to Portland, Maine.

Following the advice of Gen. Lee, the War Department took into account the Cuban rainy season and chose cavalry, infantry, and light artillery. (Heavy artillery would not work in the wet weather, according to Lee.) They issued orders for the concentration at 4 points in the South of 6 regiments of cavalry, 22 regiments of infantry, and the light batteries of 5 regiments of artillery. The four sites would be in Chickamauga, New Orleans, Tampa, and Mobile. This represented the largest proportion of the army to be mobilized since the Civil War. The South would prepare the troops for tropical Cuba.

The Navy Department also had an active day. It assigned the Naval Reserves of New York, New Jersey, Massachusetts, Maryland, and Michigan to five auxiliary cruisers to be known as patrol boats. The ships would be assigned to the Atlantic coastline, forming a general plan of coastal defense. The plan was to assign one vessel to each of the five divisions being prepared for the mosquito fleet under the command of Commodore Horace Elmer.

The Navy Department also announced a broader role for the Naval Militia. The militia had been formed to protect American seacoasts, but the navy stated that the men would be sent, if needed, to Cuban waters, or to the Canaries, the Mediterranean, the Bay of Biscay, or the Philippines.

Meanwhile, Madrid was not focused on war. They hoped peace could prevail, especially if President McKinley would be allowed to exercise full authority. The Madrid correspondent of *The Standard* telegraphed from London: "The dispatches announcing the resolutions proposed to the United States Senate and those passed by the House of Representatives caused more indignation and displeasure in Madrid than even the Presidential message. Not a single paper admits the supposition that such pretensions could be tolerated by any Spanish Government desirous of keeping in harmony with the unanimous feelings of the nation. . . .

"The watchword in official circles is to remain on the defensive firmly awaiting the development of President McKinley's action and the advance of American diplomacy. All sensible and far-sighted statesmen in Spain understand perfectly that the declarations of their Government and of President McKinley do not by any means make impossible a peaceful and conciliatory solution if circumstances permit. Besides, they fancy that the European powers, particularly Austria, France, and Russia . . . may yet have something to say and do amicably to check President McKinley."

SATURDAY, APRIL 16: The Senate session ended after 11 hours and addresses by 30 Senators. After all the rhetoric and the animated debate, the chamber declared for the freeing of Cuba, withdrawal from Cuba by Spanish forces, recognition of Cuban independence, and disavowal of all intentions to annex Cuba to the United States.

Undoubtedly, a conference would be required to settle the disagreement between the houses on the matter of recognition. More legislators were becoming agreeable to McKinley's plan, in particular non-legislative recognition. In addition, the House Speaker was an avowed anti-jingoist.

The debate once more spotlighted the trio of anti-war Senators: Donelson Caffrey of Louisiana, George L. Wellington of Maryland, and Steven White of California. True, the time for intervention had arrived, said Caffrey, but the thought of "turning loose the dogs of war and letting them lick their chops dripping with human gore was abhorrent to all civilization."

As for the President himself, he was said to be hopeful that an agreement could be reached with Spain, which would even withdraw from Cuba in a year or two. "We cannot afford," said a Presidential supporter, "to rush into a war without thinking what is to come after the war has been opened. To make war will be easy enough. Everybody is for it until you ask them what it is to be prosecuted for. After Havana is bombarded and the flag of Spain lowered on Morro Castle, what then?

"Nobody questions that the insurgents are a fragment of the island. There has been no proof offered to show that anything like a majority of the people favor the Cuban Republic. . . . It will be repellent to every sound American to advocate the erection of a minority republic in Cuba."

The Treasurer of the Longshoremen's Union, Bolton Hall, was extremely displeased about the prospect of war because it would seriously damage the Union's trade. Addressing branches in New York, Jersey City, Hoboken, and Weehawken, Hall asked, "What could be more disastrous to the spirit of universal union than war?" He argued that war would lead to burdensome taxes, monopoly, and bickering for subsistence among members.

Meetings had already been held on the theme of war revenue. A bill was under consideration calling for a tax on proprietary and patent medicines of 2 cents on packages or bottles retailing at 25 cents or under and 4 cents on those above that price. Duties on tea and coffee could bring $28 million.

Chicagoans were not concerned about war costs, but rather when the war would commence. The decision would be relayed to Chicagoans and those in nearby areas by long blasts from more than 200 whistles and the clanging of a host of bells. The whistles would blow if any of the following happened: declaration of war by Spain, declaration of war by the United States, or the authorization of armed intervention by means of a Presidential signature or resolutions passed by Congress. Chicago General Superintendent Robert Zeublin assured all that every portion of the city and every town and village in the county would hear the "good" news.

The mood in Madrid was changing quickly from resolution and peace to the inevitability of war. Having studied McKinley's message more carefully, the Madrid correspondent of the *London Times* stated: "If President McKinley by issuing his last message has set his seal upon his country's claim in Cuba, so do the Spanish Ministers respond by setting their seal upon this country's flat rejection of that claim."

The Madrid correspondent of *The Standard* in London captured Spain's disappointment in Congress: "The vote in the Senate has caused a most unfavorable impression in Madrid as closing the door to an understanding of any kind being arrived at between the Spanish and American Governments. . . . The votes of the Senate and House of Representatives are considered likely to paralyze both the mediation of the Pope and the friendly interference of the European powers in the interests of peace."

London was optimistic; Berlin, anti-American. Whatever their sources, British bankers were satisfied that the crisis would be resolved without going to war. Germany desired neutrality and had favored the United States until McKinley's message. According to the liberal *Tageblatt*, "For a long time such an important enunciation of the head of a State has not met with such general disapproval. President McKinley's humanitarian phrases render the disagreeable impression even more lasting."

SUNDAY, APRIL 17: For the second consecutive Sunday, the Cuban crisis dictated a day of no rest. Members of the House and Senate kept in touch to coordinate an approach for Monday's session.

Connecticut Republican Senator Orville Platt expressed confidence that McKinley would be supported and the House would not recognize independence. "I believe," he said, "that it is the part of wisdom, of sound Republican Party policy, and of the highest patriotism to stand by the President. He has been much abused and maligned by his critics for what they call his lack of energy in bringing the serious Cuban matters to a more speedy settlement. George Washington and Abraham Lincoln were abused after the same fashion, but now history has justified their acts. I believe President McKinley has acted with great courage and tact, and has been guided wholly by a patriotic purpose."

The *New York Times* called on the legislators to reject recognition because "recognition of a foreign revolutionary government is exclusively a question for the Executive and cannot be determined internationally by Congressional action."

Former President Benjamin Harrison, Assistant Secretary of the Navy Theodore Roosevelt, and Papal Ablegate Msgr. Giovanni Martinelli were among the day's newsmakers. On his way to Cincinnati on legal business, Harrison spoke freely about the war, confident that if war came, America would win quickly: "I don't see why the war, if we have one, should last more than a month if the results are as favorable to American arms as I think they should be."

Roosevelt was evasive about reports that in case of war he would resign his post and receive a commission with the fighting forces. He spoke highly of Gen. Lee, willing to serve with him.

Speaking to the Roman Catholic clergy of Pittsburgh, Msgr. Martinelli called on the clergy to be loyal to America. "I am an American at heart," he said, "and I believe the Cubans should be given their liberty."

Judge H. W. Rives, chairman of the Supreme Council of the Young Men's Catholic Institute of the United States, directed every council to designate a member to wire in case of war and to enroll at once all willing to serve as soon as the President asked for volunteers.

Organized labor lined up behind America by announcing it would boycott the goods of any country siding with Spain. The federation of organized labor in Chicago passed a resolution that when any country took up Spain's cause, it became the duty of all citizens "to abstain from the use of or traffic in any article, natural or manufactured, which is produced by such nation."

A week after McKinley's message, U.S. Minister to Spain Stewart L. Woodford still was sanguine about the possibility of peace. It was learned that even if the U.S. Congress agreed on a resolution along the lines passed by the House of Representatives, neither Woodford nor Señor Polo Y. Bernabe, the Spanish Minister in Washington, would be recalled from their posts.

MONDAY, APRIL 18: As the international community waited for the decisive session on Capitol Hill, both favorable and unfavorable reports circulated in foreign capitals. Press dispatches from Spain looked to the inevitability of its rupture with America. "The nature of the intervention appears to be immaterial," wrote the Madrid correspondent of the *London Times*. "It is the principle which the Spanish Government now pledges itself to resist. . . . The drastic decisions of the council are taken by the public at what will probably prove their true value."

The Rome correspondent of the *London Daily News* reported that, in the interest of peace, the Queen Regent, the Pope, and Emperor Francis Joseph I of Austria favored abandoning Cuba if that would prevent war.

A feeling of irritation toward America was growing among Englishmen. "At some future time," continued the *London Times*, "it is thought England may rue her neglect to cooperate with the other European powers in creating a precedent for united European opposition to American high-handedness."

TUESDAY, APRIL 19: Spain must end its rule over Cuba, Congress insisted, adopting the following resolutions at 1:30 in the morning: "Joint resolution for the independence of the people of Cuba, demanding that the Government of Spain relinquish its authority and government . . . and withdraw its land and naval forces from Cuba and Cuban waters, and directing the President of the United States to use the land and naval forces of the United States to carry these resolutions into effect.

"Whereas, the abhorrent conditions which have existed for more than three years in the Island of Cuba, on or near our own borders, have shocked the moral sense of the people of the United States, have been a disgrace to Christian civilization, culminating as they have in the destruction of a U.S. battleship, with two hundred and sixty-six of its officers and crew while on a friendly visit to the Harbor of Havana, and cannot longer be endured, as has been set forth by the President of the United States in his message to Congress of April 11, 1898, upon which the action of Congress was invited."

Before adjourning, Congress adopted the Teller Resolution that America claimed no "sovereignty, jurisdiction, or control over said island, except for the pacification thereof" and pledged that once Cuba was free, the United States would "leave the government and control of the island to its people."

With the signatures of House Speaker Thomas ("Czar") Reed and Vice President Hobart secured, the resolution was rushed to the Oval Office, arriving at 1:15 p.m. Disappointed legislators learned, however, that McKinley would not sign the document until the following day. Regardless, cabinet officers insisted that the President would not withhold his signature. The delay was based on his desire to frame a course of future action and to shape the ultimatum in the appropriate diplomatic phraseology.

The scenario called for an answer by Spain within 48 hours after delivery. In other words, Spain would have until Friday, April 22, to prepare and deliver to the U.S. Minister the reply directed by the Spanish Constituent Assembly.

Full details were not immediately forthcoming, but one unidentified cabinet member said no halfway reply from Spain would be acceptable. If Spain's response was not satisfactory, a blockade of Cuba and aid to Gen. Máximo Gómez were planned.

While America was prepared to wait until Friday, a flurry of military readiness was set in motion. Chairman John A. T. Hull of the House Committee on Military Affairs said a bill would be introduced the next day authorizing the President to call up to 10 million men. Secretary of War Russell A. Alger issued the first call of 80,000 men, to be filled only by the National Guard. The total strength of the Guard was fixed at 113,764. Officials prepared a table showing the number of men required from each state.

Recruiting tents were set up at eight New York City parks: Battery, City Hall, Union Square, Madison Square, Tompkins Square, Abingdon Square, Greeley Square, and Cooper Union Park. The recruiting would be organized by Captain James McMurray of the Old Guard.

"Tennessee awaits your call for volunteers," Governor Robert L. Taylor telegrammed McKinley. "The blue and gray will march together into battle under Old Glory, keeping step to the music of 'Yankee Doodle' and 'Dixie.' . . . Fur will fly and the earth will tremble."

South Dakota Attorney General Colonel Melvin Grigsby stopped in Chicago on his way to Washington as a spokesman for the "cow punchers." He said he would urge McKinley to authorize the raising and equipping of a regiment made up of cowboys. Grigsby had served in the Civil War in a regiment of Wisconsin cavalry. He was known as a "smoked Yankee" and had experiences in Confederate prisons.

Everything was in readiness at Chickamauga Park to receive several thousand troops and the arrival of General John Brooke. A cheering, holiday spirit, and great emotion were the motifs at the sites of troop departures.

In New York, the 21st Infantry started from Plattsburg, the 13th from Buffalo, and the 9th from Sacket's Harbor. A great farewell demonstration had been prepared to cheer the five companies of the 13th U.S. Infantry in Buffalo, but a heavy downpour of rain forced cancellation. Not so in Plattsburgh, where the band played "The Girl I Left Behind" as some 4,000 residents bid farewell to friends and neighbors. Along the route—at Willsborough, Whitehall, and Saratoga—the regiment was cheered at every station. A much-celebrated regiment, the 21st had drilled before the President when he and Mrs. McKinley were in the area the previous summer. Mrs. McKinley and other cabinet wives presented them with the most handsome stand of colors in the army.

In San Francisco, Market Street was lined with an estimated 200,000 people who came to cheer the Light Batteries C and F, departing for Chickamauga via the Southern Pacific Road.

The first troops—in Chickamauga, Tampa, New Orleans, and Mobile—would total only 16,000, the army confident that these veteran soldiers would be able to repel any Spanish army that might be encountered before the arrival of reinforcements. It was also hoped that the 16,000 might besiege or even capture Havana.

The mood at the Navy Department was more subdued. Waiting for orders to fight, the department authorized the purchase of seven more auxiliary vessels and was considering the purchase of additional ships and several more war vessels. Capt. Sampson assured that the navy was in great condition and might even move against Havana on Friday. Commodore Schley announced he would hunt out the Spanish Fleet.

2

Ultimatum Issued

WEDNESDAY, APRIL 20: Washington was jubilant with the announcement that the President had signed the Congressional Cuban resolution. Simultaneously, he had signed an ultimatum to Spain and sent it to Madrid to be delivered by Minister Woodford. Unless Spain withdrew its troops and warships from Cuba by April 23, American military and naval forces would drive them out.

Now that war was all but official, concrete strategies were needed. Naval men were unhappy about reports of a planned blockade of Havana and other ports, feeling that a blockade would not produce a "short, sharp, and decisive" war. Said an unidentified experienced naval officer, "Havana cannot be considered our objective. Under the instructions of the Congress, the President must compel Spain to relinquish her authority in Cuba. . . . As long as the Spanish fleet exists and can be kept together in its present formidable condition, Spain will refuse to acknowledge the authority of the island.

"Our objective is the fleet. To crush Spain beyond any possibility of prolonged resistance, the power of its naval force to do mischief must be removed. . . . The talk about a blockade alone is absurd. . . . A blockade to carry out the expectations of Congress must be supported by a landing party . . . large enough to overcome the land forces of Spain. . . . An all-summer blockade would provoke . . . dissatisfaction in the United States . . . cause discomfort in Cuba, and . . . prove more fatal to our forces than a desperate attempt to . . . fight the Spanish Army in Cuba."

President McKinley convened a conference for the immediate passage of a Volunteer Army bill. The Secretaries of War and of the Navy and Col. Wagner, Chief of the Information Division of the War Department, were all present at the meeting. It was decided that Col. Wagner would tell the Senate the exact condition of America's military forces and of the total inability to invade Cuba with the regular army alone.

A report completed on the directive of New York Gov. Frank Black showed that some 80 to 85 percent of the 8,000 men in New York City had volunteered their services, bringing the militia strength of New York State to 14,000. Since the quota was 6,000, men with families would not be required or expected to enlist. Although Maj. Gen. Charles Roe, State commander of the National Guard, was delighted with these numbers, discord was evident. In the case of hostilities, the men wanted the retention of their regular officers.

Meanwhile in Chicago, Lieut. Commander Joseph Hawley announced that about 400 members of the Illinois naval militia would be drafted to defend the Atlantic Coast, taking their places on auxiliary cruises being rigged for coast defense in the government yards.

Maj. Gen. John R. Brooke and his staff from the Department of the Lakes formally settled at the Chickamauga camping ground. They set up headquarters at the Reid House hotel in Chattanooga, which had been a hospital for both the Union and Confederacy during the Civil War. Thousands of enthusiastic soldiers had arrived by 5 p.m. The *New York Times* reported, "When the second section came in with the coaches filled with brawny blue-coated warriors from the West, cheer after cheer went up from the crowds. The soldiers cheered in return, while a bugler on the platform . . . sounded the call to arms, and as the trains slowly pulled into the station, the outstretched hands of the troops were filled with flowers by pretty girls."

THURSDAY, APRIL 21: "The War Has Come," announced a *New York Times* headline. Spain did not accept America's ultimatum and gave passports and dismissal to Minister Woodford. Spanish ships were reported to be at the Cape Verde Islands with banked fires.

As soon as Assistant Secretary of State Judge William Day received the cable from Woodford, he hurried to the White House. The President, who was about to accompany Mrs. McKinley to the railroad station for a short trip to New York, bid his wife a hasty good-bye. Then he and Day conferred. Afterwards, Secretary Horace Porter went to the Capitol to communicate the news to the Senate Committee on Foreign Relations and leading House members.

American fleets awaited orders to move. McKinley readied to issue a call for 100,000 men to form a volunteer army. The Stars and Stripes fluttered throughout Washington along with the triangular field of red and single white star of the Cuban republic.

As soon as word of Woodford's dismissal was given, the army and navy began actual operations of war. The Navy Department sent orders to the three fleets: one to sail for Havana, another to move on the Philippines, and another to move out of Hampton Roads. The American military sought to deliver Spain a crushing blow.

"The United States cannot, in the opinion of military and naval experts," wrote the *Times*, "rest upon an almost bloodless victory in Cuba. Not only must Cuba be freed, but the war must be terminated by a decisive victory and by the submission of Spain."

The President planned to ask Congress for absolute authority to enroll the 100,000 men; the House and Senate had already passed a temporary bill giving him that authority. Republican Senator Francis Warren steered through an amendment enabling the mustering of cowboy regiments from the West.

In New York, Cubans flocked to Cuban Delegation headquarters on New Street.

The men were eager to join the insurgents in the field and fight under the flag of Cuba Libre, in full view of the Stars and Stripes.

Across America, states, businesses, and schools put themselves in war mode: Massachusetts Gov. Roger Wolcott issued orders directing commanders to increase the strength of their companies to 100 men; the Delaware Legislature placed its National Guard on a war footing; the Rhode Island Assembly adopted a resolution appropriating $150,000 for military equipment.

In Indianapolis, officials, judges, and deputies petitioned McKinley to request 500,000 men, concluding that, "No such opportunity will present itself soon to impress upon the world a concept of our resources in time of war and . . . nothing would more conduce to a speedy peace"; and Postmaster Richard Von Cott announced that he would issue orders placing the New York office on war footing and orders requesting all National Guardsmen and employees intending to enlist to notify him so replacements could fill their places while they are in service.

Pledges were made to keep places for those employees who volunteered for service by companies such as: the Brooklyn dry goods firm Abraham & Straus; the Philadelphia and Reading Railway; American Insurance in Newark; and the John Good Cordage and Machine Company of New York and New Jersey. Bert Reiss, receiver for John Good, promised to personally pay the salaries in full of those with families who served at the front; the money would come from commissions he accrued as receiver and not from company assets.

Ceremonies and parades at Dartmouth and Wesleyan burned Cuban Gen. Weyler in effigy. "Weyler sunk the *Maine*," declared the Dartmouth banner.

FRIDAY, APRIL 22: The ultimatum would not expire until the next day: the President was withholding his proclamation for volunteers until that time and no declaration had been issued. Still, a *New York Times* headline shouted, "War Begun in Earnest."

How does one define the "beginning of war"? President McKinley issued a blockade proclamation, announcing the closing of Cuban ports to commerce and cited the joint Congressional resolution of April 20, which called for Spain's withdrawal from Cuba. Then two developments, one at 10 a.m. and another at 11, clearly proved that hostilities had begun. The *Times-Citizen* and *Union* of Jacksonville, Florida, reported "the first battle of the war" off Boynton, Florida, 25 miles south of Palm Beach. Fishermen off Lake Worth heard heavy firing and ran to the beach to see a U.S. monitor chasing a Spanish man-of-war or gunboat conveying a coal or transport ship. The chase was a standoff, and the Naval men disclaimed any firing orders.

An hour later the gunboat *Nashville* captured the Spanish merchant steamship *Buenaventura*, in the Key West waters. "The whole population is frantic with enthusiasm," reported the *New York Times*. After the *Nashville* fired a blank shot at the *Buenaventura*, bound for Holland with lumber, the American vessel intensified the action by launching a six-pound shot across the bows of its target. The Spanish ensign was hauled down immediately. The commander of the *Nashville* was Washburn Maynard. The American vessel, with its 1,371-ton displacement, "steamed proudly out of the harbor late this afternoon, having achieved the first victory of the war."

There were many developments on the unofficial first day of war, although of a less sensational nature. In recognition of continuing demands, the Secretary of War promised to retain the organizations of the National Guard as far as possible, and both houses agreed with little difficulty to the Volunteer Army bill and sent it to President McKinley for signature.

As America awaited the President's proclamation, throughout the land there was recruiting, drilling, and other preparations. Adjt. Gen. Whitney Tillinghast announced that commanding officers of regiments reported between 70 to 100 percent of their men willing to volunteer from their respective National Guard groups, and after meeting with Gens. Plume, Stryker, and Donnelly, and the colonels of the different regiments, New Jersey Gov. Foster Vorhees designated the 1st Regiment of Newark as the first to go to the front.

New York Congressman George B. McClelan offered the services of the 12 companies of the 1st Regiment of the Irish Volunteers and, in anticipation of Gov. Black's call for volunteers, state commander Maj. Gen. Roe said he favored Van Cortlandt Park as an assembly point for the troops.

In New York City, Secretary of Lafayette Post Allan C. Bakewell announced that a diverse group of close to 2,800 railway employees, clerks, messengers, and mechanics had enrolled at 256 Broadway, and about 250 men came to Third and Ninth to enlist for three-year terms. A number of policemen applied to the City Police Board for a leave of absence, perhaps none as colorful as John C. McGee of the mounted squad attached to the High Bridge Station. An accomplished horseman who spoke Spanish and Portuguese fluently, he was an old-time cowboy and served as a government scout on the plains for many years.

All employees who joined the New York State militia would continue to receive their salaries, announced Abraham & Straus. Each employee received this letter: "We are informed you are a member of the State militia. In case your regiment should volunteer to go to the front and should you decide to join, you can do so with the assurance that you will be reinstated in your position on your return, and that your salary will be continued. . . . Kindly notify to whom to pay your salary . . . and [may you] return in health and honor to resume your position with our firm."

Even in London, U.S. Ambassador John Hay was flooded with applications for enlistment in the American military. He could not accept them because of the British Foreign Enlistment Act—although Spanish officials were secretly enrolling British volunteers for the Spanish Army.

Final exams were only a few weeks away, but Princeton University undergrads met at Alexander Hall to set up a committee to receive enlistments for a Princeton company. Gen. Daniel Butterfield gave a patriotic address at Union College in Schenectady, New York, and after offering to equip a battalion of Union students, three-fourths of the audience offered their services. The President of Bowdoin College in Brunswick, Maine, William De Witt, presided at a meeting to discuss the military situation, resulting in their formation of a company with F. A. Thompson '98, who spent some years at West Point, selected as captain.

Although no company was organized at Columbia University, a large patriotic rally was climaxed by a trumpet call to arms by Michael B. Conroy, a trumpeter for five years in the U.S. Cavalry, and the University issued a statement that no student would be penalized academically if he volunteered for service.

Several men were in the news, including Capt. Olmstead and Gen. Lew Wallace. From his home in Sedalia, Missouri, former-Confederate officer Olmstead revealed that his personal friend Gen. Fitzhugh Lee had offered him the position of Chief of Scouts, assuming Lee would command U.S. troops in Cuba. Although, for many, the fame of Lew Wallace rests on his best-selling novel *Ben Hur*, this versatile American, a 2nd lieutenant in the Mexican War who attained the rank of Major-General in the Civil War; served on military commissions, including one on Lincoln's assassination after the war; and became Governor of New Mexico Territory and later Minister to Turkey was, according to the *Chicago Tribune*, willing to leave his comfortable home in Crawfordsville, Indiana, abandon his campaign for U.S. Senator, and join the campaign against Spain at the age of 71.

Also in the news was Secretary of State Sherman. With great military minds and planning needed, Washington became anxious when word got out that his health was so impaired he would be of little value to the President in these times of crisis. Unfortunately, there was little diplomatic experience among the assistant secretaries.

Back on the military front, it was a scrambled, nonimposing departure when Capt. Sampson, temporarily appointed Rear Admiral—a promotion that would become permanent if the war endured—left Key West in the early dawn with most of the vessels of the North Atlantic Squadron. The flagship *New York* led the way for the Florida Straits and Cuba, followed by the *Iowa* and *Indiana*; cruisers *Cincinnati* and *Detroit*; gunboats *Wilmington*, *Castine*, *Machias*, *Nashville*, and *Newport*; the monitor *Amphitrite*; the *Mayflower*; and torpedo boat *Foote*.

Three thousand arrivals, almost all from the West, checked in at Chickamauga—15 train loads of infantry, cavalry, and artillery. Chickamauga Park was renamed Camp George H. Thomas for the Civil war hero who led the 14th Army Corps in the campaign of middle Tennessee.

Tampa was transformed into a bustling military post, with trains arriving throughout the day from all over America to swell the number of men in camp to 3,000. Headquarters were set up at the Tampa Bay Hotel under the command of Gen. James F. Wade, whose role would include command of all volunteers.

In its editorial "The War and the People," the *New York Times* voiced widespread sentiment that the present conflict was unlike the Civil War, which was a "vital conflict. . . . With Great Britain at Gibraltar, apart of the peninsula itself, it is mere nonsense for Spaniards to talk about the possession of an island 3,000 miles from home as a necessity of national existence. . . . [While America does not belong in Cuba, the issue is that] *Spain* has no business in Cuba, and . . . Spain . . . has prevented the United States and Cuba from being as good neighbors and . . . customers as nature meant them to be. . . . [With American sentiments aroused by the sinking of the *Maine*, and] the cause of the war is just and honorable. It fulfills Burke's definition of justifiable war—'The blood of man is well shed when it is shed to redeem the blood of man. The rest is vanity; the rest is crime.'"

SATURDAY, APRIL 23: From Key West came a report that the *New York* captured a Spanish steamer at 2:20 a.m., sailing between Havana and Puerto Rico. Added to the capture of the day before, officials pondered the necessity of making a formal declaration of war. The President was said to feel that war could be waged without the declaration; others insisted on Congress passing a resolution recognizing a state of war.

America experienced its first attack between 5 and 6 p.m. in the harbor of Matanzas. The U.S. torpedo boat *Foote*, Lt. W. L. Rodgers commanding, was fired on three times by the Spanish. All shots went wide, and the *Foote* returned to the *Cincinnati*.

The President issued a proclamation calling for 125,000 troops to serve two years, in accordance with the Congressional resolution of April 20. The drafts would be furnished by the states and territories in proportion to their populations.

The War Department issued the formal order of a Grand Army Corps highlighted by headquarters at three Gulf ports. The corps at Camp Thomas, commanded by Maj. Gen. John R. Brooke, would consist of one division of cavalry, one division of infantry, and one brigade of light artillery. Infantry regiments at New Orleans, Mobile, and Tampa would be commanded by Brig. Gen. William R. Shafter, Brig. Gen. John J. Coppinger, and Brig. Gen. James F. Wade, respectively.

Congress concentrated on a war revenue measure. Republican Maine Congressman Nelson Dingley, Jr., introduced a bill in his role as chairman of the Ways and Means Committee. Annual revenue estimates were between 90 and 100 million dollars, excluding such previously designated items as coffee, petroleum, railroad tickets, and tea. Included were fermented liquors ($35 million); tobacco ($15 million); tobacco licenses ($5 million); cigars ($5 million); tonnage tax ($2.5 million), stamp tax on documents, telegrams, wines, mineral waters, chewing gum, and so on ($30–40 million).

The rush of volunteers continued, with more than 10,000 enlisting in Greater New York: At 1 Broadway in Manhattan, headquarters of the Volunteer National Reserve, enrollment reached 6,000 (the roll nationwide already passed 200,000 and was quickly approaching 250,000); at West 36th Street a group of colored Guardsmen committed to raising a regiment of 1,000 men; Col. P. J. Cody announced the raising of a regiment of young Irishmen with registration underway at 372 Third Avenue; and Yen Sing and 50 of his compatriots from Mongolia came to the recruiting office at 19 Bowery promising 100 more men (the recruiting officer was not very receptive, however, because the men did not meet the naturalization and English-language requirements).

The Spaniards of New York wanted no part of American patriotism. Hundreds rushed to the Spanish Consulate responding to a circular, issued by Consul Haldasone, directing them to present themselves "for the preservation of their interests." They were fearful of war, had no interest in fighting for America, and were clearly disappointed that they could not leave for Spain immediately.

The National Volunteer Reserve announced that Dr. Elizabeth Johnson would coordinate a branch recruiting office for female nurses. In Boston, Gov. Wolcott reported that State Regent Sarah E. Hunt offered the services of women in any capacity through the Massachusetts Society of the Daughters of the Revolution.

The members of Manhattan's Sunbeam Club, all under nine years of age, met every afternoon to make linen bags in which they placed a Bible and needles, thread, and a thimble. On the flyleaf of every book they put the name and address of the sender so that each sailor would know who his little friend was.

Southern belles streamed to the South Railway train station at Charlottesville, Virginia, to see off the more than 4,000 men. When the men left, many had buttonless coats, the women having cut them off as mementos. These scenes were repeated, said railway officials, at Lynchburg and Alexandria.

The war's first shortage: flags and buntings. Dealers declared there would soon be a dangerous absence of patriotic symbols and emblems. Every office building in New York City flaunted the Stars and Stripes. Those without flagstaffs improvised and erected one. Three out of five tenement houses displayed some patriotic symbol, and hotels competed with one another for patriotic decorations, adorning every facade and balcony. Schools and municipal buildings were decorated, and the Police Department ordered all stations to hoist flags.

It was the season of flags. The lone star of Cuba waved happily alongside the Stars and Stripes, especially in districts with noticeable Cuban representation. Along the North and East Rivers, the green flag of Eire and the Union Jack were put up by commission merchants of Irish and English heritage.

SUNDAY, APRIL 24: The President, Assistant Secretary Day, Attorney Gen. John Griggs, U.S. Senator Cushman Davis from Minnesota (Chairman of the Committee on Foreign Relations), and Senator Eugene Hale from Maine met at the White House and approved a resolution to be sent to Congress Monday, calling for a formal declaration of war.

It was announced that Washington would have its first camp of citizen soldiers on the next day. The 1,600 men of the National Guard of the District would be under the command of Gen. George Harries, who would become Brigadier General in World War I. They would be housed on the grounds of the soldiers' home.

For the duration of the war, the religious pulpit would be a forum for American patriotism. The *New York Times* reported on the "remarkable patriotic demonstration" at the morning service of the Lafayette Avenue Presbyterian Church in Brooklyn. The Rev. Dr. David H. Gregg's sermon was titled "The National Crisis; or God's Purpose as Wrought Out Through International Relations." In full view of a large American flag, the congregation heard the minister call war with Spain a struggle for humanity and liberty. As the assemblage began to file out, Presiding Justice William W. Goodrich of the Appellate Division of the Supreme Court rose and, coming into the aisle, asked the pastor if the sermon could be printed in pamphlet form. Responded the clergyman, "Not the least." Added the jurist: this would be one of the most righteous wars in the history of humanity.

With those words finished, an old gentleman, whose name has never been recorded, jumped up with indignation to shout that the war was unrighteous and unholy. Furthermore, the conflict was being advanced by the Cuban Junta, who, he maintained, gave orders for the sinking of the *Maine*.

The man's protests were drowned out in a cascade of boos. When the boos stopped,

Goodrich asked, "Dr. Gregg, as an offset to that speech, do you have any objection to three cheers for the flag and for the Government?" When the minister bellowed, "No, give them," the judge faced the audience and led the cheering. According to the *Times*, "The walls of the church rang and echoed with three hearty cheers."

Throughout the war, the *New York Evening Journal* presented "new war ideas" from its readers. William E. Russell suggested temporary war armor; Joseph Giroux advised on protecting harbor mines; and Frank Nearing called for improving the present system of artillery. Said Mr. Nearing: "The plan consists of a system of railway artillery of the various sizes and descriptions . . . necessary for defense of seaports or offence against fortifications. As railways now reach all important points where defense is necessary in this country, and the principal points of attack in any other country we may have trouble with, [we should have a] system which would allow one good battery to cover a large territory."

3

WAR OFFICIALLY DECLARED

MONDAY, APRIL 25: As expected, the House and Senate unanimously declared war on Spain. The House passed the bill almost immediately after its introduction; the Senate said yes after a two-hour closed session.

The volunteer army was being organized throughout America; nevertheless, the invasion of Cuba would not be delayed and would begin before the end of April, early May at latest, with as large a body as the regular army could muster at that time. It was thought that the most suitable point for landing was Cabañas or Bahía Honda, both west of Havana, accessible for American land forces, and the easiest to defend against Spanish attacks.

The Secretary of War sent a dispatch to the Governor of each state and territory informing them what would be expected under the President's call for troops. The largest quotas were those of New York (12 regiments of infantry and 2 troops of cavalry) and Pennsylvania (10 regiments of infantry and 4 heavy batteries).

Utah Gov. Heber M. Wells issued a call for 500 volunteers, to consist of one troop of cavalry and two batteries of artillery. The recruits would rendezvous at Salt Lake City through May 5, at which time they would be mustered into service. Secretary Russell A. Alger sent the Governor a dispatch authorizing the enlistment of 85 "good shots and good riders," as part of the Rough Riders, "to form a company in a mounted rifle regiment."

Wells appointed seven of Utah's most illustrious citizens, mostly from Salt Lake City, as recruiting officers. Many of these officers were from the family of the legendary Brigham Young, founder of the Mormon Church. The seven were Richard W. Young, Willard Young, Frank A. Grant, Joseph E. Caine, John Q. Cannon, George F. Downey, Ray C. Naylor.

In response to orders from Adjt. Gen. C. Whitney Tillinghast, New York City National Guard regiments assembled at their respective armories. The most colorful scene was at the 71st Regiment Armory at 34th Street and Park Avenue. To the cheers of a large throng, the men trooped into the army—the older members in fatigue uniforms and the new recruits in civilian dress. After a roll call, the fife and drum corps played a march, as the colors were carried in and the regiment presented arms.

Having reviewed his troops, Col. Francis Greene—later the City Police Commissioner—advised the men that they should not feel compelled to enlist, especially if they were family men. "To those who have families dependent upon them," said the Colonel, "I would say they are perfectly free to refuse to enter the service, and they can do so without prejudice to themselves."

Quotas were being filled quickly across the city and several special-interest regiments were being organized. Chaplain Frederic Rotzier founded the American Rescue Army and sermonized nightly in Madison Square Garden. He also organized the American Wanderers Brigade and attracted 200 homeless men, with the goal of reaching 1,000.

The Bankers and Brokers Regiment opened its office on 15 Broad Street, headed by brokers Charles F. Quincy and Washington F. Conner. One of their former employees, clerk E. S. Fitch, 45 years old, with much military experience, was the first to enroll. Second was H. A. Lawrence, 32, an engineer with the Otto Gas Engine Co., who had placed the engines in the Holland torpedo companies. The first broker to enroll was J. J. Lutkin of 5 Broad Street. By day's end, 110 had enrolled at 15 Broad and an additional 85 at other locations on Wall Street. Their efforts would continue, aided by Commodore James D. Smith of the New York Yacht Club, who was named chairman of the General Organization Committee.

The *Jewish Daily News* and *Jewish Gazette* opened a recruiting office on 185 East Broadway for Jewish immigrants on the Lower East Side. Many of them had served in the armies in Austria and Russia, and they had already formed three miliary companies. Some signed up on the first day and, according to editor Sarasohn, "We have also received applications . . . from Jews in Newark, Philadelphia, and Baltimore, and . . . almost every large city." He added that many of the volunteers belonged to Russian Jewish benefit societies that agreed to pay them $25 for enlisting and to retain their status in the societies until war's end.

Five Spaniards, only one claiming to be an American citizen, applied for the National Volunteer Reserves. They were sent to City Hall to declare their intentions of becoming citizens.

Enlistees came from all walks of life. John Logan, son of the late U.S. Illinois Senator John A. Logan, notified the War Department that he had raised a cavalry regiment that he offered to command. Arthur Draper, a Harvard postgraduate student, enlisted as a private in Battery A; his father, an ambassador, had enlisted as a private in the Civil War and went out as a commissioned officer. Harvard's Varsity Crew would have difficulty rowing competitively; four enlisted in the militia and three others, including ex-captain Goodrich, left for Washington hoping to get commissions for service in the auxiliary fleet.

Frank Brito, son of a Yaqui miner, was working for $30 a month as a rider with the Circle Bar near Silver City, New Mexico, when his father told him to come home. "When I got home after riding 10 hours, it was late at night, but our house was all lit up. I thought for sure somebody had died. My dad came out and said . . . war had been declared against Spain and they wanted volunteers, especially cowboys. He told [my brother] Joe and me to go to Silver City and enlist. In those days you didn't talk back to your father. [Since] I was a few months short of 21 . . . the recruiter looked me over pretty good. Then he turned to another man and said, 'Hell, I haven't got the heart to turn him down.'"

Who was the first volunteer accepted by the War Department? *Jews in American Wars* (Friedman and Falk 71) identifies him as Col. Joseph M. Heller of Washington, who left a thriving medical practice to become acting Assistant Surgeon in the army. He was cited for "perseverance, patience, and fidelity to duty" in the Philippines by Gen. Elwell Stephen Otis.

The cold realities of war came to nonvolunteers in varied forms. An order to the shipping men in New York Harbor, given by Col. H. M. Adams of the Engineer Corps, stated in part: "Submarine guns having been placed in position in connection with the defenses of New York . . . no vessel will be allowed to pass Sandy Hook or the Narrows between the hours of sunset and sunrise. During this interval vessels must not approach within three miles of Coney Island, Gedney Channel, Sandy Hook, or the Narrows."

The defense of the powder works in Wilmington, Delaware, concerned company officials, who feared the Spanish would assail that center. For many years the Dupont Powder Company employed one watchman by day and another at night. Six men would now guard the center until the mills turned out all powder contracted for by the government.

TUESDAY, APRIL 26: President McKinley expressed confidence that America would succeed in the war. Strategy was laid out in a meeting with the commander of the army, the officers of the Naval Strategy Board, and two retired military heroes, Capt. John Schofield and Capt. Alfred Mahan, considered the greatest living authority on naval strategy.

The first move would be securing a base of supplies and operations in Cuba and, later, a similar base in the Philippines. The President also issued a proclamation concerning captures already made by Admiral Sampson's fleet. Interpretation varied although the intention seemed to fix policy from April 21, the official day of the war's beginning. Most thought that previous seizures such as the *Buenaventura* would be left to the U.S. Court; however, the President was in a quandary. International public opinion would not look kindly on the seizures; yet he did not want to criticize the zeal and dedication of his officers.

The enlistments continued steadily. In New York, Maj. Gen. Roe reported a large number of recruits for the National Guard. Plans called for five regiments from New York City, three from Brooklyn, and one from Buffalo. Four regiments and twelve separate companies would be left in the state for defensive purposes; and volunteers would camp on Hempstead Plains. In Peekskill, Col. Joseph Story, in charge of preparing the state camp for volunteers, said nearly all the tents were erected for the 4,000 scheduled to arrive on April 28.

Pennsylvania Gov. Daniel W. Hastings and Adj. Gen. Stewart left for Washington to petition the Secretary of War to reverse his decision that wiped out five of the fifteen regiments that were supposed to be mustered into service.

In Chicago, large numbers marched out of the city headed for war. It was a scene not viewed in the armories since 1861. The troops that left for the camping ground at Springfield were the 1st, 2nd, and 7th Regiments of Infantry and the 1st Cavalry. It was estimated that 5,000 people followed each of the regiments to the trains. Reported the *New York Times*: "For hours before the time set for the troops to move, the streets in front of the armories were . . . absolutely impassable to vehicles. At times the pressure was so great that detachments from the regiments were compelled to clear away the throngs . . . women clung to such of the blue clad boys as they could lay hands on . . . and those people who could not reach the ranks cheered and waved handkerchiefs and flags."

The scene was duplicated in Detroit, where 2,700 from the 4th Regiment departed for Island Lake, 50 miles west of Detroit. The patriotic fervor had not reached this intensity since the days of the Grand Army of the Republic. Members of the local militia company at Port Huron were presented with a five-dollar gold piece; two officers were given horses. The Bay City Common Council pledged to retain positions for those enlisting. Cheering send-offs were visible in Bay City, Grand Rapids, and Saginaw.

Enthusiastic crowds were at every station along the route to the State Fair Grounds near Indianapolis, where members of the Indiana National Guard encamped. The first troops responding to the President's call were from Company K of Frankfort, 600 men under the command of Capt. Ben Allen.

Michigan's charismatic Gov. Hazen Pingree, a prisoner of war during the Civil War, a shoe manufacturer, and a former Detroit Mayor, offered to take command of the state's 2,700 troops while they were in camp awaiting call-up and examinations.

In Charleston, South Carolina, Col. Coward addressed the 56 remaining cadets at the Citadel Academy, the others having been recruited to meet the quota. The cadets passed a resolution to defend their country in any way possible. While it was not likely they would see active duty, they might yet serve in the preparatory work of forming regiments.

Future Lincoln biographer Carl Sandburg eagerly became Private Sandburg upon enlisting in Company C, 6th Infantry Regiment of the Illinois Volunteers: "When I quit my job, and told the family . . . they were a little sad and somewhat puzzled," he recalled in *Always the Young Strangers*. "[My brother, Martin] spoke for the family, 'We'd like the honor of . . . a soldier in the family, but we don't want you to be killed.' I said it might not be a real war . . . I might not get shot . . . some soldiers always come back home. And besides, having seen the West I would now see the East and maybe the Atlantic Ocean and Cuba."

Hundreds of families said their farewells with Sandburg at what became known as "Burlington Station." "The whole city [Galesburg] was aroused as it had not been since the days of the Civil War," wrote *The Annals of Knox County*. "10,000 or more of our citizens, gathered first at the armory, where the men of Company C were assembled, and again at the Burlington station, where they were to entrain, to give them last messages of farewell and God-speed." The company would drill for 10 days in Springfield, which gave Sandburg an opportunity to visit the state capital and President Abraham Lincoln's gravesite.

For another American man of letters, Sherwood Anderson, this was his second day of service. Why did he leave a position in business to enlist in Clyde, Ohio: "Can it be that it was not patriotism that brought me home from Chicago to enlist? I was, like the others of our company, a middle western small town boy, and the island of Cuba was far away. . . . We were farmers' sons, merchants' sons, sons of workers . . . young roughs, gentle quiet boys, frightened ones and many, like myself, who wanted only to appear brave and indifferent. . . . our hearts did not ache for the suffering people . . . of Cuba. . . . they ached for adventure."

WEDNESDAY, APRIL 27: It was a problem how best to effect a blockade with the advent of bad weather, in particular the rainy season in Cuba. Intense consultations were held between Maj. Gen. Nelson Miles, chief in command for America, and Gonzalo de Quesada, chargé d'affaires of the Republic of Cuba in Washington.

Headed by the flagship *Olympia*, the American fleet left at 2 p.m. for Manila. On board was Emilio Aguinaldo, who led the Filipino insurrection against the Spanish and would become president of the provisional government. Plans called for his taking charge of the insurgent forces. Admiral George Dewey's primary goal was the capture of the Spanish fleet, which he considered much more important than the capture of Manila.

Secretary of War Alger issued a directive on immediate measures to recruit the regiments of the regular army and the battalion of engineers. Within the next two or three months, the army would increase from 27,000 to 186,000—61,000 regular troops and 125,000 volunteers—with the help of the Hull bill. Alger also spoke out strongly to amend the present volunteer law so that America could recruit at least six regiments of yellow fever immunes, totaling 6,000 men. He sought these recruits in the Gulf states and asked the aid of Louisiana's U.S. Senator Donelson Caffrey who said he could raise 20,000 just in New Orleans, since nearly all natives there had already contracted yellow fever.

Quotas were being filled throughout the land, but recruiting did not end. The Lafayette Post Brigade, at 256 Broadway, surpassed 5,000, with at least 70 percent expected to pass their physicals. A large building at 5th Avenue and 14th Street had been donated for use of the brigade, with a nominal rent of $1 a month. Lyman J. Bloomingdale opened a recruiting office in his store and promised to donate uniforms for the Lafayette Post Brigade. He quickly enrolled 100 men, and Capt. Levy of West Point drilled them on one of Bloomingdale's floors.

Active recruiting began in Salt Lake City, and it was announced that recruiting officers would be at Provo, Bountiful, Price, Springville, Lehi, Nephi, Eureka, Farmington, Mount Pleasant, Park City, Manti, Richmond, Bingham, Ogden, Salina, Brigham City, Tooele, Heber, and Richfield over five days. The armory of the National Guard on South Temple Street served as Salt Lake City's recruiting center. L. W. Calhoun, an employee in the freight department of the Union Pacific Railroad Company, is credited with being the first Utah man to enlist in the war. However, he enrolled in his old home in Mississippi, so the honor of being the first Utah man to sign up with a state organization was given to Arthur L. Thomas, Jr., son of the Postmaster.

A patriotic spirit pervaded all of Utah, as described in an article by D. O. Rideout in *The History of the Utah Volunteers*: "[T]hrough the State there was the greatest enthusiasm. Brass bands . . . public meetings . . . patriotic speeches . . . and the boys, as they enrolled . . . were already spoken of as heroes. . . . Many of the hardy sons of the settlements signed away their liberties and laid their lives upon the altar of their country.

"Mormon, Gentile and Jew; Republican, Democrat and populist; high, low, rich, and poor—all were swept away by the wave of patriotism. . . . The lawyer gave up his practice; the tradesman laid aside the tools of his craft; the student forsook his books; and the farmer forgot his harvest . . . ; the delicately reared city girl gazed fondly in the eyes of her affianced and bade him go; wives surrendered their husbands, and mothers, with streaming eyes, heard of their noble boys' enlistment and did not say them nay. . . .

"[T]he Latter-day Saints . . . [urged] its communicants . . . to fly to arms in so worthy a cause, while from . . . [other] churches came similar words. Employers gladly gave up their most trusted aides . . . holding their places . . . until the war was over" (Prentiss 29–30).

Omaha, Nebraska declared a municipal holiday and closed its stores, as 2,000 citizens, civic societies, semimilitary groups, and bands paraded volunteers to the special trains that would take them to Lincoln. "There were many pathetic scenes," reported an observer, "where mothers broke down and cried as their young ones passed out of sight."

Sherwood Anderson and his fellow volunteers were still savoring the reception that came to cheer them as they boarded the train for Toledo. All factories were closed, as were the schools. As he observes in *A Story Teller's Story*: "I was received with acclaim. Never before that time or since have I had a personal triumph and I liked it. When . . . [we] marched away to the railroad station to entrain for war, the entire town turned out and cheered. Girls ran . . . to kiss us and old veterans of the Civil War— they had known . . . of battles we would never know—stood with tears in their eyes. To the young . . . [like] myself, . . . it was grand and glorious" (278).

In the headlines was former Assistant Secretary of the Navy Theodore Roosevelt, who met with Roger D. Williams, Vice President of the National Fox Hunters Association, to raise a company of 100 Kentuckians to join his cowboy regiment. Needed: Men who could ride, fight, shoot, and obey orders.

Applications had been flooding his desk, so Roosevelt made it known that the recruiting would be coordinated by Col. Leonard Wood, a former assistant surgeon in the U.S. Army. Recruits do not need prior training or manuals in endurance, said Roosevelt. "Wherever they strike, they will make things hum . . . inhabitants will think that several circuses and several kinds of disaster have broken in upon them."

Although a former President of the New York City Police Board, Roosevelt did not want New York's finest, nor was the Police Board willing to part with its men. Of 25 requests for leaves, the only one given the nod was Mortimer L. Stover, who had been a gunner for four years before joining the force. The Board issued the following statement: "The question of granting . . . leaves of absence to members of the police force is different from . . . other departments of the City Government. There is no [way] . . . we could fill the places of those . . . excused, and it is . . . necessary that an efficient police force . . . be had during war."

Not seeking to join forces with Roosevelt and Wood, wealthy rancher Jay L. Torrey of Wyoming said he would ask permission from the President to raise one independent regiment of frontiersmen who would be skilled horsemen and marksmen. And Manhattanite F. James Gibson announced plans to form a regiment of Canadians to serve in the war.

The mood was not jubilant at the Pimlico race track site in Baltimore, where the 1st Brigade of the Maryland National Guard was encamped. The Secretary of War called on Maj. Gen. Wilmer to provide one regiment and four batteries of heavy artillery to leave for the front. Wilmer selected the 5th Regiment, under the command of Col. Frank Markoe, and asked Col. Willard Howard and officers of the 4th Regiment to make up part of the batteries. The 4th, being senior to the 5th, were stunned by the decision. They vehemently protested and were told by Howard that the men must be enlisted to go to the front or they would not go at all. Because of their protests, Wilmer ordered the men to return to their armory in the city. The men cheered Col. John Howell when he told them he and Lt. Col J. Frank Supplee would go tomorrow to protest their mistreatment to the Secretary of War and offer the command as a regiment of volunteers.

THURSDAY, APRIL 28: Let's strike at once was the consensus of a meeting among the President, the Secretary of War, and advisors of the Chief Executive.

The landing division would be formed during the next three days. Eight transport vessels were selected to take the invading regular forces to Cuba: the *Florida* and *Olivette* of the Plant Steamship Company; the *Decatur H. Miller, Berkshire,* and *Allegheny* of the Merchants and Miners' Company; the *Comal* and *Alamo* of the New York and Texas Company; and the *Arkansas* of the Southern Pacific Company. While not determined, the landing was likely to be made on the northern coast, with the goal to surround the Spaniards in Havana and Matanzas.

Gen. Wade and his staff met for half an hour with Clara Barton, who helped organize and served as President of the American Red Cross. They sought her counsel in dealing with yellow fever.

As decisions were being finalized, Admiral Sampson ordered the firing upon fortifications at Matanzas, most likely to reduce Spanish works on the Cuban coast before Havana was reached. Did he exceed his authority? Regardless, naval authorities felt the attack could keep Spain from mounting big guns to defend the Havana harbor.

The War Department gave Judge J. L. Torrey authorization for a second regiment of Rough Riders. Another cowboy regiment would be commanded by South Dakota Attorney General Melvin Grigsby, a cavalry officer during the Civil War. The three cowboy regiments would be known as the 1st, 2nd, and 3rd Regiments of the U.S. Volunteer Cavalry, to be made up of 12 troops each.

Torrey said he would leave for Wyoming shortly to round up the impatient cowboys. He himself would take command: "The Superintendent of my ranch in Wyoming has ready for me a horse which has been in training now for about two years. . . . All the boys will bring their own animals, branded, and accustomed to many a trick of the owner. . . . There is no difficulty about the climate . . . [these] men can live anywhere on earth. The horses, although tired in a high altitude, will be able to travel with speed unheard of in Cuba. . . . [T]he Wyoming rough riders will make very smooth records if they get but half a chance."

Among the Illinois Volunteers newly arrived at Falls Church, Virginia, was Carl Sandburg. During his nearly two-month stay, he visited the White House, the Capitol, Ford's Theater, and the Peterson, where Abraham Lincoln passed away.

Spies, sabotage, treason—there was cause for concern. A Spanish plan to wreck bridges and blow up trains carrying soldiers to Key West was revealed by Dr. James L. Long, a physician of Good Hope, Georgia, in a letter to his friend, Georgia Gov. W. Y. Atkinson. Two Spanish spies, according to the physician, passed through Walton County. "I hope you will not let this go unnoticed," he wrote the Governor, "as they blew up our battleship [the *Maine*]. Please inform the department officials . . . also . . . they intend to employ Negroes to work in front."

Near New Orleans, the government engineer officer at Port Eads arrested John Walsh, believed to be a Spanish spy. On his person were found several undeveloped films and maps of the government works at the port.

The most sensational news was the seizure of a letter mailed at Santa Clara, California, addressed to Señor Praxades Sagasta, Spanish Prime Minister, offering detailed information about the fortifications and defenses of the California coast. The letter was snatched by the Post Office in Washington to conform with the Postmaster General's order to suspend forwarding of mail to Spain. The letter, mailed several days before the order was promulgated, with no return address given, revealed meticulous details about the submarine mines and torpedoes in San Francisco, pinpointed the location of batteries and forts, and cited the distances between points and other strategic information. The writer, said to be a feminine hand, advised the Spaniard to capture Monterey and march by land to San Francisco because of the mine torpedo protection of San Francisco.

FRIDAY, APRIL 29: Brig. Gen. William R. Shafter was selected to lead the expeditionary troops that would land in Cuba from Tampa, where they were now forming. The exact point of landing for the 6,000 troops was a secret although possibilities were Cabañas, Bahía Honda, Cárdenas, Matanzas, and even Santiago de Cuba. It was decided that no attack on Havana would be made for some time.

Troops began moving to Tampa from Mobile, New Orleans, and Chickamauga. The 10th and 22nd Infantry Regiments received orders to leave for Tampa. The train for Mobile, the Louisville and Nashville Railroad, carried quartermasters' supplies, 15 escort wagons, 21 ambulances, and 75 mules. Three regiments had arrived in New Orleans only two days ago, when they were ordered to leave for Tampa. Wild enthusiasm greeted the soldiers along Espanada and other avenues as they proceeded to the trains. At Chickamauga, activity was frenzied as artillery, the 24th Infantry, and 9th Cavalry were hurried to Tampa.

New York State's first body of National Guard soldiers to go into active service was

Company H of the 71st Regiment. Comprising 84 men and 3 officers, they left the armory at 34th Street and Park Avenue for Hempstead Plains in Long Island.

An explanation for the bombardment of the Matanzas batteries on April 27 was offered by Admiral Sampson. The unexpected engagement was the first in which the U.S. Navy participated in some 30 years. Sampson said that there was never any thought of capturing the city but only to stop the erection of batteries. Mission accomplished: the explosion of shells tore up the nearly completed earthworks and fortifications.

On the Presidential agenda were the appointments of Major Generals and Brigadier Generals for the war effort. Connecticut U.S. Senator Orville Platt lobbied McKinley for Gen. Stewart L. Woodford and Col. Fred D. Grant, both seeking commissions in the volunteer army. Gen. Fitzhugh Lee was still uncertain of his war role; he was in the news because the Lees hosted Miss Cisneros, the young Cuban girl rescued from Cabañas.

Harvard University continued as a thriving center for enlistment. At Faneuil Hall, Capt. Quinton of the U.S. Army recruited for the regular army while clerk George Fred Williams signed up students for the volunteer regiment. The enthusiasm had been sparked by a patriotic address by Prof. Albert Bushnell Hart, head of Harvard's American History Department. "The war with Spain was inevitable," he said. "For 91 years, the Spanish misrule has inflicted untold suffering on Cuba, and. . . . By intervention, the United States only fulfilled her duty as the protector of a weaker American people."

In Cincinnati the Right Rev. William H. Elder instructed his priests to deliver an address on patriotism to their congregations on Sunday, May 1. He called for the recitation of one "Our Father" and one "Hail Mary" "for the souls of those who die in the contest, including the brave victims of the *Maine*." But the essence of the sermon was to deal with obeying the government: "Society must have civil government, hence God requires that the civil government must be obeyed. . . . The power of declaring war is an essential attribute of sovereign authority. Consequently, Catholics understand . . . every one must do his full duty to his country . . . under pain of sin. . . . [T]here is one service which everybody owes to his country, and that is prayer."

4

VICTORY AT MANILA BAY

SATURDAY, APRIL 30: One of the great American successes at sea began to unfold. In the evening Admiral Dewey's six ships, the Asiatic Squadron, slipped past the Corregidor fortress and entered the harbor of Manila, the Philippine capital. Excitement was high and anxiety even greater. The President gave assurances that there would be no bombing of undefended or unfortified settlements, only firing in response to guns from Spanish ships or forts.

The administration was looking forward to a victory at sea and also anticipating a landing in Cuba. "The officers who served in the war of the rebellion," wrote the *New York Times.* "are as frisky as the youngsters who have recently come from West Point and have yet to smell powder in action for the first time."

However, Maj. Gen. Brooke injected a worrisome note in an address to the Young Men's Business League in Chattanooga. He said the government was shortsighted in not maintaining a larger standing army. There were not enough men at Chickamauga, and invasion could be delayed because of inadequate preparation.

Meanwhile, a great transportation operation was in full swing in New York. Gov. Black designated Gen. Howard Carroll to coordinate the transportation of the various military groups to the state camps. Some 13,000 men would have to be transported. Headquarters were set up at 34th Street and Park Avenue.

The Governor assured the men that arrangements would be made "to have refrigerator cars containing meats and other edibles transferred directly to the camp . . . to furnish the men luxuries of some kind . . . in a sufficient degree to keep them in good spirits and not make them feel too homesick."

The men from Poughkeepsie were going—an unexpected joy. The 15th Separate Company had been overlooked in the assignments announced several days ago. Ninety-three privates—nine more than the company's full quota—had volunteered. The company would form part of the 1st Regiment, heading for Hempstead Plains under the command of Col. Barber.

In New Jersey three regiments of infantry, the state's quota, were leaving for the state camp at Sea Girt. Reports circulated that the camp would be called Camp Vorhees to honor the popular Governor. Vorhees said that he would set up headquarters in the camp, starting May 2.

The Newark Board of Education called upon schools to give students a half holiday on May 2 that so the children could see the soldiers leave. They also decided that all who enlisted for service would remain on the payroll; the city Aldermen extended the rule to all city employees.

Dissatisfaction, however, pervaded Bergen Troop A, a new cavalry company organized by townspeople in Westwood, New Jersey. Kirk Falker was elected captain, but after a few drills, some of the men checked his background. He was a member of Troop A of Colorado Springs, but when he could not show discharge papers, he was voted out.

Private Michael J. Byrne of Company D 1st Regiment was another unhappy New Jerseyite. He was prevented from going to the front because his wife had accused him of desertion, and he was ordered to appear for examination in Bloomfield. Byrne maintained that all the fuss was a "put-up job" to keep him home.

These New Jersey stories were atypical of volunteers across the land. Russell Harrison, son of former President Benjamin Harrison, personally applied to Secretary Alger for assignment in one of the staff departments of the army, expressing preference for the Pay Department. And the honor of the first Negro volunteer regiment was credited to Company A, Colored Volunteers, when Alabama Gov. Joseph F. Johnston accepted its services and appointed officers J. H. Bone, who was a Captain in the Federal Army, as Company Captain, and F. Morse Taylor, whose father was Surgeon of a Wisconsin regiment, as First Lieutenant.

A corps of nurses was being organized under the auspices of the National Society of the Daughters of the American Revolution. Dr. Anita N. Mcgee headed a committee that planned a two-class corps—one would be called "Daughters," and the second would be trained nurses or hospital assistants. Surgeon Generals Van Reypen of the navy and George Sternberg of the army welcomed the offer but said that the nurses would not be sent to Cuba. Regent Floretta Vining of the John Adams Chapter of the Boston Chapter of the Daughters of the American Revolution offered Massachusetts Gov. Wolcott the services of the chapter, its funds, and the company grounds at Hull for any military use.

Elsewhere in New England, seniors and graduates at Yale University designed the Yale Horse Battery, which attracted 100 students and faculty at the drills. The battery would go to the front with Connecticut's quota of troops. The students had first planned a machine-gun battery but changed to a battery of horse artillery. A full complement of 275 men would be required, and the armament would be six 3.2-inch rapid-fire guns. The training would be severe, and drilling was scheduled for the near future at the Niantic state grounds.

War enthusiasm was great in the Halls of Ivy, fortified when the naval authorities named a new cruiser the *Yale*. Every night during the past week hundreds of students marched down the main streets of New Haven singing college songs, "burning red fire," and displaying effigies of Spanish Gen. Weyler, "the Butcher."

Next year in Jerusalem? Perhaps, but for the moment the 25,000 Russian Jews of Chicago had decided on Cuba. The goal of the city's 12 to 15 colonization societies, called Zion groups, was to settle in Palestine. Spokesman Dr. A. P. Kadison explained the change: "Our people do not forget that it was Spain which banished 1 million Jews, and treated them with inhuman barbarity. It will be to avenge this that we go."

Also in Chicago, 3,000 congregants came to Anshe Knesseth Israel for a special service that prayed for the health of and guidance for President McKinley in the war with Spain and for the continued welfare and prosperity of the American Government. Before an audience of many Russian refugees, William Zoloktoff, an officer of the synagogue, told the congregants that only in a land of liberty did the Jews have the chance to bear arms against a nation that had persecuted their ancestors.

On the Lower East Side of Manhattan, a company of Russian Hussars, all Jewish, and 250 other Jews signed applications for enlistment. And in Woodbine, New Jersey, the Baron de Hirsch Colony of Russian Jewish farmers, offered their services to Gov. Vorhees.

Synagogues read a Hebrew prayer, "The War Prayer," formulated by the Jewish Ministers Association in New York. Its translation: "O Lord, thou art the God of battle and the God of peace. . . . In Thine hands are the destinies of the nations and the lives of all men. We implore Thy help and mercy. . . . Protect, O God, our nation, guide and counsel its chief magistrate and all his advisers . . . and let the cause of liberty and justice come forth triumphantly. . . . Sustain with Thy strength the arm of those who hold the sword in defence of our land and its free institutions. . . . Let tyranny vanish against smoke, and let all dwellers on earth recognize that Thou alone art King. Let . . . the trumpet of war be silenced forever, and may all nations be united in love and peace. . . . to Thy name may be glory and honor forever—Amen."

A day did not seem to pass without a spy story. In Dover, New Jersey, two supposed Spaniards were arrested at the Forcite Powder Company. The watchmen spotted the prowling suspects and placed them under arrest after a desperate battle. They refused to give their names and would not explain their presence at the works.

SUNDAY, MAY 1: Who won the battle of Manila, and what was the extent of the victory—or defeat? Facts would later reveal that American guns overwhelmed the Spanish fleet; when all ended, some 170 Spaniards were killed and all their ships destroyed while only one American was a victim—to heatstroke. But for now, reports were sketchy.

The first reports, attributed to the Spaniards, *were* of an American victory, and if the enemy wanted to lie, wouldn't they have distorted the report in their favor? So although McKinley honestly expected a Spanish victory, he accepted the report.

The press waited past midnight, but there was no official confirmation: "It looks, however, as the news must be about straight," Secretary Horace Porter told them. And while they waited, the Secretary of the Navy, his Assistant John Long, and Theodore Roosevelt all went to sleep. Secretary Alger waxed enthusiastic, calling it a "glorious victory."

The battle of Manila was about the only item commanding front-page headlines on this quiet May Sunday. Chickamauga Park experienced its quietest day since mobi-

lization began: No troops came, none left, no orders were received for further movement south, and the only order of any interest was for the Assistant Quartermaster and
his aides to search middle Tennessee for badly needed horses and mules.

New Mexico met its quota for a Rough Riders Regiment, in the form of a cavalry
unit, before most other states. George Curry, later to become an important force in
New Mexico's campaign for statehood, enlisted right after President McKinley's call.
As a commissioned first lieutenant, he organized one of four companies from the territory. He and his second lieutenant, Charles Ballard, and their men arrived in Santa Fe,
then left with other New Mexicans for San Antonio as local citizens cheered.

In Staten Island, large crowds entertained themselves by getting a glimpse of the
new cruiser *Topeka* which arrived, 12 days out from Falmouth, England. She was not
a trim, formidable American-built craft although she had stability and endurance.

To show support for America, the Congregation of St. Paul the Apostle decided at
its meeting to send one of its Paulist Fathers to the front. Behind the idea was the Rev.
Father Deshon, Superior General of the community, a West Point graduate and
classmate of Gen. U. S. Grant. Selected was the Rev. Frank Brooks Doherty of their
newly established community in San Francisco.

Well-known black military leader Col. William Murrell of West Asbury Park, New
Jersey, contacted Secretary Alger with the offer of raising a regiment of colored men.
He had been wounded three times during the Civil War while in the 54th
Massachusetts Regiment and after the war had commanded the 4th Regiment,
Louisiana National Guard.

In Jersey City, 40 Cubans accompanied by two surgeons boarded the 8 p.m.
Pennsylvania Railroad. Their destination: Cuba, where they intended to fight for the
country's freedom.

Today's spy story: Carpenter's Steel Works in Reading, Pennsylvania, beefed up
its guard with a 12-man staff, in response to reports of Spanish spies in the vicinity of
other companies involved in government work. The guards were instructed to shoot
any suspicious loiterers who did not leave after being warned.

MONDAY, MAY 2: Washington was now satisfied that Dewey had led America to
a decisive victory, although exact details were still not available. A volume of praise
was directed his way.

From Indianapolis, Admiral George Brown took especial pride in his prodigy,
having known Dewey since he entered the Naval Academy in the mid 1850s. "The
fight at Manila," rejoiced Brown, "was his Trafalgar. More fortunate than Nelson, he
will live to enjoy the honor he has won. The moral effect of this victory in Europe is
incalculable. The demoralization of Spain cannot be computed. . . . I would have been
greatly disappointed if Dewey had not accomplished everything he was sent to do.
With fine ships, with a splendid corps of officers, with as good fighting sailors as there
are in the world, with modern guns, it was with me a foregone conclusion that Dewey
would win."

"Well done, Dewey," shouted the assemblage at the Worth Monument in Madison
Square. The *New York Journal* sponsored a free concert and fireworks to celebrate his
triumph. The fireworks included many rockets and single bombs and set pieces

displaying the words, "Red, White, and Blue Fire" and "Remember the *Maine*."

At New York's Windsor Hotel, the quarterly meeting of the Friendly Sons of St. Patrick adopted a resolution praising Dewey.

On this day other military heroes received good news: Gen. Fitzhugh Lee received a telegram at his Richmond home from Adjt. Gen. Henry C. Corbin congratulating him on his appointment as Major General. In San Francisco, Col. John S. Mosby received a letter from Gen. Miles that the President had recommended his appointment in connection with raising troops in the South.

Not so exuberant were reports from the camps in New York. True, mail service would be provided on Chickamauga and Long Island (Maj. Gen. Charles Roe of the New York militia had telegraphed Postmaster Gen. Charles Emory Smith to establish a military postal service for the 9,000 troops in the state); however, conditions were very unpleasant in Peekskill (renamed Camp Townsend in memory of the late Adjt. Gen. Frederick Townsend, who had reorganized the state militia into a military organization). The 8th Regiment, under the command of Col. Henry Chauncey, Jr., started arriving at 5:15. Camp Townsend now had three regiments: the 8th, 9th, and 12th. They were welcome to the hard facts of military life. The 9th was assigned to suitable quarters in the old camp ground. However, the 8th and 12th were placed in the North Parade Grounds. They slept on straw spread on damp earth. There were no cots or mattresses except in the officers' tents. Most of the soldiers were city folk, not used to outdoor sleeping, so surgeons prepared for night calls.

The mess hall was under the direction of Duncan & Odell. The consensus was that the meals were fairly good. Maj. E. C. Roessele, in charge of the commissary, signed contracts with a number of provision dealers, leading to a daily diet of fresh beef, bread, and coffee, and an occasional dish of prunes "or some such luxury."

Spirits did sag, especially on the raw recruits. Wrote the *New York Times*, "Many appeared much depressed in spirits when the comparative loneliness of their positions forced itself upon them, this being especially true of the recruits. Every pretext for excitement was eagerly seized."

To brighten things, camp commander Peter C. Doyle, Brig. Gen. of the 4th Regiment encouraged the opening of a canteen and "knapsack," where one could purchase anything from a shoestring to a stove. On the outskirts of the camp appeared a barbershop, slot machines, cane ringing outfits and the like, giving the camp an air of Coney Island. This ambiance did not fully please Doyle: "This is a camp of instruction and preparation, and we are on a war footing," he insisted. "This will be no summer game and mighty little fun. It will be camp life with all that that means, and while the boys will be well fed as long as we have charge of them, there will be no frills. I think that as soon as they come to an understanding that they are soldiers in every sense everything will go swimmingly."

Across the river in New Jersey, matters were proceeding smoothly. The work of mustering the state's quota had begun. The following had responded on time to the President's call: The 1st, 2nd, and 3rd Regiments; Companies, A, C, and G of the 6th; and Company E of the 7th. Children of the Manasquan public schools, with fife and drum corps, marched on the lawn of Camp Vorhees and lined up inside the fence between the railroad and the Governor's headquarters. The regiments marched by as the children sang "America." The troops were reviewed by Gov. Vorhees, Maj. Gen. Joseph W. Plume, and Col. Oliphant.

There was uneasiness in Port Tampa. A number of the troops—the 5th Infantry and all of the cavalry—drank water and were taken ill. The cause was placed upon an identified Spanish spy. An analysis of the well water was underway by the Surgeons of the several regiments encamped here.

TUESDAY, MAY 3: Details began to emerge about the thriller at Manila. According to the Department of the Navy, Dewey's mission was to seek out and destroy Spain's squadron in the East. Once done, Dewey was to check with the Navy for further orders. The destruction was effected, but Dewey had not yet reported back.

The difficulty was that the cable connecting the Philippines with Hong Kong, which starts from a point about 50 miles from Madrid, had been cut. By whom? Madrid hinted that Dewey had cut the cable; Washington felt Spaniards at Manila cut communications to avoid Madrid's being aware of the military disaster.

The story of the battle reached the British Colonial Office in London through two cable messages from Lieut. Col. Sir C.B.H. Bennett, Governor of the Straits Settlement. As the American ships entered Manila harbor, a fort opened fire. The American fleet switched position to one near Cavite, in Manila Bay. Dewey's squadron destroyed the enemy in two hours, suffering only one disabled vessel. Dewey contacted British Consul E. H. Raison Walker to transmit a message to the Spanish Governor General: Surrender all torpedoes and guns at Manila and possession of the cable offices or face bombardment of Manila. The Spaniard refused and prevented the agent of the telegraph company from conferring with Dewey. The Americans then initiated a four-hour combat and once again routed the Spanish vessels. Spain sent the following dispatch to the *London Daily Mail*: "The Americans are now moving on Madrid, but there has been no capitulation yet . . . Gen. Augusti will probably defend the Plaza of Manila. . . . The Spanish Ministers admit that the battle ended in the utter rout of the Spanish fleet, but they are resolved not to spare any efforts in the defense of the country. . . . The Spanish warships *Reina Maria*, *Cristina*, and the *Castilla* have been totally burned. One vessel was purposely sunk, and the rest were damaged."

Reports from Manila also claimed that Dewey's fleet had taken up a position in front of Manila, establishing a blockade of the port as the population started to flee. The bombardment of Manila was expected today. The *New York Times* was grandiloquent in praise of Dewey and the American Navy in its editorial "The Fleets at Manila": "The exploit of Commodore Dewey in destroying the Spanish fleet at Manila was characterized by the calm confidence of a commander . . . thoroughly acquainted with the power of the force under his command and who knew exactly how to use it. Bold and brilliant it . . . was for a commander to penetrate in the blackness of a night a harbor . . . only imperfectly known to him and . . . protected by fortifications, a numerous fleet . . . presumably by some submarine mines. But it is evident that . . . Dewey had fully measured the force to which he was opposed, and . . . knew how to meet it. The attack on the harbor of Manila was no foolhardy feat . . . but a wisely planned naval maneuver. His results might have been wholly different had the American fleet been unskillfully handled, but no one expected such. . . . The victory . . . [demonstrates] that our naval officers know what to do with our navy."

As impressive as the fleet was, American sea power would be even more impressive with more vessels. According to the *Cleveland Leader*, Ohio's Jews would raise enough money—$10,000—to purchase a warship for America. Three prominent Cincinnati Jews came to Cleveland to meet stalwart Harry Bernstein to plan for the raising of funds. Bernstein was confident that the goal could be reached by the Jews of the Fifth Ward alone: "Spain has mistreated the Jews in times past, and although the Jews are not a warlike people, they are ready and willing to fight if necessary. . . . That we will buy a warship for the Government may be stated as an assured fact. The Jews are heart and soul in sympathy with this war because they know what humanity means."

When it came to flag waving, it was hard to outdo the *New York Evening Journal*'s campaign to "float from window and housetop the American flag as a mark of our love and faith in the banner which our army and navy are upholding." The paper saluted the effort of St. Patrick's Cathedral whose "titanic" flag—40 feet long and 35 feet high—was flying 500 feet above the street. "It was flung from the [twin] church spires," said the paper, "in honor of Archbishop Corrigan's silver jubilee and as a symbol of patriotic sympathy for the brave boys who are upholding its folds at the risk of their lives upon the sea."

While the Manila victory gave the naval component of the war a stunning start, the expedition to Cuba still had no set date. With 10,000 troops already in Tampa and 6,000 due in camp before the next night, the men awaited orders. The troops now at Port Tampa were the 1st, 4th, 5th, 6th, 9th, 10th, 13th, 17th, 21st, 22nd, and 24th Infantries, all of the light batteries in the army, and the 9th and 10th Cavalry. However, since only three of the eight transports chartered by the government had arrived, the troops would not be able to leave until May 7 at the earliest.

Meanwhile, work went on equipping and organizing the new army of 186,000. The glory of being the first regiment to be mustered in belonged to an Arizona regiment of mounted riflemen under the command of Col. Leonard Wood. Reports came in from New Mexico that it would soon be mustered, and Massachusetts would be the first state east of the Mississippi to begin the process.

In the Plains, mustering was expected to begin in Sioux Falls, South Dakota. Col. Frost arrived and met 800 of the men he would command in the 8th Cavalry. Grigsby received instructions from the War Department to recruit his regiment immediately and to take five troops from South Dakota, four from Montana, two from North Dakota, and one from Nebraska.

Critics felt that setting up camp in Washington, D.C., would bring meddling by Congress. Still, Congress and the President were leaning toward a decision to set up a camp for 50 to 60 thousand men, sending an unmistakable message that a major war was underway.

The Quartermaster General's department announced it was to complete the order for 10,000 canvas uniforms for those serving in Cuba and regulation blue uniforms for the other servicemen, and the Postmaster General issued an order to set up postal service in the first Cuban port to be occupied by the United States, appointing Eben Brewer of Pittsburgh as the department's special agent to organize the plan.

Unfortunately, even though companies of colored soldiers were being recruited to the cheers of crowds, there was no concealing the fact that the Civil War was only 40 years earlier and that blacks were still treated as second-class citizens. An ugly incident unfolded in Mobile, Alabama, over payment for a bottle of soda. It involved a Negro named Lewis Reed and an unnamed member of Company K, 3rd Regiment, Alabama National Guard. Reed pulled a pistol and shot twice into the crowd. One shot hit Hugh Collins of Company K, Birmingham Rifles, in the temple, leading to his death that evening.

After the shot, Reed fled, waving his pistol in the air. Some 500 soldiers and citizens pursued him, finally spotting him under a doorstep. The potential posse was stopped as police arrived, followed by Adjt. E. W. Johnston, who drew two pistols and said that he was commissioned by Commander Higdon to have the accused arrested and given a fair trial. Reed was then put in the patrol wagon by the police. An extra detail of 40 men was assigned to the camp, and all was peaceful.

In place of a spy report is other news: The American jingoist press had played a major role in creating the climate that had led to the Spanish-American War, so, appropriately, coverage of the war was to be the most extensive in American military history. Secretary Alger announced that 145 papers were given passes permitting correspondents to accompany the army and that many other applications had not been acted upon yet. Only one female correspondent—Mrs. K. B. Watkins, representing a Toronto newspaper—was included.

5

THE LONG WAIT

WEDNESDAY, MAY 4: It was now agreed that the Spaniards had been beaten badly at Manila and Cavite. According to a correspondent of the *London Daily Telegraph*, one more such defeat could end the war: "Those who are best informed as to the Government's view allege that if the Spanish arms suffer another reverse like that of Cavite, the Government would informally request the great powers to lend their services to arrange the best possible terms of peace. Many Liberals consider that Spain, having maintained her honor and justified her chivalry, can now afford to yield to superior force, but it is doubtful whether public opinion would approve this line of action. I am assured that the Government would be content to cede Cuba to the United States, but would not be able to pay indemnity because unable. Well-informed politicians regard the war as practically terminated, and that toward the end of May it will become history. What will follow, however, it is difficult to foresee."

Europe was in a "sullen mood" about American victory in the Philippines, and rumors of intervention by Emperor William of Germany and Nicholas of Russia abounded. America barely averted an incident with France when the gunboat *Annapolis* seized the French steamer *Lafayette* near Havana after the Americans concluded that the *Lafayette* had intentionally decided to run the blockade despite warnings to desist. The Americans released the naval prize after U.S. Assistant Secretary of State John Moore and Secretary of the French Embassy Thiebaut announced that the incident was the result of miscommunication.

And a report to the *London Daily Mail* from Key West—sent via Tampa to avoid censorship—claimed that Admiral Sampson would sail for Puerto Rico either to destroy or occupy the coaling station before the Spanish fleet arrived, after which he would sail for battle with the fleet at Cape Verde.

Dewey won highest praise from the celebrated English admiral, inventor, and author Philip Howard Colomb, who told an interviewer: "I doubt if there ever was such an extraordinary illustration of the influence of sea power. A superior fleet has attacked and beaten a Spanish fleet supported by batteries and, it now appears, it passed those batteries and has taken up an unassailable position off Manila. The boldness of the American Commander is beyond question. Henceforth, he must be placed in the Valhalla of great naval commanders. Nothing can detract from the dash and vigor of the American exploit, or dim the glory which Dewey has shed upon the American navy."

The Commodore's squadron would be joined by two vessels, the *Australia* and the *City of Peking*, loaded with coal and supplies. The inclusion of troops was undecided.

While all America was proud of Dewey, Rochester, New York, boosted its own favorite son, Oscar F. Williams, U.S. Consul at Manila. During the engagements in Manila Bay, the Consul was on board Dewey's flagship, the *Olympia*. Rochester credited Williams with informing Dewey of the obstacles to overcome in the battle and the weak points in the fortification of Manila harbor, which, "may have contributed largely to his brilliant victory."

A potential hero of another kind emerged. Manhattan florist Joseph Fleischman suggested to the Secretary and Assistant Secretary of the Navy that by using a balloon at a height of 1,000 feet or more, America could greatly increase the distance that can be seen by the lookout of a war vessel from the present distance of 30 miles to the view to a minimum of 100 miles. The balloon would be fastened to the ship by a cable so that, should an approaching fleet be seen, the lookout in the balloon could communicate with the vessel and provide the opportunity for action. Gen. Carroll enthusiastically endorsed the idea.

The *New York Evening Journal* continually sought to encourage inventive genius for the war effort, so they offered $1,000 for the best new war idea. The paper was inundated by inventions of every degree of practicality. Among the ideas: a wire-bound torpedo; a bomb so powerful that it would destroy a city in a few hours; a floating bomb filled with high explosives operated by electricity; a monitor designed to destroy the entire Spanish fleet; a cigar-shaped machine propelled by either steam or electricity and provided with wings; an electrically propelled torpedo; and two raid-firing guns, one projecting from the bow, another from the stern. John J. O'Neill already had a patent for his Telegraph Transmitter, but he proposed its widespread use in the war since it was easy to send, simple to make, and accurate in every letter. He wanted the $1,000 so he could leave for the front and provide for his family of seven.

Five army officers had their names put forward by New York Gov. Black, who asked McKinley to promote them to General: Charles Roe to Maj. Gen. and Peter C. Doyle, Robert Shaw Oliver, McCookry Butt, and George Moore Smith to Brig. Gens.

Meanwhile, soldiers sweltered day and night in tents on Tampa's sand. They could not depart for Cuba until the Spanish squadron was swept from the sea, so six regiments of infantry, one of cavalry, and the light artillery were told to be patient.

At Camp Vorhees, the weather was gloomy and rainy, but spirits were high. Quartermaster Gen. Donnelly saw that two extra tents were erected on each company street. Medical examinations were administered to the 1st Regiment, under the direction of Assistant Surgeon W. C. Gorgas of the regular army. Col. Henry Allers of Harrison had the distinction of being New Jersey's first accepted volunteer.

In Connecticut, 50 Yale University athletes formed a major component of artillery recruits and became the first college company to go into camp as enlisted volunteers. Known as the 3rd Platoon, Connecticut 1st Artillery, commanded by Herbert T. Weston of Beatrice, Nebraska, they left for the state encampment at Niantic with the Connecticut state troops.

Joseph Mullady never made it through the physical examination at Camp Townshend in Peekskill. A private in Company M of the 8th Regiment, he was taken from camp and sent to the insane pavilion at Bellevue Hospital for treatment. The 28-year-old plumber from Long Island City had appeared at the tent of Surgeon Herman F. Haubold, making ludicrous statements that led the surgeon to consider him either drunk or crazy. He told the surgeon he was sentenced as a Spanish spy and would be shot at sunset. At first, Haubold placed him in a hospital tent, but his condition grew so bad that he had to be strapped down in the vehicle to Bellevue. The Surgeon concluded that the recruit had not recovered from a prior illness and that conditions at the new camp aggravated the condition.

Camp Black had its share of problems. First, Edward H. Gillespie, 18, of Albany, was caught removing money from letters. Believed to have stolen several hundred dollars before being nabbed by Corporal Van Wagnen, he was brought to New York by Secret Service men to be arraigned before the U.S. Commissioner in the Federal building. A second soldier was headed for court, to face martial law at Camp Black, as a result of a barroom brawl at Matthew's Long Island Hotel. In a drunken rage, Private Irving of the 69th Regiment bombarded the crowd with bottles and glasses, cheering the flag and opening up with rapid-fire soda bottles. One struck Private Hagelganze of the provost guard and cut his scalp. A contingent of local police was brought in and grabbed Irving. Gen. Roe said discipline would be tightened in the camp and other soldiers who had been rowdy recently would join Irving to face martial law. He repeated camp regimen: The hours of miliary exercise are from 5:25 a.m. to 5 p.m. daily.

Volunteer Isidore Weill, who later became commander of the Hebrew Veterans of the War With Spain, recalled his experiences the *Jewish Veteran*: "I enlisted in the Volunteer Signal Corps, where my services as an electrician were most useful. The War Department had no signal equipment. My captain, a West Point graduate, was dispatched to Albany, New York, to purchase . . . equipment from the National Guard. . . . A few days after I volunteered, I met . . . a distant relative, who had fled from Germany in 1848. 'I am happy that you have enlisted,' he said to me, 'as the horrors of the Spanish Inquisition are still fresh in my mind. If I were [younger, I would] sacrifice my life to free those enslaved people.'" Weill went on to point out that, in 1898, Jews made up about 1.4 percent of the entire U.S. population, yet more than 2 percent of the armed forces were Jewish. "Had . . . Jewish young men . . . known more of the expulsion of Jews from Spain . . . the [number of] Jews in the American Army would have multiplied five-fold."

THURSDAY, MAY 5: Why had Commodore Dewey filed no report? The Navy Department reasoned that after defeating the fleet and forts together, Manila must have yielded to American bombardment—perhaps a day or two's work. And a report was being prepared, to be received by week's end.

According to Naval Constructor Philip Hichborn, "Supposing that Dewey bombarded the town Monday [May 2], it may have been Tuesday before [he] . . . took possession. Then he would . . . take some time to get a boat ready to send to Hong Kong with dispatches, the presumption being that all his vessels were in action and that they were all more or less damaged. . . . [And] he could not afford to send a hastily prepared report [because it] would be necessary to compile very carefully a list of the killed and injured, all of which would take at least a day . . . it will surprise me if we hear from him by way of Hong Kong before Saturday [May 7].

With that in mind, the administration began formulating plans for the civil government of the Philippines pending the future of the islands at the close of the war.

No news was forthcoming from Sampson either. The Navy Department anticipated news comparable to the Manila triumph. Officials expected that he had carried out instructions—reducing the batteries and forts at San Juan and occupying the Puerto Rican city in a few hours—since the Spanish fleet, if it did appear, would offer little opposition.

The men at Vorhees and Townsend experienced different moods. At Vorhees no new recruits arrived for the first time since the camp opened; every company had been filled; six companies of the 1st Regiment had been examined; and there were no complaints and no grumbling as the recruits were put through very exhausting preliminary drills. At Camp Townsend, however, onlookers were distressed; something must be done, according to the *New York Times*, to prevent it from being "a disgrace to the Empire State"; shoes, stockings, underwear, shelter tents, shovels, axes, hatchets, meat cans, coffee mills, overcoats, trousers, fatigue caps, service hats, leggings, canteens, meat cups, and eating utensils were among the supplies lacking and, according to the *Times*, "many of the officers in the guard were outspoken in their condemnation of the state authorities in failing to sooner supply these necessities." Problems notwithstanding, physical examinations began. The regimental surgeons were the first to pass the inspection of the mustering-in officers. About 400 men could be examined each day, meaning the process would take 10 days. The examinations, promised the *Evening Journal*, would be "as rigid as that of any life insurance company."

Physical examinations also began at Camp Black, but the main news from Long Island was a fight between two adjoining camps: the 24th Separate Company and the 69th Regiment. Men from the 24th stood on line and called their neighbors "harps"—a derogatory term for Irishmen—and the like. In one incident, the 24th grabbed a 69th man who had on a service overcoat they swore was stolen from one of their men. A melee broke out and when the dust cleared, the 24th had the overcoat and the 69th grabbed their recruit back, sans coat.

In Ivy League news, the report from Yale was excellent, with all Yale students in the machine-gun battery—members of the state quota of volunteers in Niantic—passing the physical examination; however, at Princeton only 8 of 18 were accepted into Battery A of the Pennsylvania National Guard because, according to the commander, Barclay H. Warburton, he had no "place for them." As he told the *Princetonian*: "Every man . . . would have been acceptable if I had a place for them.

As it is, I can only send them back to their Alma Mater, and say that if we need more men, they shall be the first accepted."

FRIDAY, MAY 6: The administration did not expect news from Dewey—and received none. The House of Representatives turned its attention to the annexation of Hawaii. The majority on the Foreign Affairs Committee strongly favored the action. Michigan's William Alden Smith argued that the island was necessary for war operations and past questions of ownership in the West Indies were shortsighted and unwise.

The minority view was offered by Missouri Congressman James Clark, who reasoned that it was against our policy of territorial ownership outside the continent.

The *New York Times* spoke out strongly against annexation: "Existing conditions strengthen the argument against annexation. . . . Our ships, men of war, transports, and merchantmen can go from side to side and end to end of that vast sea without the slightest danger from what, officially, it is still necessary to call the enemy. We need no intermediate station between San Francisco and Manila or Hong Kong. But if we did . . . we should have it by the action of the Hawaiian Government, which has put the islands . . . at our disposition."

There was good news and bountiful delivery headed for Chickamauga. Two million rations—including four trainloads of bacon, hard bread, sugar, coffee, beans, salt, pepper, and vinegar, the bacon alone totalling 27 carloads weighing 900,000 pounds —would be transported to the troops from Chicago.

A near brawl erupted at Hempstead Plains as the 13th Regiment of Brooklyn inscribed their names in disgrace. When word got around of the possibilities of mass refusals to volunteer, General Headquarters issued an order directing all officers and enlisted men who "do not intend to volunteer to proceed at once to Brooklyn and report to the commanding officer of the 2nd Brigade N.G.N.Y." Realizing the possible disgrace that awaited them, the men called company meetings to air out the issues. Those advocating staying brought up "sacred duty" and the imperative to "follow the flag." Arguments on the other side included the unlikelihood of the Regiment retaining its organization and identity, hardships of family, neglect of business, and the unproven need to call the troops to service. The deserters won 330 to 220.

The vote completed, the men were ordered to pack and leave. As they filed out of camp, members of the 14th Regiment of New York and the 65th of Buffalo shouted "cowards," "traitors," "tin soldiers," and hurled bread and tin cans at them. Col. Frederic D. Grant, commander of the 14th, stepped forward and called for attention. "Now, boys," he said. "Let us show these men what good soldiers are. Fall back and remain quiet." They were quiet but not silent. Dozens of men softly whistled the "Rogues' March." The departees left, accompanied by Col. Watson. As they got on the train, the sentries, assigned so that no one could leave the camp without permission, joined for a collective jeer.

In its report, the *New York Times* painted the scene of the "Gloomy March from Long Island Station" of the group, which had grown to 350: "Gloomily, with furled flags and silent drums, what was left of the fraction of the 13th Regiment . . . left the Long Island Station . . . and marched to the armory, at Jefferson and Sumner Avenues.

. . . A sorrier and more dismal homecoming could not be imagined. . . . Not a cheer greeted them as they left the station. Not a ripple of applause sounded anywhere on the long march to the armory. Through the drizzling rain the men dejectedly jogged on, apparently not displeased that their arrival attracted no notice. A few small boys . . . ran along with the men and [even their] demeanor . . . was not as respectful and admiring as usual. . . .

"At the armory . . . at last the returning wanderers got the applause which had been denied them on the march."

In his remarks, Watson told the men and their friends: "You boys understood the question and acted as you saw fit, according to your conscience and independent preference. . . . We stand today willing to do all that is required of us to the extent of volunteering in the service of an organization, taken as it stands."

An uproar at the Lafayette Brigade on East 14th Street concerned the opposite problem—men who had enlisted and had not been sent to camp and eventual service. They complained they were being shoved into the National Guard to replace the men at the camp. Speaking for the 1st Battalion, Sgt. Henry Schmalz said, "Many of these men gave up good positions to enlist. Now they have no work and not enough money to pay their board. They cannot be blamed for this exhibition of indignation, and they will all desert if not ordered into camp at once." Maj. Washburn pacified the men by assuring them he was expecting orders to send them to camp.

Other happy folk included five Americans who arrived on the *Abudos* safely from San Juan, Puerto Rico, where they had business. Among them were the Borda family, who owned a large stock farm and a sugar-grinding plant. When hostilities broke out, Spanish soldiers were quartered on the farm, their cattle were killed, and their possessions were snatched without compensation. A friend of the Bordas, Consul Hanna, also fled to save his life.

Carl Sandburg, too, was pleased. He was 10 months short of 21 but had passed himself off as 21 to qualify for soldierhood. On this day he put on his uniform: heavy blue-wool shirt, coat of dark blue with brass buttons, pants of light-blue wool. Gen. Grant and Robert E. Lee had worn the same uniform, beamed Sandburg: "I felt honored to wear the uniform of famous Union armies. . . . I could say when asked my rank . . . 'I'm a high private in the rear rank'" (Sandburg 405).

In the sizable Jewish community of New York City, debate raged. Many felt their history with Spain, symbolized by the Inquisition and expulsion, coupled with its savagery in Cuba, was enough to condemn Spain and join in war. But Solomon Solis-Cohen reasoned that the present conflict was a war of aggression and would take its place along with the barbaric Mexican War of 1849. His traditional Jewish response was, "If thine enemy hunger, give him food, and if he thirst give him to drink." Solis-Cohen further argued, "The expulsion or ill-treatment of my fathers by . . . Spain gives me no right to murder Spaniards . . . even though I . . . march beneath a banner bearing stripes and stars."

Another pacifist, Cyrus Sulzberger, was incensed that God's name could be invoked in a war of such immoral exercise. In his article "God and War" he writes: "So long as our plowshares are made into swords and our pruning hooks into spears, it would be well to keep away from God's holy mountain. Rather than set apart occasions for prayer . . . let us close our houses of worship until we shall be cleansed . . . [and] fit to enter them."

But whether the war was barbaric or not, the soldiers deserved our concern and good deed, declared Mrs. Cyrus Sulzberger, chairman of the new auxiliary of the American National Relief Committee of the Red Cross Society formed at Temple Emanu-El to "alleviate the sufferings of the soldiers and sailors."

In the Spanish intrigue of the day, California Gov. James H. Budd was warned by a Southern California Pacific brakeman that Spaniards were plotting to kill him. According to the brakeman, three Spaniards were agitated about the Governor's organizing troops to fight Spain. While the Governor's associates were concerned, the executive made light of the incident.

SATURDAY, MAY 7: The report finally came. How sweet the victory of Dewey! The naval hero sent two dispatches: May 1 from Manila, and May 4 from Cavite. He reported that his squadron destroyed 10 vessels, a transport, and water battery. The squadron was "uninjured" and only a few were "slightly wounded." As for the Spanish toll, Dewey estimated 150 killed and 250 sick and wounded, including the Captain of the *Reina Cristina*. (Governor General of the Philippines, Gen. Augusti, later placed Spanish losses much higher, at 618.) America was in total control of the bay and could capture Manila at any time.

Dewey received his deserved reward for his "splendid achievement and over-whelming victory." The hero was now Acting Admiral. A thankful Congress might elevate him to Rear Admiral.

Washington was besides itself with joy. "Rejoicing in Washington," shouted the *New York Times* headline. "There had been flags in abundance everywhere before . . . confirmation . . . of Dewey's victory arrived. With the reception of the details . . . more flags . . . were hung out at windows."

How did Dewey do it, many wondered. Some thought he caught the Spaniards napping, ran past their batteries undetected, and poured broadsides when they were literally sleeping. "One officer thought the Spaniards had failed to keep banked fires, so that they had no steam on and could not move . . . while Dewey's ships . . . [fired] first from one side and then another," said the *Times*.

Others attributed the success to the "superb judgment" of Dewey, who "absolutely smothered the fire of the Spanish batteries and ships under the weight of his metal before they had opportunity to make any effective response." On May 3, at the golden wedding anniversary of the Admiral's brother, Charles Dewey, and his wife, the Dewey family revealed a letter from Hong Kong dated April 2. In it, Dewey said he had not slept more than an hour a night for a month to prepare the fleet for attack.

Next on the agenda for Manila, 10,000 troops would be sent to aid Dewey; 2,000 might be sent by May 12. Volunteer troops from the West, possibly Idaho and Colorado, would be attached to the army of occupation.

In Puerto Rico the administration was still looking to Admiral Sampson to bring a Dewey-like triumph at San Juan. The Key West fleet might even be in front of the San Juan harbor by tomorrow. Little opposition was expected from the Spanish, so once Cuba and Puerto Rico were attacked, the Canaries and Cadiz could be attacked until

Spain's power was dissipated.

On a much lesser scale, the cruiser *Montgomery*, under the command of Capt. Converse, drew raves for being the first warship to capture two prizes in one day. Cruising 50 miles off Havana, the *Montgomery* first captured the *Frasquito* and later the *Lorenzo*. Both were taken easily with their two cargoes of beef.

Spain had some attack power left, at least according to its dispatch. It told of the capture of the Island of Panay in the Philippines, thought to be headquarters of the insurgents against Spain. The report claimed that Panay was defended by 4,000 and that 172 were killed on the spot; 500 more while retreating.

In another battle, a report from Havana spoke of two American warships pursuing the Spanish schooner *Santiago*, bound for Yucatán with salted fish. The *Santiago* fired six shots, carrying off the smokestack and one of the masts of the lead American cruiser. One shot fell on the deck of the other cruiser.

Back home, at Camp Black, which was named for the New York Governor, there was still a bitter taste from the Brooklyn regiment that went home in disgrace. Adjt. Gen. Whitney Tillinghast made his first official visit, accompanied by Surgeon Gen. Marshall O. Terry and Maj. Burbank of the 3rd U.S. Artillery. An impressed Tillinghast observed, "It is a matter for sincere congratulation to see this great body of men, the majority of whom have never had an hour of camp life, taking so kindly to their present surroundings and keeping up so well under the disadvantages to which they have been subjected. . . . They are a sturdy, well-behaved lot of fellows and will no doubt make splendid soldiers."

Camp Vorhees, on the other hand, witnessed an ugly scene. Seven timid men of the 1st Regiment who had failed in the final muster were marched from the guardhouse to Col. Campbell's tent for further orders. Jeers and taunts greeted the downcast rejects as they walked to the tent. They were pelted with mudballs until Col. Campbell restrained the soldiers. "Now, boys," he said, "you are going with me and I am going with you, but these fellows want to stay home. Let them go there."

A heartening development at Camp Vorhees was the report of Sea Girt's probable selection as permanent headquarters for New Jersey and Pennsylvania volunteers. Toward that end, a rigid and official inspection of the camp grounds and surrounding country was made by Lieut. T. Bently Mott, aide-de-camp on the staff of Maj. Gen. Wesley Merritt.

Meanwhile, a tract of land in the vicinity of Falls Church, Virginia, was selected as a camp for 20 to 30 thousand soldiers of the volunteer army. Gen. Fitzhugh Lee was considered a top choice to command this detachment.

At the Rough Riders camp in San Antonio, Theodore Roosevelt made his dominant presence felt. Curry had impressed him by securing—through nonofficial channels—urgently needed feed for the Riders' horses. He had actually commandeered a train and ordered it ridden into the camp. With a touch of sarcasm, Roosevelt complimented Curry: "Why the hell did you wait so long to act?" The New Mexicans were awed by Roosevelt's leadership and named their mascot, a golden eagle, Teddy. Curry was superb as a supply officer and before leaving camp was promoted to Captain.

The rush to enlist was still enthusiastic throughout America: In Chicago, announcement was made of a proposed Irish brigade of three fully recruited regiments from

Chicago, Boston, and New York, and the men sought an Irish officer from the regular army who would serve as their brigadier general; the Post Office Department reported numerous applications from employees seeking leaves of absence; and at Colgate University in Hamilton, New York, triweekly drills were being held in the gymnasium for the 27-man company of students from the Theology Department.

SUNDAY, MAY 8: It was sermon Sunday, with oratory about the Spanish American War ringing from the pulpits. The Rev. Dr. R. Heber Newton delivered a sermon on "The Ethics of the War" at the All Souls' Protestant Episcopal Church at 66th and Madison in Manhattan. He said that America had assumed the role of executioner of Spain for its evil deeds.

The war was a "holy uprising," sermonized the Rev. Dr. A. E. Kittredge at the Madison Avenue Reformed Church. The issue was to eliminate the sufferings in Cuba, "a wronged and downtrodden people." The sermon called on Americans "to end the reign of brutality which for centuries has ruled over the most beautiful island in our hemisphere and . . . has caused the death of more than 200,000 women and children."

Spanish behavior had justified the war, preached the Rev. Dr. Samuel McComb at the Rutgers Riverside Presbyterian Church in Manhattan. It was a struggle of principles between America, "the home of freedom and defender of right," and Spain, which "belongs to the sixteenth century, is corrupt, moribund, eaten through and through with fraud and chicanery."

There was a positive aspect of the war for America, opined the Rev. W.F.F. Anderson of the Washington Square Methodist Episcopal Church. Above the singing of national airs, at a church decorated with the Stars and Stripes, he said, "The men of the Blue and the Gray, who once faced each other . . . with the bitterest hate . . . will now march side by side against a common foe . . . and under one battle flag . . . under . . . Gen. Lee—a confederate soldier."

With his theme "Science and God," the Rev. Henry Frank of the Metropolitan Independent Church spoke at Berkeley Lyceum: "The first great battle of the war has been fought and won. The name of Dewey is immortalized. The name of our dear old Columbia stands once more for victory and human hope."

Dewey's victory was God's doing, reflected the Rev. A. L. Beller of Washington Methodist University, filling the pulpit at Cavalry Methodist Episcopal Church. And Divine intervention would come again in the next great battle, "leading finally to the crushing defeat of Godless Spain."

The navy suffered a setback when the Spanish set a trap for two American vessels off Havana, the *Vicksburg* and the cutter *Morrill*. The Spaniards sent out a schooner, and Commander Lillie of the *Vicksburg* and Capt. Smith of the *Morrill* went in pursuit. The schooner ran for Morro Castle and led the American warships directly under the guns of the Santa Clara batteries. America's ships were battered for half an hour but had no major damage although shrapnel shells from eight-inch guns exploded all about them. Poor Spanish shooting spared the vessels from becoming another ill-fated *Maine*.

American enlistees knew that the Cuban rainy season would be an unpleasant experience, but they didn't expect horrid weather conditions in the camps. Saturday night and Sunday morning brought misery to the Eastern camps. Camp Hastings in Mt. Gretna, Pennsylvania, was in deep mud as 9,000 soldiers and recruits endured the worst weather conditions in the history of the Pennsylvania National Guard. Furious winds blew over many of the tents. The 1st Brigade lay in the lowland, and the rain turned their places into swamps. When the rain combined with the cold, thoughts of sleep disappeared. Three companies without supplies on hand went hungry all day.

The Guardsmen of the 8th Regiment shivered in the rain and dampness at Camp Townsend, with nothing but blankets on bare ground. However, the men of the 9th Regiment were better prepared because of past tours of duty at the camp. They were well prepared, as their wooden doors kept out all unwelcome elements.

The rain was relentless at Camp Vorhees. Regimental surgeons were kept busy distributing quinine. The enemy was the elements: "Not to be defeated, however, by the watery batteries from the sky," wrote the *Times*, "the boys made ready to meet the enemy. Such a driving of stakes and hasty preparation for the flood was never witnessed in a peaceful camp."

All this made the campers more anxious to leave the scene for actual warfare. They were all in tune with Captain Charles H. Jones, chaplain of the 2nd Regiment, who led a service of song and preached the motto of the regiment, "I am ready," taken from Romans I:15. The visit of U.S. Senator William J. Sewell, appointed Major General in the volunteer army, raised hopes that the day of departure might be near.

Camp Black was hit mercilessly by the storm. Soldiers spent a night of suffering and torment, many without shelter, exposed to the rain and winds. About 20 tents in each regiment were blown away. The men had no breakfast or anything warm to cheer them. The day's provisions had become soaked and unusable. The lead in the *Times* told a tale of woe: "All the elements seem to have entered into a huge conspiracy against the occupants of Camp Black, for as if the measure of their woes were not yet complete, the worst storm that Long Island has seen for many years, broke over their heads last night, and the camp this morning was the sorriest, most desolate-looking place imaginable. Tents turned inside out, great pools of water, broken beams, and tent poles were everywhere in evidence, while the men, shivering in clothing, wet through and through, hungry and sleepy, stood in groups, nestling close to each other and vainly endeavoring to protect themselves from wind and weather that chilled them to the very bone."

The storm went past dawn and into the early morning hours. This did not deter some 1,000 visitors, notably 200 from Port Jervis and 60 from Binghamton, who came to visit and cheer the men. The most touching scene was a woman from Binghamton who was very anxious about the condition of her son in the 20th Separate Company. With a heavy basket filled with provisions, she had to travel a mile in horrid conditions, marked by gullies and ankle-deep mud. "Well, this is pretty tough," she said, "but that poor boy of mine had it worse last night, and I've at least brought him some fresh socks."

MONDAY, MAY 9: No major naval battles were fought today. The conclusion concerning Admiral Sampson's fleet was that no engagement had taken place. It was reasonable to assume that the fleet was lying quietly at the Canary Islands or at Cadiz.

The battleship *Oregon* arrived at Bahía, Brazil, drawing comments that a part of Sampson's mission would be to protect that ship.

With America still basking in the Dewey triumph, Secretary Long released the text of the orders sent to Dewey on April 24: "War has commenced between the United States and Spain. Proceed at once to Philippine Islands. Commence operations at once, particularly against the Spanish fleet. You must capture the vessels or destroy them. Use utmost endeavors."

The victors would be rewarded with medals and a lucrative bounty. According to Section 4.635 of the Revised U.S. Statutes, each man would receive $100 in bounty for each person on board any "vessel of war belonging to an enemy at the commencement of an engagement which is sunk or otherwise destroyed . . . by any [U.S.] ship or vessel." Under the statute, the men and officers of the Asiatic Squadron would receive an estimated $185,000, with Dewey receiving one-twentieth of the sum, or approximately $9,300.

Congress adopted a vote of thanks to Dewey and his men on the recommendation of President McKinley. A bill was passed increasing the number of Rear Admirals from six to seven to accommodate a promotion for Dewey. Massachusetts Republican Senator Henry Cabot Lodge introduced a resolution that Dewey be given a sword of honor. And McKinley released a message: "On the 24th of April I directed the Secretary of the a to telegraph orders to Commodore George Dewey [commander] of . . . the Asiatic Squadron, then lying in the port of Hong Kong, to proceed forthwith to the Philippine Islands, there to commence operations and engage the assembled Spanish fleet. Promptly obeying that order, the . . . squadron, consisting of the flagship *Olympia*, *Baltimore*, *Raleigh*, *Boston*, *Concord*, and *Petrel*, with the revenue cutter *McCullough*, as an auxiliary dispatch boat, entered the harbor of Manila at daybreak on the first of May and immediately engaged the entire Spanish fleet."

Assistant Secretary of the Navy Theodore Roosevelt became Lt. Col. Roosevelt and all bureaus, some reporting with all their members present, stopped by his office to bid him farewell and best of luck with the Rough Riders. Many of the employees joined in presenting him with a very impressive silver-mounted cavalry sabre, which he proudly showed well-wishers coming by his office.

Having been mustered into U.S. service, Roosevelt and a group of 31 left Washington with travel rations from the U.S. Subsistence Department. A group of Rough Riders, 280 strong, were waiting at their Riverside Park Camp in San Antonio. According to observers, "a hardier, handier lot never set foot in stirrup." The Arizona group came first, with 30 half-broken animals from Fort Sam Houston.

Activities were underway assembling an army capable of capturing and holding the island of Cuba. The right number was 50 to 60 thousand: larger would be unwieldy; fewer would not be successful. The War Department was busy sending messages to the camps to find out how quickly the volunteers could be mustered and moved to Chickamauga, the rendezvous nearest Port Tampa, from which the army would sail to Cuba. One army officer later commented, "Napoleon took two years to get together transports for the . . . 100,000 men with which he proposed to invade England, and we were expected to get together transports for . . . 50,000 men in two weeks."

To clarify plans, Secretary Alger announced the three points where the greatest number of troops would be received, each point having a distinct purpose. The first regiments mustered in and ready for service would go to Chickamauga to be licked into shape and would then proceed to Tampa, New Orleans, and Galveston before embarking for Cuba; the second division of regiments would leave for Washington and form a grand reserve, ready to reinforce the Cuban Army or man American coast defenses as needed; and group three would remain in their respective states, available for call to the Philippines or for general reserve assignments.

Unfortunately, confusion seemed imminent at Tampa, where it was announced that Gen. Wade would replace Gen. William Shafter. The change was necessitated by law: Since both were stationed at the same camp, both became Major Generals on the same day, but Gen. Wade, having served longer, would take over the command. The officers' staffs were demoralized because every department would have to undergo great change.

In other news of the day America would receive "unexpected" assistance in battling Spain. The *New York Journal* headlined the story "Noble Red Men Will Fight Dons," reporting how, instead of battling the government on the frontier, Big Hump of the Sioux offered the War Department himself and 600 trained warriors for service in Cuba. If he and his men were landed, they could aid the insurgents in seizing Havana. The Cherokees, experienced as U.S. warriors from the Civil War, were also available.

Famous names on the list of nominees whose appointments as officers in the volunteer army were sent to the Senate by the President included: John Jacob Astor, the only son of wealthy financier William B. Astor, for Inspector General with the rank of Lieutenant Colonel; Charles A. Whittier, a wealthy merchant and relative of poet John Greenleaf Whittier, for Inspector General; and former New York City Police Commissioner Avery D. Andrews for Chief Commissary of Subsistence with rank of Lieutenant Colonel.

Finally, reports of smiles at Camp Townsend! The sun shone beautifully and the day was enhanced by visits from wives, mothers, and sweethearts. The day was nearly destroyed when 51 men, rejected at their physical examinations, lined up to be sent home. The other soldiers, thinking the group were quitters, began beating on tin basins, whistling the "Rogues' March," and slinging mud. Order and harmony were quickly restored when the truth became known. The rejected and depressed patriots received a resounding cheer from their fellows.

Msgr. Giovanni Martinelli, the Apostolic Delegate in Washington, released a cablegram from the Vatican expressing concern over the Pope's alleged bias to Catholic Spain: "Some journals, especially English, are diffusing insinuations, with regard to the Holy See, in the present Spanish-American conflict as though the Holy See were taking the part of one or the other of the conflicting parties. It is superfluous to deny such foolish talk; the perfectly proper attitude which the Holy See has maintained and will maintain toward the two nations being known to all; the Holy See has no other desire than that for peace."

6

ON THE WAY!

TUESDAY, MAY 10: Movement to Cuba was finally under way. The first invasion force left Tampa on the steamer *Gussie* at 2 p.m., with an expected landing on the northern coast. Commanded by Adjt. Gen. Joseph Dorst, the force—whose numbers were not pinpointed—consisted of Companies E and G of the 1st Infantry. They were accompanied by a full medical corps with two hospital nurses and four medical assistants. The two companies guarded a cargo of munitions: On board were 7,000 rifles and 200,000 rounds of ammunition bound for the Cuban army in Pinar del Rio.

At first, the force would be small, 10 to 12 thousand. However, the number would jump in a short time to 50,000 regulars, as Maj. Nelson Miles announced he would leave the Tampa front on the following day. The increased hurry and haste was evident in the office of Adjt. Gen. Corbin. Telegrams were going out *to* governors and mustering officers pleading for haste in the preparation of troops of the National Guard while telegrams *from* governors and mustering officials in other states, detailing the progress of the enlistment of the volunteer army, were flooding the office.

Maj. Gen. Brooke, commander of the U.S. regular provisional army corps at Chickamauga Park, received orders from the War Department directing him to send all 6,000 cavalry and infantry troops currently at Chickamauga to Tampa, posthaste.

Calling itself the first state to have all its volunteers mustered in, Minnesota was also the first regiment mustered in. According to telegrams received from Washington by Capt. Swogert, mustering-in officer at Camp Ramsey, and Col. Bobleter, senior colonel in charge of the brigade; "Minnesota troops will be sent to Tampa on the instant they are uniformed and armed."

Several other states received orders from Secretary Alger: Massachusetts Gov. Wolcott was to send his state troops to Chickamauga rather than Camp George H. Thomas; Illinois Gov. John R. Tanner was to dispatch two regiments of infantry, one regiment of cavalry, and a light battery to New Orleans no later than noon on May 12; and Wisconsin Gov. Edward Schofield was told to direct the 3rd Wisconsin Regiment to Tampa instead of to Chickamauga.

U.S. mustering officer Captain Schuyler announced that the 71st Regiment in Camp Black would be the first New York regiment to go to Chickamauga. The 14th Regiment would probably be second.

While the Cuban land invasion moved ahead, the Sampson plan was placed on hold. "Official information has been received that four Spanish cruisers and three torpedo boat destroyers have returned to Cadiz," read a State Department cable. Sampson had orders to seek out and destroy the Spanish fleet—hopefully at or near San Juan—but not to go to Cadiz. The alternative now was to reduce the San Juan fortifications and render the harbor useless to the enemy in the event that the entire Spanish naval force advanced toward Cuba.

Adjt. Corbin received reports that 35,354 men from 13 states had been mustered into the volunteer army. Despite the totals, the army medical corps voiced concern about the large number of rejections due to heart trouble attributed to cigarette smoking. Dr. Benjamin King of Philadelphia, who was an examining surgeon in several Eastern states during the Civil War, noted, "most of the men who failed to pass the medical examination have weak hearts or lack the vitality necessary to make a good soldier."

Lt. Col. Roosevelt was hoping the Rough Riders could go with the first expedition to Cuba. It all depended on how soon the men received their equipment. Meanwhile, Maj. Gen. William Sewell, who was assigned to command the camp near Falls Church, Virginia, was facing the possibility of having to give up his tenure as a U.S. Senator, and Maj. Gens. Fitzhugh Lee, Joseph Wheeler, and John Wilson, who were all assigned to Chattanooga under Gen. Brooke, faced tough decisions in appointing their staffs. The popular Lee, for example, had 20 applications for every staff opening.

Chaplain Eugene Griffin, First Vice President of the General Electric Company, announced the opening of a recruiting office in Schenectady, New York, for those mechanics, practical electricians, artisans, and line and construction men wishing to sign up in the volunteer engineer brigade. Part of the brigade would go with the invading army to Cuba; the remainder would be used in coast defense work.

The House Committee on Foreign Affairs voted 10 to 4 on the resolution of Nevada's Democratic Congressman Francis Newlands to "Annex Hawaii." Mississippi's Democratic Congressman John Williams offered a substitute resolution of independence, which was voted down. The majority felt a protectorate involved more cost, more responsibilities, and more complications.

Praises for Admiral Dewey filled newspaper columns. The *Baltimore American*, a newspaper serving a black readership, featured a poem: "Dewey, When Yo' Comin' Home?"

> Mistah Dewey, like to know
> When yo' comin' home?
> Reckon day yo' mus' go slow,
> When yo' comin' home?
> Sence de startin' ob dis war
> Yo' is mighty popular,

Name yo' got done traveled far—
When yo' comin' home? . . .

Mistah Dewey, yo' has spunk,
When yo' comin home?
Made dem Wienerwurstes shrunk,
When yo' comin' home?
Made dem Phillupeeners tame,
Made dem fo'iners walk lame,
Made Ol' Glory glad she came–
When yo' comin' home?

Mistah Dewey, ef yo' please,
When yo' comin' home?
Swung dat banner to de breeze
When yo' comin home?
Ef dey 'sists to get too gay,
Nail it to de mast to stay,
Den just telyfone an say
When yo' comin home?

The Christian temper of the war was noted twice on this day: at a convention of the Protestant Episcopal Church and in a plea by the International Medical Missionary Society. The keynote speaker at the 114th annual convention of the Protestant Episcopal Church told the audience, "The [U.S.] is at war with Spain. I believe it is a just cause. . . . [T]o put an end to unspeakable barbarities practiced under the name of government. . . . [As] our people demanded the . . . powers of Europe should [have done] for Armenia, and which we censure them for not doing."

Those who choose to minister to the sick and wounded servicemen ought to be devout Christians, claimed the International Medical Missionary Society, noting in its appeal for missionaries for the Army and Navy Hospital Corps that it had formed special committees to examine and train men, provide Christian literature and varied supplies, and fund the operation.

WEDNESDAY, MAY 11: Spain would not be so thickheaded to try to regain the Philippines by using its squadron now at Cadiz, analyzed the Navy Department. To do so, Spain would have to move its entire fleet to the Philippines and expose it to American assault. Once fortified with the *Charleston* and *Philadelphia* and 10,000 troops, Dewey would overcome any Spanish effort. If Spain were reckless, Commodore Schley would seize upon the vulnerable Spanish ports.

Dewey's squadron had nothing new to report, but those wounded in the Manila battle received dainties such as clam juice, lemons, jellies, and beef extract, purchased via the Surgeon General with monies contributed by the National Relief Association of the National Society of Colonial Dames of America.

America experienced its first loss during the conflict. The torpedo boat *Winslow* entered the harbor at Cárdenas and was met by fire from an enemy gunboat and light guns on shore. The revenue cutter *Hudson* towed the disabled *Winslow* out of the harbor. One line officer and four enlisted men were killed.

President McKinley and Secretary Long were distressed at the news that *Winslow* Ensign Worth Bagley and others—unidentified—were killed and that the *Winslow* was badly crippled. America did not have a large supply of torpedo vessels.

The only other violent death at sea during the war was also connected with a torpedo boat. Ensign Breckinridge was swept from the deck of the *Cushing* during a trip from Key West to Havana.

While the administration felt Lieut. Bernadon should have exercised better judgment than wandering into enemy territory, he would not be censured for his daring spirit. Life is dangerous and lonely on a torpedo boat, wrote the *New York Times*: "The men and officers cannot escape the stuffy little rooms . . . the noise of the engines, and the [constant] vibration. . . . It is a relief . . . to be engaged in a brush with the enemy, but the vessels . . . are liable to serious accidents from stray projectiles."

Back home, impatience hovered over Tampa. The men still there were no closer to leaving for Cuba than yesterday or the day before. Officers were heard saying, "If we ever go." The latest news was that May 15 would be the earliest departure. The men were tired of hearing *mañana*. They were anxious, and they could not be asked to be stoical in the face of camp conditions. Tampa was not a resort in May. The heat and glare were torturous, and there was no shade at the artillery and cavalry camps and only little at the infantry camps. Even Cubans agreed that conditions would be better in Havana.

Looking for answers to the delay of the invasion, analysts pointed to the army's lack of readiness. The issue was not just landing in Cuba and taking on the men of Blanco. Perhaps a greater enemy was the potential ravage of sickness and disease, and the army did not have adequate supplies of hammocks and tents, rubber blankets, canvas uniforms, and other tropical paraphernalia. The Surgeon General of the Navy had already received a report, from the surgeon of the gunboat *Vicksburg*, that there were five suspected cases of yellow fever aboard the captured *Aragonaufa*. (It turned out to be ephemeral fever, endemic in West Indian latitudes.)

It was expected that Gen. Nelson Miles, commanding the army, would arrive in Tampa by May 13, accompanied by clerks and a great mass of papers, charts, and logistic materials already packed in his trunks. His most distinguished companion would be Lieut. Col. A. L. Wagner, chief of the Bureau of Military Information, a premier authority on military movement and military armament and author of a widely used book on tactics.

In the meantime, New York Gov. Black was telegrammed by Secretary Alger to dispatch two state regiments to Tampa immediately, the assumption being that they would go to Cuba with the first expedition.

The men at Camp Black, knowing that six regiments would go to Chickamauga and Washington, continued to watch the bulletin board for assignment. While the men waited, they were assured of better treatment, thanks to a good fairy, Mrs. Charles F. Roe, wife of Maj. Gen. Roe. When she heard of shortages at the camp, she approached J. Pierpont Morgan, who said, "Just send me the bill. Get the boys what they need." The men of the 69th Regiment received 200 gray woolen shirts, 200 suits of thick underclothing, and 200 pairs of stockings.

The mood was upbeat at Fort McPherson in Atlanta, where the day's highlight was the visit to the post barber by 16 prisoners of war, starting with Gen. Weyler's brother-in-law, Col. Cortejo, who grunted and scowled at what they considered an indignity. But by day's end, all were clean-shaven and well groomed.

In South Carolina's capital, Columbia, people jammed the streets to cheer the soldiers marching to service. Wrote the *Record* of Columbia: "At last the troops of this state have been put on the march, and if all are to be of the kind that came yesterday, no one need fear for an instant that the glory of the [state] flag . . . will be tarnished in the slightest degree. . . . Yesterday was unquestionably the most eventful day in Columbia since . . . the '60s. Old veterans—some minus a leg, some carrying an empty coat sleeve—stood by to see the boys pass, and their war spirit rose until their friends hardly recognized them."

A very practical offer was made by Gen. Roy Stone, director of the Road Inquiry Bureau of the Agricultural Department. His offer of service was advanced by Gen. Miles because it was imperative that the armies of invasion and occupation be fully equipped with supplies and the most up-to-date machinery for the construction of roads and railroads and also be fully versed in the use of such machinery and construction.

No one, however, was excited about the offer of New York magnate O.H.P. Belmont, who was willing to build and equip a torpedo boat for government use during the conflict. Without intending any comment on the donor, the Navy Department said no because Belmont stipulated that he himself command the boat. That was against precedent and smacked of privateering.

In another story of sabotage, an unidentified man, seen by members of the 19th Infantry, was trying to poison the creek that served as the water supply at the Mobile, Alabama, camp. The man escaped and was still unnamed and unapprehended.

THURSDAY, MAY 12: The death aboard the *Winslow* was quickly avenged by the cruiser *Wilmington*. The ship shelled the battery that fired on the *Winslow* and then directed its fire to other forts and to the town of Cárdenas. In the first Spanish battery, 113 bodies were found. Some 300 Spanish died in the bombing of Cárdenas. Not one Spanish shell hit the *Wilmington*.

In the Philippines, Dewey waited for another possible challenge. According to special dispatches from Madrid, 40,000 reserves have been ordered to rejoin the Spanish Army and a major expedition was being organized for the Philippines.

Meanwhile, a dispatch to the *New York Times* from Singapore read: "The Philippine refugees here are preparing a congratulatory address to Rear Admiral Dewey. They also express a desire for the establishment of a native Government and for American protection. They deprecate the restoration of the Philippines to Spain or the transfer of the islands to any Continental Government."

Gen. Wesley Merritt was the man of the hour, having been named to command the invasion of the infantry upon the Philippines and having assumed the title of Governor General of the Philippines. In conjunction with this expedition, the Navy Department sent the *Charleston*—a protected cruiser of 3,730 tons displacement, built of steel, with 8 guns mounted in her main battery, under the command of Capt. Henry Glass— on a relief mission to Dewey's fleet in Manila.

Concern—perhaps unjustified—focused on the Eastern United States. Spanish torpedo boats were now off the New England coast, according to reports received by Assistant Secretary of Navy Charles Allen. Himself a Massachusetts man, the newly appointed Allen had many offers of assistance from New Englanders. To meet the possible threat, the Navy Department assigned monitors and vessels of the mosquito fleet to patrol the coast and alert Commodore Schley's squadron at Hampton Yards.

The concerns took on more alarming tones when the British ship *Menantic* reported foreign torpedo-boat destroyers hovering about the coast off Nantucket Shoals. Some officers believed U.S. cruisers might have been mistaken for Spanish vessels. *Menantic* officers and Admiral Erben, commander of the Atlantic Coast patrol system, were, however, convinced that the vessels were Spanish and that the Atlantic Coast was threatened. Erben met with *Menantic* Capt. Alfred J. Mann. Later, the Navy Department communicated with all commanding officers regarding the fortification and harbor defenses on the coast. Contact mines were laid in the harbor to protect New York.

Perhaps Spanish treachery was on the minds of the administration in light of the George Dowlings alias Rawlings case. Arrested on May 8, accused of spying for Spain, he was discovered hanged in the Washington Barracks with a towel and silk handkerchief. A native of England, Dowlings, 33, had been a yeoman on the *Brooklyn* before being discharged on suspicion of disloyalty and because he could not get along with his mates. Vowing revenge, he came to Washington, where it was alleged he communicated with a Spanish attaché who employed him to provide information for Spanish Consul Polo.

Chief Wilkie of the U.S. Secret Service suspected Dowlings and traced him to Toronto, where he had turned over information to a member of the former Spanish Legation in Washington. His letter addressed to Montreal promising further information was intercepted. A search of his room revealed added evidence, leading to his arrest. On May 11 Dowlings broke down and spoke of his impending trial, certain conviction, and lack of friends. He collapsed completely and wept. He became calm after a talk with the commander of the barracks, who said he would allow him to write to his mother in England. He was under continued surveillance and was last seen reading a magazine on his cot. He was discovered hanging from a bar across the top of his cell. The knot was just below the ear, done with the expertise of a professional hangman.

The mood at Camp Vorhees was genial. It was a beautiful spring day, and hope reigned that the men would move on May 13. A first was recorded when the Young Men's Christian Association erected a tent within the lines of the 2nd Regiment. It was the first tent at Vorhees dedicated to religious purposes and was supplied with books, papers, and pamphlets.

7

ATTACK ON SAN JUAN

FRIDAY, MAY 13: In terms of action, this day matched the action although not the excitement of the battle at Manila. Admiral Sampson led an attack on San Juan, trying to intercept the Spaniards. To reduce the means of defense should the Spanish arrive, he bombarded the city. Among the casualties were one killed and four seamen wounded on the USS *New York*. Among the wounded was Comrade Samuel Feldman, who remained confined for decades to the Brooklyn Naval Hospital.

"Is America any better than Spain?" asked Chaplain George W. Prioleau in a letter to H. C. Smith, editor of the *Cleveland Gazette* (Gatewood 27–29), relating the treatment of the black regulars in the South en route to Cuba. The letter spoke of the dedication of "these sable sons of Ham," the men of the 9th, 24th, and 25th infantries and eight batteries of artillery.

"The American Negro," said the chaplain, "is always ready and willing to take up arms, to fight and to lay down his life in defense of his country's flag and honor. All the way from northwest Nebraska this regiment was greeted with cheers and hurrahs. . . . While the 9th Cavalry would play some national air, people would raise their hats . . . wave their handkerchiefs; and the heavens would resound with their hearty cheers. The white hand shaking the black hand."

The cheers stopped at Nashville and remained silent at Chattanooga. Hadn't segregation ended? wondered the chaplain: "[T]here was not a cheer given us, the people living in gross ignorance, rags and dirt. . . . Had we been greeted like this all the way . . . there would have been many desertions before we reached this point."

As cold as the reception was in Tennessee, it did not compare to the prejudice encountered in Tampa. The white chaplain was outraged: "Here, the Negro is not allowed to purchase over the same counter in some stores that the white man purchases over. The Southerners have made their laws and the Negroes know and obey them. . . . You talk about freedom . . . fighting [to free] poor Cuba and of Spain's brutality; of Cuba's murdered thousands, and starving reconcentrados. . . . Has [America] not subjects in her very midst who are murdered daily without a trial . . . whose children are half-fed and half-clothed, because their father's skin is black? . . . He is a noble creature, loyal and true. . . . Forgetting that he is ostracized . . . considered as dumb as driven cattle . . . he answers the call to arms with blinding tears in his eyes."

SATURDAY, MAY 14: Three American warships battled several thousand Spanish troops at Cienfuegos and San Juan. Attacking with only a portion of his fleet, Sampson withdrew after three hours of fighting and headed for Key West. He did not capture San Juan, but that was not his intent. His goal: "Administer punishment," which he did to the forts and the city. One American sailor, Frank Widemark, was killed, and seven were injured.

The navy received two cables: From St. Thomas, Sampson wrote, "The attack lasted about three hours and resulted in much damage to the batteries and . . . the portion of the city adjacent to the batteries. The batteries replied to our fire, but without material effect." Expressing satisfaction from the *Iowa*, mighty Sampson exulted, "I am satisfied with the morning's work. I could have taken San Juan, but I have no force to hold it. I only wanted to administer punishment. This has been done. I came for the Spanish fleet and not for San Juan."

From the Associated Press dispatch boat *Dauntless* came this report: "The remarkable feature of the bombardment . . . was the bad marksmanship of the Spanish gunners. Hardly a shot from the forts struck the ships, while the forts were hit repeatedly. Most of the Spanish projectiles fell very wide."

Under fire from several thousand Spanish troops, three American warships—the cruiser *Marblehead*, gunboat *Nashville*, and auxiliary *Windom*—cut the cable connecting Santiago and Havana. Seaman Patrick Regan of the *Marblehead* was killed; six others received serious injuries; two might never recover. The task was carried out by volunteers who responded to the calls of the ships' captains, Maynard of the *Marblehead* and Lieut. Cameron Winslow of the *Nashville*. Both were wounded in the fighting.

The Navy Department was busy planning the next moves, which would involve both Sampson and Schley. They would join forces to confront the Spanish warships in West Indian waters, a naval battle that could end the war.

The Spanish squadron was sighted near Martinique, 600 miles from Puerto Rico and from Sampson, who was at Puerto Plata, a small seaport on the northern Dominican coast. The impatient Schley felt frustrated in being out of the action, so when he got the command at 3:45 to leave Hampton Roads, he hastened out before the administration could change its mind. He left aboard the flagship *Brooklyn*; the *New Orleans* and *Minneapolis* remained behind for further orders.

Schley's orders were sealed. Even without any help, Sampson's fleet could overcome the Spanish squadron, as long as they were out of reach of fortifications. Still, Sampson's fleet was slower than the Spanish squadron, and Schley's men could make it easier to corner the Spaniards and force the battle.

So what were the Spaniards planning? The cruiser *St. Paul*, Capt. Charles D. Sigsbee commanding, was sent to overtake Schley's squadron and give him the latest movement on the Spanish fleet. The consensus was that if the enemy sailed into any

Cuban port, they would be overmatched by the Americans. But Admiral Pascual Cervera could try to decoy Sampson to Puerto Rico, then move to Havana and wipe out the ships left there. Or, most undesirably, once he learned that two squadrons were in pursuit, the Spaniard would sail for Charleston and bombard the Southern port.

Naval strategists huddled throughout the day. Had Sampson overtaken the Spanish vessels or resumed the blockade of Havana? They concluded that Schley would be heard from next in Havana and he would then proceed toward the east as far as Cárdenas to alert the blockading vessels of the approach of Spanish warships. This would seem logical given reports that Sampson was not headed for Havana but keeping to the south of Haiti and onto the track of the Spanish warships.

What was happening in Tampa? Gen. Joe Wheeler arrived to assume command of the cavalry forces in the army of invasion. He set up headquarters in the Tampa Bay Hotel. Meanwhile, an amazed 71st New York regiment and 2nd Massachusetts regiment wondered why they were not heading there. By midday they were on board the steamships *City of Washington*, *Seneca*, *Vigilancia*, and *Saratoga*, anchored in the Bay off Liberty Island, destinations—uncertain!

The supposedly "official" reason for the delay in heading toward Tampa was that Admiral Erben had notified the navy that Spanish vessels were off the coast. That being so, it would be unwise to dispatch troopships to sea without convoys. Since plans were suspended, Gen. Miles postponed his departure for Tampa to take command of the army in the field.

A magnificent ceremony at Camp Townsend mustered in the men of the 12th Regiment New York Volunteers. The campgrounds, wrote the *New York Times*, "have never been . . . a more impressive sight. . . . The sun shone brightly, the lawn . . . was like a carpet of green velvet . . . contrasting [with] . . . the blue of the uniforms and the bright toilets of the many women who graced the occasion. . . . Not a man . . . wavered; there was not a backslider . . . each one is anxious to see active service and do his best . . . to upholding the honor of his country."

Nobody knew for sure where and when, but according to Recruiting Headquarters, by the end of next week, all regiments of the National Guard at Camp Black would be mustered into the Federal volunteer army. The glory lost some edge by several incidents: Edward Rock and Burt Lyons of the 9th Separate Company of Whitehall, both 22, passed their physicals and then refused to enlist. Rock even told the physician he suffered from shortness of breath, heart palpitations, and so on. Reported the physician, "From this man's statement it seems he has not been well for years. It is [my] opinion that it is a simple case of cowardice." Lyons conceded to the Captain that he was fearful of fighting in Cuba; Rock delightedly said he had failed the physical, but his face flushed when he saw the physician's report. First Sgt. John Hobson was told by his superior to "cut the buttons off these men's uniforms before they further disgrace them," after which the Captain roared in disgust, "Now, get out of my sight, you damned cowards."

In contrast, 12 other men of the same company were in near tears because they failed their physicals. After begging for a reexamination, Capt. Greenburgh interceded, but they failed again. Most notable, Quartermaster Sgt. Clarence A. Jillson, had been a member of the company 17 years but was now slightly deaf.

The Jewish community continued to debate the war's wisdom, as reflected in the *American Hebrew*. Charles Brand was distressed that an article, "An Unholy War," in the previous issue, might be taken as mirroring "the feelings of the Jews." How dare Dr. Cohen compare the present conflict to the Mexican war? "The object" of the Mexican war, he reminded, "was to entrench slavery more firmly in our country, whilst the Cuban war is waged to release the suffering inhabitants of the Island of Cuba."

Solis-Cohen had agreed that the Cubans deserved liberty and independence, but they should fight to achieve it; Americans should not "interfere." Mr. Brand's response would be echoed by world Jewry 50 years later during the Holocaust: Fifteen years earlier, hundreds of thousands of Russian Jews were forced to flee their homeland in the face of the Czar's savagery, as the world watched and did not interfere. "I well remember with what shame and despair the Jews of the world recognized the apathy of the civilized powers . . . if [only] Germany had . . . said to Russia, 'Hold! You have no right to drive these people from their homes . . . to curtail their liberty, confiscate their property, and violate their most sacred feelings.' [I doubt] that if Dr. S. Solis-Cohen had been . . . in Germany, he would have said, 'The Jews are entitled to their liberty . . . but it would be a monstrous crime to shed one drop of German blood.' No! No! . . . no Jew, or for that matter no liberty-loving Christian would have ever subscribed to such unholy, unpatriotic sentiments."

According to Sam Greenbaum, Dr. Cohen has misread history; Spain will never listen to reason. As for the Bible's admonition, "Thou shalt not kill," Greenbaum rebuffs Cohen because the prohibition is only in relations between individuals: "Standing on the platform of justice, of truth, [the Jew] can give but one answer to his country's call."

The last words of fireman G. B. Meek of the *Winslow*, killed during the bombardment of Cárdenas on May 11, were "Tell them I died like a man." It became a song, written by Paul West, composed by Monroe H. Rosenfeld, and sung by Leona Lewis:

> On *Cárdenas'* sunny bay
> In the thickest of the fray,
> Was the *Winslow*, fighting bravely, but in vain.
> For the foeman aimed too well
> Every shot and every shell,
> But still the Yankee showed her teeth to Spain
> Then we heard a sudden cry:
> "Help us! Save us, or we die!"
> Upon her deck had burst a murderous shell.
> And we saw her heroes fall,
> But above the noise and all
> Came a moan from one poor lad as he fell.
>
> [Chorus:]
> Tell them I died like a man!
> That I fell in the battle's van!
> Tell them not to grieve or cry.
> I was not afraid to die
> 'Twas my turn and I died like a man!

As we drew our boats away,
Torn and bleeding there he lay—
By his side were other comrades gone to rest.
In the flag he loved so well
Did we wrap him where he fell.
And crossed his wounded hands upon his breast.
Ne'er again will call to arms
Summon him to war's alarms.
His soul has gone to seek its rest on high.
And when other heroes fall
Answ'ring to their country's call.
That brave lad's words will cheer them as they die.

SUNDAY, MAY 15: Sunday papers were filled with attention-grabbing, "mendacious" news. There were reports of mysterious firings in Provincetown, Massachusetts. Another report spoke of the capture of the *Yale*, a U.S. auxiliary cruiser formerly known as the American line steamer *Paris*; the Associated Press, however, reported that the *Yale* had arrived at St. Thomas in the Danish West Indies.

The Navy wondered when super seamen Sampson and Schley would join to close in on Spain's warships. Schley and his four-vessel squadron arrived in Charleston, South Carolina, and the U.S. torpedo boat *Porter* and the storeship supply sailed to join Sampson's squadron near Haiti. The Navy Department hoped the *Oregon*, *Marietta*, and *Buffalo* would join them as well.

One of those wounded at Cienfuegos, Ernest Suntzenich, a seaman first class on the *Marblehead*, died in the Marine Hospital in Key West. Shot through his left leg while helping cut a cable, he died after the limb was amputated. His father said Ernest liked fighting Spain.

The Queen Regent of Spain asked Señor Sagaste to form a new ministry after all her Cabinet members resigned. No one considered the changes part of a peace initiative; in fact, the new Cabinet was expected to prosecute the war with added vigor. The Spanish fleet was at Curacao. The *Maria Teresa* and *Vizcaya*, with coal, provisions, and medicines, were admitted to the port; *Almirante Oquemdo* and *Cristobal Colón* waited outside.

The Manila blockade continued to be effective and was expected to bring an early surrender. Dewey filed this dispatch: "Maintaining strict blockade. Reason to believe the rebels are hemming in the city by land, but have made no demonstration. Scarcity of provisions in Manila. Probable the Spanish Governor will be obliged to surrender soon. Can take Manila at any moment. On May 12 captured gunboat *Callao*, attempting to run blockade."

The ground forces for the Manila expedition remained at the Presidio camp in San Francisco; the 3,000 men, drenched by an all-out night rain that made the camp an ocean of mud, continued to endure. The *City of Peking* and steamers *Australia*, *City of Sydney*, and *Ohio* were being readied for use as transports. Gen. James A. Smith, commander of the 1st Cavalry, was ordered to leave on the *City of Peking* on May 16, but an inadequate supply of arms and general field equipment made it impossible.

The woeful state of affairs among Manila's populace was reported by the Associated Press. People were reduced to eating horseflesh. The insurgents asked Dewey for permission to attack the city. He agreed, as long as there were no atrocities. When told they had few arms except machetes, he responded, "Help yourselves at the Cavite Arsenal."

Conditions in Havana were as pitiful as those in Manila, if not more so. When the American gunboat *Machias* captured two fishing boats off Havana and offered them money for their catch, the Cubans said they preferred bread because they were starved. The reconcentrados and rebels had been expelled from the cities to die in the suburbs.

The situation was also described by a Havana refugee, a surgeon in the Spanish Army before the war, who was visiting New York. All hospitals and asylums were filled with Spanish sick, stricken especially with *palodismo*, a Cuban malarial fever. Except for packages marked Red Cross, all food and medicines intended for reconcentrados were seized by the Spanish Army.

Our soldiers in the northeast were not faring that well themselves. The weather had been cruel during May, and it was no better on this Sunday. Thousands of visitors to Camp Vorhees fought their way through mud and ankle-deep water. The all-day rain depressed Camp Black's soldiers and visitors. The weather, however, did not diminish the elation of three wedding ceremonies celebrated by Chaplain Daly of the 69th Regiment. The couples were John J. Keely of Company D and Margaret G. Ensko of Third Avenue, Manhattan; Edward S. Brown of Company K and Birdie Nelson of Granite, Maryland; and Michael Murray of Company C and Mary Foley of 87th Street, Manhattan. As wedding presents, the couples were granted 24-hour honeymoons. The Browns and Murrays went to Hempstead; the Keelys to Garden City.

Utah's 85 Rough Rider recruits arrived at Fort Russell and were mustered in by Col. John Q. Cannon, later to become Lieutenant-Colonel of the regiment as Captain of Company I of the 2nd Volunteer cavalry. Like the other Rough Riders, they were unequalled in military history. According to Utah Volunteers: "As horsemen, they were the equals, if not superiors, of the Mongolian Tartars, who had been bred to the saddle for, perhaps, 10,000 years . . . as marksmen they surpassed the Parthian horsemen in effectiveness, and the Balearic slingers in accuracy."

The Spanish-American War put a premium on the nonprofessional soldier. From the start, President McKinley realized the professional army of fewer than 30,000 could not defeat Spain. In the words of Gerald E. Linderman (*The Mirror of War*), "the hometown National Guard company became the prism [through] which many Americans viewed and interpreted the . . . War."

Officers and soldiers viewed themselves as representatives of their communities first, and many pledged they would not serve except with their own officers. When Sergeant A. I. Robinson of the same Ohio company as Sherwood Anderson learned the War Department was increasing the size of the companies, he wrote home, "The boys were hoping the . . . new men will all be from Clyde. . . . [They were] very much chagrined [when news came of the appointment of a] Toledo man [as captain of Company I]. But like good soldiers they made the best of it."

MONDAY, MAY 16: The Navy Department offered a report of the movements of Admiral Sampson, Commodore Schley, and the Spanish fleet: Sampson was off Cape

Haitien and thought to be guarding the Windward Passage or sailing for Cienfuegos; Schley was cruising southward along the coast to receive orders at Key West; and the Spanish warships disappeared in a westerly route after leaving Curaçao.

The Naval Strategy Board was concerned about getting the *Harvard* out of St. Pierre Harbor without risk from the Spanish boat destroyer *Terror*, still laid up at Martinique. The *Yale* and *Montgomery* had been assigned to keep their eyes on the *Terror* for any hostile move.

Anxiety was also raised about the safety of the *Oregon*; last seen off Brazil, all hoped she would avoid the routes of the Spanish squadron and eventually join Sampson's fleet. In addition, concern of a much lesser sort surfaced when a list was published of American yachts presently in the Mediterranean. Yachting men, however, were convinced the Spaniards had a more important agenda than seizing pleasure craft. Among the millionaire owners of the yachts were Messrs. Vanderbilt, Walters, Weaver, Drexel, Stuyvesant, and Day.

The first officer killed in the war was buried with military honors in Raleigh, North Carolina. Ensign Worth Bagley, whose grandfather was Governor of Virginia, was killed on the *Winslow* at Cienfuegos. The ensign's mother's home, where his hat and sword lay upon his casket, was filled with floral offerings. Civil War hero Maj. Gen. Joseph Breckenridge sent palms to memorialize his son Cabell, a classmate of Ensign Bagley's. The citizens of Savannah sent a floral North Carolina flag. Still more flowers were sent from the people of Key West and from the men and officers of the *Winslow* and the *Cincinnati*. An estimated 10,000 people—government officials, veterans, schoolchildren, family, and friends—attended the services, during which all businesses were suspended. The procession to Oakwood Cemetery was witnessed by 15,000.

On a more positive note, an agreement was reached to exchange two American prisoners of war—newspaper correspondents, Charles Thrall and Hayden Jones—in exchange for Spanish prisoners in the United States. *London Times* correspondent Knight was chosen to negotiate the exchange.

Maj. Gen. Wesley Merritt, who had been appointed to command American forces mobilized on the West Coast for an expedition to the Philippines, was unhappy about the mobilization process. "It is by no means a settled fact that I will depart for Manila at any time," he said. "The command they propose to give me is not adequate for my rank. . . . [The] 15,000 men, including 1,000 regular troops, which it is proposed shall constitute the expedition, is [not] at all sufficient for such an undertaking . . . [and] I am unwilling to undertake the command . . . unless it shall include at least 5,000 trained and disciplined troops of the regular army, no matter how many volunteers will be sent." He also still wanted a larger volunteer contingent for service elsewhere. An entire volunteer corps of 13,000 was expected at Camp Black next week, as a reserve force to man the coast fortifications if needed.

Camaraderie was evident at Chickamauga. While no date for departure had been set, the volunteer army, already numbering 8,500 men from six states, was blending well.

Most enlistment quotas were full, but offers still came in. Connecticut's Col. Burple offered the government a state regiment, but Secretary Alger told him the Nutmeg State needed no more. On the other hand, newsworthy offers were accepted: The President agreed to find staff appointments for the sons of Brig. Gen. George Pickett, who led the charge at Gettysburg, and Brig. Gen. James Longstreet, Commander at Bull Run. Gen. Walker, who presented the two men, wanted to fight at the front himself, but McKinley thought he might be of better service in Congress.

Father Edward J. Vaitman, post chaplain at Fort Sheridan, was asked by Gen. Miles to be in charge of all Catholic army chaplains, as sanctioned by authorities in Rome. Having served the army more than any other chaplain, he would be in charge of three chaplains in the regular army and 15 among the volunteers.

The 4th Regiment of the Missouri National Guard welcomed *its* new chaplain, the Rev. Thomas Ewing Sherman of the Society of Jesus, affiliated with St. Ignatius College. The son of famed Civil War hero Gen. W. T. Sherman, Father Sherman told his almost all-Catholic regiment, "Duty will lead us on many long, hot marches [and] compel us to wade swamps, stifle hunger, scale parapets heavy with hostile guns [and] grapple with death . . . trusting in God, we . . . march steadily onward till victory is won."

Gen. Fitzhugh Lee appeared at the religious service for troops at Camp Lee accompanied by Virginia Gov. James Hoge Tyler. "Speech, speech," shouted the soldiers upon instant recognition. Although Lee was a name worshipped in Virginia, the Rev. Moses D. Hoge flatly refused: "This is a place of worship," he said, "and there must be no speech making." However, Charles Algernon Sartoris, the grandson of Gen. Grant, and Fitzhugh Lee, Jr., did made good use of family connections; although lacking military training, both would serve on Gen. Lee's staff.

Signs of patriotism proliferated: The bunting mills in Lowell, Massachusetts, were besieged with orders for flags and tents, and a frustrated representative of the National Equipment Company at 10 East 23rd Street, Manhattan, told the Quartermaster General he would fill the order of 500 flags and a number of tents as soon as humanly possible; the Women's War Relief Association met at the Windsor Hotel, elected officers, and pledged to raise funds to aid soldiers in the fields; and there was much seriousness, but also a little "pun," at the Republican Convention for the Fourth Congressional District of Kansas, which adopted as a platform a series of resolutions, including the following: "As Americans we are especially proud of . . . McKinley as a statesman, Fitzhugh Lee as a diplomat, and Dewey as a fighter, and we are firm in the conviction that when the South Atlantic community comes, we will 'Schley' the Spaniards with 'Sampsonian' vigor. . . . [However, we] desire to call attention . . . to the fact that the Populists who . . . were loudest in condemning President McKinley for his slowness in beginning the war, have . . . made Kansas the last state to get its troops into active service."

TUESDAY, MAY 17: The first "I was not quoted correctly" of the war surrounded Gen. Merritt's apparent refusal to lead the expedition into the Philippines. To defuse matters, he telegrammed Secretary Alger: "[T]he interviews published in the New York papers this morning are in every way incorrect and unauthorized."

Not one official believed that a professional like Merritt would publicly refuse to follow orders although they agreed that fewer than 5,000 regulars would not do it in the Philippines. "He is too good a soldier," said one Major, "to be threatening to refuse to obey orders."

Interestingly, Gen. Shafter announced that Gen. Merritt had been named Military Governor, with responsibilities to 8 million Filipinos. Also appointed was Col. Babcock as Adjutant General of the Department of the Pacific.

The movement of troops to Chickamauga continued. The 8th Massachusetts Regiment passed through Jersey City: 850 men under the command of William Pew, Jr. When they bid farewell in Boston, there was much weeping and presentation of cash and other keepsakes. "I hope you'll come back," said many a voice. The men boarding the train sang "Farewell," which only brought on more tears.

Surprisingly, new regiments continued to be organized. When Camp Ellerbee witnessed the mustering in of a company from Newberry, South Carolina, a reporter for the Newberry *Observer* recorded his impressions: "A finer body of young fellows never faced a mustering officer. . . . These men have made many sacrifices to the call of duty. . . . They have left pleasant homes . . . for the precarious living of the tainted fields, caresses for hard knocks. . . . Captain Langford and his officers have worked earnestly to furnish . . . an entire company . . . rent almost in twain by rigid medical examinations. Undismayed, . . . [they] redoubled interest; obstacles only served to increase their zeal."

In Nebraska, Gov. Silas A. Holcomb authorized William J. Bryan to organize the 3rd Regiment of Nebraska Volunteers. Thousands had previously offered their services; with the news of a new regiment, predictions were the state would establish a record for most volunteers in proportion to a state's population.

At Camp Wood, life had settled down. Camaraderie flourished between the Western cowboys and the Eastern "la de dah boys," as the Westerners called the Eastern Rough Riders. They drilled on the heat-scorched prairies, curried their horses, and rustled for forage and supplies. During infrequent leaves, they drank beer and attended band concerts. The regiment's unofficial anthem became "There'll Be a Hot Time in the Old Town Tonight." The New Mexicans, in particular, were so eager to fight that they even looked forward to breaking up intracamp skirmishes. The Rough Riders wrote a fight song: "Rough, tough, we're the stuff. We want to fight and we can't get enough."

Little news came from the fighting front. The damage to the *Winslow* was greater than first thought. One shot smashed a starboard cylinder and another traversed one of the boilers. The ship had to return to Norfolk for repairs.

Supposedly, an agreement had been reached to exchange Spanish prisoners for American journalists Charles H. Thrall and Hayden Jones, but a dispatch from Havana claimed the reporters were spies, having in their possession revolvers, cartridges, a camera, and implicating documents. A third newspaper correspondent, Freeman Halstead, was arrested at San Juan in the act of taking photos of the fortifications.

WEDNESDAY, MAY 18: The location of the Spanish squadron remained a mystery. Schley was perhaps somewhere off the coast of Cuba, having joined forces with Sampson. The *Oregon*, which left San Francisco six weeks earlier, had traveled more than 13,000 miles and was seeking to join the other American ships.

If the Spanish fleet tried to avoid America's vessels, Sampson could trap it. Said one naval officer, "We are bound to come up with [the enemy], unless he decides to run for our coast. But that will only defer the inevitable . . . a few days. The longer he . . . dodges, the shorter becomes his supply of fuel. Once that is exhausted, he has [to go to] San Juan or Havana. . . . If it be Puerto Rico, Sampson would return and resume the bombardment. I do not, however, believe . . . Cervera will permit his fleet to be bottled up in a harbor and shelled where it cannot maneuver."

The Naval War Board offered no information whatsoever on Sampson's location. Let the Spaniards guess. However, for publication, it reported that he was bound for Cienfuegos, news probably intended to dupe the enemy.

The cruiser *Charleston* sailed for Manila from Vallejo, California, with a large supply of powder and projectiles for Admiral Dewey's fleet.

Gen. Merritt was scheduled to leave Governors Island in New York for San Francisco to take command of the American army preparing to occupy the Philippines. Brig. Gen. Royal T. Frank was arriving tomorrow in New York to succeed Merritt as Chief of the Department of the East. Maj. Gen. E. S. Otis, was ordered to head for the Philippines as second in command to Merritt.

The *New York Times* agreed that Merritt had not stated his views about the adequacy of America's Philippines force for print. However, "there could not have been a madder scheme than to compose an invading army . . . of amateurs, commanded by amateurs. The efficiency of the National Guard differs very widely in different states . . . [even the] best of the militia, commanded by professional soldiers, would have to go through additional [training and the] militia of the Pacific states is not . . . equal to the best."

A more imminent question than a Manila landing was the Cuban invasion. The goal was still 50,000 competent men to take on the forces of Blanco. The 16,000 regulars at Tampa could depart at any time. Most of the volunteers at Tampa, New Orleans, Mobile, and Chickamauga were not yet uniformed, armed, equipped, or trained. Military experts believed a month would be required to ready 35,000 volunteers to join the regulars to invade Cuba. Of necessity, without delay, was the dispatching of Tampa regulars to the Cuban coast to clear the way for the army later on.

Because of future actions in the Philippines and Cuba, military officials were convinced that the priority was now to get the 125,000 men already called out mustered in and equipped. Rather than calling for more volunteers, the regular army should be increased to 104,000, as was envisioned by the original bill. Reports revealed that 95,000 volunteers had been mustered in other states; the physical examination stage was under way.

The 9th Regiment at Camp Black would be next to head South once their last two battalions were sworn in. A touching ceremony honored Col. William Seward, who received a loving cup from the men and officers of the 9th upon his resignation after 40 years of service.

Joy reached new heights for Sherwood Anderson and his fellow volunteers, as he remembers in his *Memoirs*: "[N]ow we were in the South, in that very fabled land where so many of our fathers had fought. . . . What a trip it was for me, crowded as we were . . . we boys from . . . places of bitter cold winter mornings [with] chores to be done, stores to be swept out, fires to be built and, for myself, heavy barrels of apples to be . . . piled in an icy cold warehouse. . . . After that, the long hours of drilling, [and] of marching and counter-marching, with gun, knapsack and blanket roll, seemed as child's play to me. . . .

"[T]he excitement of the journey south . . . [wiped out] my guilt . . . [about deserting] my brothers and sister to go help save my country . . . [which] did not look as though it needed saving.

"And on down to . . . Chickamauga Park. . . . Here, on this very spot, stood grim Sherman . . . [and] Grant, clad in the uniform of a common soldier, a fine horseman, dashing across a field."

The war already well into its second month, the press reflected on the motives of the war. True, America wanted to avenge the *Maine* and end the inhumane conditions in Cuba, but it was time to glorify the virtue of patriotism, proclaimed the *New York Times*: "It is a grand, patriotic impulse that unites [us] . . . ; for the dominant thought is that this is our country's war, 'our country—right or wrong.' It is this impulse, which does not [look back] for the establishment of the righteousness of our cause, that moves the majority . . . to uphold the action of the National Government. . . .

"The present generation has never witnessed such an outpouring of . . . patriotism. . . . Never before have the National colors been so profusely . . . displayed in city, town, and village . . . [nor] the younger generation . . . so profoundly stirred by allusions to the country's cause."

THURSDAY, MAY 19: Orders were issued for regular troops to be sent to Manila via California. The near 5,000 troops under Merritt's command would consist primarily of the 5th Cavalry and 18th and 25th Infantries currently stationed at New Orleans and the 19th Infantry, now at Mobile. They would be joined by the 14th Infantry, already consisting of several batteries of the 3rd Artillery, now at San Francisco.

Of especial note was the handpicked 25th, a colored regiment which was expected to be very effective should interior fighting take place in the Philippines. Fortifying the regulars would be the cream of the National Guard, who would match up with any group of regulars in the country in terms of training, equipment, and efficiency. Personifying the volunteers was the 10th Pennsylvania. The use of all these troops for the Pacific Expedition would not interfere with the planned Cuban invasion.

Further details of the cable cutting at Cienfuegos focused on the great losses of the Spaniards: The American ships had concentrated their fire on an improvised fortress manned by 1,500 Spaniards where 300 were killed and several hundred wounded; the Spanish forces were hit by 450 five-inch shells and 700 shots from the *Marblehead*'s second battery; the *Nashville* launched over 400 shells and 1,500 shots from her second battery; the hospitals at Cienfuegos were filled; and fear reigned that American warships would return and finish the job of destruction.

Other updates included an Associated Press story of *Winslow* survivor William O'Hearn of Brooklyn, an 18-year Navy veteran who was cited for bravery in 1897 for preventing the *Puritan*, then in the Brooklyn Navy Yard, from being blown up when its boiler room caught fire. His intriguing story included the tale of a now-famed parrot, which was next to O'Hearn as he spoke to the Associated Press: "Beside him, in a bright tin cage, was the *Winslow*'s parrot, which made himself famous on the day of the battle by shrieking and chattering like a demon. . . . 'He has been mighty quiet since the fight,' said O'Hearn, 'and I sometimes think . . . [he] is mourning for the boys who were killed. He was very fond of the black cook, Josiah Tunnell [for whom O'Hearn thought of naming the bird], and when the poor fellow lay dying on the dock calling for water, the parrot screamed and shrieked as if he were mad. Tunnell used to feed him every day, and I think he actually understands what has happened.'"

O'Hearn described his view of the battle in his role as water tender. When the shells started landing, he went on deck to report to the captain, Lieut. Bernadou. "'I went back into the boiler room and in a few minutes I went up on deck again, and the fighting had grown hotter. . . . Several of the men were missing. . . . Lying all in a heap, on the afterdeck in the starboard quarter, . . . I saw five of the men, where they had wilted down after the shell had struck them. In other places were men lying groaning or dragging themselves about wounded and covered with blood. I went over where the men were lying in a heap and saw that they were not all dead.'"

One of them, John Meek, could still speak. O'Hearn narrated his last moments: "'Can I do anything for you, John?' I said, and he replied, 'No, Jack, I'm dying; goodbye,' and he asked me to grasp his hand. 'Go help there,' he whispered, gazing . . . where Capt. Bernadou was still firing the forward gun. The next minute he was dead. He was my friend."

The survivor then told of the death of Ensign Bagley: "[He] was lying at the bottom badly torn to pieces, and the bodies of the other three were on top of his. The colored cook was lying a little apart from the others, badly mangled and in a cramped position. We supposed he was dead, and covered him up. . . . Nearly half an hour after that we heard him calling and [moving slightly] under the cloth . . . '[F]or God's sake, move me. I'm lying over the burner and burning up. . . .' The deck was very hot, and his flesh had almost been roasted. He also complained that his neck was cramped, but did not seem to feel his terrible wounds. We moved him into an easier position and gave him some water. 'Thank you, sir,' he said, and in five seconds was dead."

O'Hearn said the men thought the *Winslow* would be sunk. They were saved, he felt, by the crew of the *Hudson*, who spent an hour getting them out of shooting range.

Volunteer service reached a milestone as the number of volunteers mustered into service exceeded 100,000. Twenty-one states completed their quotas: California, Colorado, Georgia, Indiana, Kansas, Maine, Maryland, Massachusetts, Minnesota, Missouri, Nebraska, New Hampshire, Ohio, Oregon, Pennsylvania, Texas, Vermont, Washington, West Virginia, Wisconsin, and Wyoming. The Adjutant General's Office reported that 57 regiments were on cars hastening to assigned destinations, including Chickamauga, which had its busiest day since volunteers began arriving. Arriving on this day, in order, were the 5th Pennsylvania (600 officers and men); 12th Minnesota (1,033); 21st Kansas (1,027); 8th Massachusetts (946); 9th Pennsylvania (630) and 12th New York (1,048). By 6:00, the camp had a total of 24,000 men.

New Jersey's U.S. Senator, W. J. Sewell, declined his appointment as Maj. General. As he wrote to the President, "I beg to decline the commission . . . with which you were kind enough to distinguish me, and which was unanimously confirmed by the Senate . . . with great reluctance and only . . . because advised that the holding of the commission while occupying a seat in the Senate is incompatible with the provisions of the Constitution."

To lighten the economic burdens of civil service clerks who serve, the President was considering a proposal to waive civil service law when appointing substitutes to fill their spots. Instead of drawing upon the eligibility list in order, a member of the clerk's family—if one were on the list—would take precedence in filling the vacant spot.

FRIDAY, MAY 20: The priorities of expeditionary forces were the Philippines and Cuba, in that order. Gen. Merritt came to the War Department and met with Secretary Alger and Gen. Miles. He later met separately with the President. He set forth his needs and demands for an expeditionary force. No announcement was made, but a top source said his expectations would be fulfilled. Pointing to this direction was the departure today of two regular infantry from New Orleans to San Francisco.

Although the invasion of Cuba fell to second priority, activities proceeded for the raising of 10,000 yellow fever immunes for the invasion force. Ideally, the army wanted men who had endured yellow fever epidemics or, that failing, who had at least lived in hot climates and in the outdoors, so recruiting would be done in the Southern coast states. Surgeon Gen. George M. Sternberg said he had appointed immune contact surgeons—those who already had yellow fever—connected with stations in the South, to accompany the force to Cuba. President McKinley sent the Senate nominations of Colonels for six of the ten regiments into which these special corps would be divided. The nominees were Cols. Robert S. Riche, Duncan N. Hood, Patrick Henry Ray, James S. Pettitt, Herbert H. Sargent, and Laurence D. Tyson.

The encampment of the 12th Regiment in Chickamauga was the first of the Camp Townsend Guardsmen to be readied for moving against Spain. Every Guardsmen was mustered into service, with the exception of the field and staff officers of the 9th Regiment, who would take the oath tomorrow. The men were saddened to hear that Frank J. Macready, Company D of the 12th, died of a heart attack while marching from Rossville to Chickamauga.

On the Ivy League campuses, different levels of enthusiasm were evident. Yale students and alumni filled College Street Hall and agreed to present to the U.S. Government two Vicar-Maxim guns and a strand of colors for the cruiser *Yale*. President Timothy Dwight, meeting chair, told the crowd to remember their alma mater's song, "For God, for country, and for Yale."

Harvard President Charles Eliot was more subdued at a somber lecture at Sanders Theater. He advised students not to enlist until the end of the academic year, unless there was an urgent necessity. "War at first," he said, "is a dull, coarse, squalid, dreary monotony, varied by infrequent spasms of intense exertion, excitement, horror, exaltation, or dejection. It cannot possibly have any attraction for any of you."

But the attraction *was* powerful for Harvard graduate and former football player, John Lorimer Worden, whose grandfather and namesake commanded the *Monitor* in her War of 1812 battle with the *Merrimac*. A member of the New York Stock Exchange like his father, Daniel T. Worden, young Worden left for San Antonio to join Roosevelt's Rough Riders. He was the first member of the stock exchange to become a trooper.

SATURDAY, MAY 21: According to an Associated Press report, twelve Spanish warships had been sunk and two American warships disabled in a skirmish off Môle St. Nicolas. The unconfirmed report was attributed to a passenger from Port-de-Paix who arrived on the Haitian steamer. While the location named was a strong possibility for a naval battle, officers discredited the news. Secretary Long was out of Washington, and President McKinley had fixed a "censorship" over the Cabinet so that war secrets would only be given to Long and Secretary Alger.

The *New York Times* published a letter received from an officer in Dewey's fleet. It was dated April 19, two days before the United States and Spain cut off relations and four days before the blockade of Cuba. It showed confidence in American superiority: "The Spanish naval power in these waters," said the missive, "is much inferior to our force and could not really make any effective resistance. . . . [T]heir vessels are already leaving Manila and scattering among the . . . [island's] small harbors and bayous."

One step closer to the Philippines: The 1st Infantry at Presidio announced they would break camp, at the latest, Sunday night, April 22, and set up quarters on board the *City of Peking*. The troops would leave for the Philippines on April 24.

Preparations were progressing quite well at Chickamauga, thereby making the availability for active service much earlier than was first predicted. Supplies were coming in so efficiently that in two weeks all men would be equipped. Assistant Quartermaster W. K. Wright announced that 4.5 million rations had been purchased and were on route. Prosper, Lazard, and Co. had begun work on a huge bakery to help meet the new contract requirement of 75,000 loaves daily.

Disappointment followed the news that Surgeon Gen. Sternberg would not use women physicians in the field during the war. Sternberg responded to an offer by Dr. Gertrude Gail Wellington of the National Emergency Association of Women Physicians, Surgeons, and Nurses.

A portion of Col. Grigsby's cowboy regiment arrived in Chicago from Sioux Falls to an ovation from a large crowd, who cheered and waved flags in appreciation of the Rough Riders. The two companies of 186 men were dressed in regulation cowboy costume, broad sombreros with long pistols strapped to their sides. Other groups from South Dakota and Montana would join Col. Grigsby at Chickamauga.

The enlisting of soldiers was of little interest to the government at this point, but New York's Italian Americans felt they would be the right choice to fight in Cuba. They claimed that, if given arms and uniforms, they could recruit 1,000 well-drilled, veteran soldiers who could fight in hot weather. New York City coroner Zucca sought to coordinate this effort with Col. Gustave Martinetti, who had served both under Gen. Giuseppe Garbaidi and in the last Greco-Turkish war. "We have very many men here," Zucca said, "who served in the Abyssinian campaign. They are thoroughly immune to very hot climates, are thoroughly drilled, and have also had experience in guerilla warfare. . . . [T]hey would be free from yellow fever and other fatal epidemics which will mow down large numbers of men who have been taken from counting houses and other peaceful occupations."

SUNDAY, MAY 22: Upon returning to Washington, Secretary Long authorized the following statement to dispel persisting rumors: "No truth . . . concerning an engagement off Môle St. Nicolas."

Encouraging news emerged from Tampa, where 25,000 regulars and volunteers were equipped in readiness for the Cuban invasion. Gradually, the force would reach 50,000, according to Gen. Shafter. The first force would be sent to establish a basis and hold it; volunteers would follow under the command of Gen. Lee.

Shafter denied reports that the transports would not be ready for a week. All 11 ships in Tampa Port were in full readiness; the 5 to 7 on their way were said to have bunks and stalls. Once embarkation orders came, two or three days would be needed to get artillery, troops, and horses aboard. Anyway, Shafter was still convinced there would be no movement until the Spanish Navy was defeated. The enlistment of the 10,000 immunes needed for the invasion was delayed by the President's slowness in naming an additional four colonels, the slowness of some Southern states—particularly North Carolina, Mississippi, and Tennessee—in filling their quotas, and the weaknesses in the National Guard organizations.

Meanwhile, the 69th was set to leave for Chickamauga next Sunday, so Camp Black had a record number of 20,000 visitors. Mothers clung lovingly to their sons, telling them to not seek uncalled-for danger, but to honor their families by being brave Americans on the front lines. Those who wanted to visit the men of the 3rd Company of Oneonta were disappointed because they were quarantined with measles.

The expedition to Manila took a big step forward when the *Charleston* passed through the Golden Gate at 8:20 in the morning, with 6,000 soldiers gathered at the Presidio to wish her bon voyage. The first vessel to be built on the Pacific Coast, the *Charleston* received an enthusiastic sendoff as never before seen in the San Francisco harbor.

Also drawing attention were two fund-raising efforts and a boycott. Unable to serve in the war, Evangelist Dwight L. Moody "arranged" for the Rev. A. C. Dixon, of the Hanson Place Church in Brooklyn, to go to Tampa. Moody took over Dixon's pulpit and was raising money to spread Christian work at the Tampa base. "Some people," he sermonized, "say to me, 'Moody, *you* want a man to be saved right away. Why don't you give him some time to think it over?' Well . . . during the Civil War . . . thousands of men . . . were going into battle in 24 hours, many of them never to return. I knew there was only once chance for those men, and I told them to take it. And I've done it ever since."

The presentation of a torpedo boat to the government by Rhode Islanders was advanced by Newport businessman F. P. Garrettson, started the subscription list with $1,000. Garrettson said the vessel, to be named for native son Oliver Hazard Perry, would be built by the Herreshoffs of Bristol as one of the fastest torpedo boats in the world. Once fully equipped, it would be turned over to Gov. Elisha Dyer and members of the state's Senate and Congressional delegations for presentation to Secretary Long.

Irritated at French hostility to America's position in the war, 75 women of prominent families in St. Joseph, Missouri, assembled at the Country Club to inaugurate a boycott of French goods. The women would neither buy nor wear French-made goods and would discourage the merchants they patronized from handling them.

MONDAY, MAY 23: Despite talk of an "immediate" invasion of Cuba, military experts insisted it would not happen until the Spanish navy was disposed of and 50 to 75 thousand men were ready. Sending an initial token force was opposed by Gen. Miles. And the question persisted: What was happening with Sampson and Schley? The prevailing opinion was that Admiral Cervera was in the Caribbean, his stock of coal depleted, with no depots in sight for refueling. His only hope: being joined by colliers and more Spanish vessels.

In the meantime, the *Oregon* reportedly arrived—at Key West. What made the unconfirmed report reliable was a dispatch—dated Key West—that the wife of an *Oregon* crewman received during her stay in Washington. The dispatch simply said he and the ship had arrived safely.

The only naval battle reported was a legal conflict. Members of the Spanish parliament, the Cortes, charged America with violating international law by flying the Spanish flag on her warships. Not so, argued naval officers, quoting the Navy Department's edition of "Snow's Naval Precedence": "The use of a foreign flag to deceive an enemy is permissible. . . . [I]t must be hauled down before a gun is fired, and under no circumstance is an action to be commenced or an engagement fought without the display of the National ensign."

The troops headed for Manila from Presidio on the *City of Peking*. Reported the *New York Times* about their departure, "As [they] proceeded through the residential district . . . the crowd grew thicker and thicker. There was one continuous roar of cheers, flags were waved . . . and people . . . rushed out and grabbed [soldiers they recognized] to say good-bye. When Market Street . . . was reached the crowd was enormous . . . nothing like [it] . . . was ever seen here before."

But alarm, not joy, prevailed when people in Washington state heard reports that the monitor *Monterey* would be sent to Manila. Citizens rushed to the Navy Department, concerned that the ship was the only remaining protection, except for fortifications, should the enemy attack the Pacific coast.

Newsworthy notes: Observers called the review of the 1st Division of the 1st Army Corps by commander Maj. Gen. James H. Wilson a "spectacular scene" with historic overtones as the first great formal movement of a sizable body of troops for the Spanish-American War and the first review of its kind since the Civil War. Adjt. Albert Dalton received a letter from Capt. E. M. Weaver, the U.S. Officer who mustered the Massachusetts Volunteer Militia into U.S. service, saying, "[Congratulations] . . . on the truly splendid regiments contributed by Massachusetts. I doubt very much whether any other state has sent . . . regiments so well drilled and so completely equipped."

Special commendations went to Private Grant Connelly of Company 1, District of Columbia Regiment, who was on guard at Camp Alger when his company accidentally left for Chickamauga without him (he was sent to join his forgetful comrades); and the first pension of the war, in the amount of $12 a month, went to the childless widow of William H. Hook, who took sick at Camp Harvey and died of stomach trouble on May 15, at age 36.

President McKinley announced the appointments of Congressman E. E. Robbins of Pennsylvania—a Major and Quartermaster of the 2nd Brigade, State Militia—as

Assistant Quartermaster of the U.S. Volunteers, and Gen. John A. Wiley, also of Pennsylvania, as Brigadier General of Volunteers. Clara Barton reported that the work of the Red Cross in Cuba was not harmed by the conflict, that the hospital at Serro, which had 60 children under care when she left, now had 160, and that "Gen. Blanco himself belongs to the Red Cross Society of Spain . . . [so] I am confident . . . the Red Cross work in Cuba will not be interfered with."

American journalists Thrall and Jones, reportedly alive and well, would shortly be exchanged for Col. Vincent de Cortijo and Dr. Isidro Julian, who were being moved to Havana from Fort McPherson Barracks near Atlanta, where they had been under arrest; and photographer, Dr. D. S. Elmendorf, who had taken pictures for the American Museum of Natural History, received 3,000 feet of film upon which he hoped to photograph the bombardment of Havana by America's 48 siege guns, making history as the first to capture a bombardment in progress.

The happiest man of the day undoubtedly was Gen. Wesley Merritt. No, he did not get delivery of his desired troops. No, there was no imminent *military* engagement. The engagement of *this* day was between the 62-year-old Governor of the Philippines and 20-year-old Laura Williams, daughter of Mr. and Mrs. Norman Williams of Chicago. Gen. Merritt's fiancée was a tall and pretty blonde, an outdoor person, who had received much attention in America and abroad. His future father-in-law was a well-known Chicago financier and a founder of the Chicago Telephone Company.

TUESDAY, MAY 24: A letter from an officer of the *New York* received in Washington convinced militarists that Sampson had returned from San Juan to Key West, probably for coal and supplies. That being so, he lost the chance, for the moment, of sailing through the Windward Passage and intercepting Cervera, who was sailing to Santiago.

A cablegram from Admiral Dewey to the Navy Department emphasized the disquieting scene in Manila and reinforced the priority of the Philippines over Cuba. "Situation unchanged," he wrote. "Strict blockade continued. Great scarcity provisions in Manila. Foreign subjects fear an outbreak of the Spanish soldiers." After meeting with the President, one Republican Senator commented, "If it becomes a matter of deciding whether troops shall be first hurried to Manila or to Cuba, they will go to the former, as the situation there is vastly more critical." The situation was corroborated by the Japanese cruiser *Akitsushima*, which reported Manila plagued by riots, burning houses, and food scarcity. Horseflesh was being sold at $1.50 a pound.

Although premature, Spain thirsted for peace, according to a Madrid correspondent of the *London Daily News*: "Rumors as to the negotiations of the powers in favor of peace are premature, but responsible Spanish statesmen are prepared to seize the first opportunity to end the war, provided it can be done on terms honorable to Spain. Should a neutral nation come forward with an honorable arrangement, its proposals would be examined here in no impractical spirit of false pride. If, therefore, America does not insist upon impossible humiliations, there is still a possibility of peace."

But America's intent was not humiliation. It was winning the war. And that involved seeing that coal cargoes did not fall into the hands of Spanish warships. The Treasury Department issued instructions that no clearance papers be given to any vessel with coal for Central or South American or West Indian destinations unless they could prove that the coal was not for Spanish consumption. In line with this order, the German steamer *Amrum* was detained awaiting instructions from Washington.

The total of volunteers mustered into service reached 112,000. Equipping the men, especially for the invasion of Cuba, was tardy because many state National Guard regiments were not well prepared; however, the Quartermaster's Department was confident it could rapidly equip all volunteers.

The plan for raising a force of 10,000 immunes was fading because those chosen to raise the regiments were focusing more on strong and seasoned men than on men merely immune to disease. A more important concern, especially for southern Senators, was voiced by Mississippi's Money, who told an executive session of the Senate that raising this force was being made nigh impossible by the selection of regimental officers from the North who had never been subjected to tropical diseases.

A more satisfying picture was shaping up at Chickamauga, where camp numbers reached 36,000 and would climb to 44,000 by May 28. Among the newest arrivals were the 1st Vermont Regiment (1,207 officers and men commanded by O. D. Clark) and the first markedly Southern troops in the park, the 3rd Tennessee Regiment (1,005 officers and men commanded by J. P. Dufee).

At Tampa, no fatalities were recorded, but daily drills were shortened because of the heat. As described by the *New York Times*, "Many of the unseasoned volunteers are suffering . . . from excessive heat. . . . From the cloudless sky the sun pours . . . light as brilliant and burning as molten brass, and from the white and gleaming [sand], comes a heating glare as dazzling as if each grain . . . were a refracting mirror. The skin tingles and burns . . . and the brain becomes dazed."

The atmosphere was more enjoyable along the Broadway route from West 22nd to Cortlandt Ferry, where thousands waited to cheer the 9th Regiment, under commander Col. G. James Greene, which traveled from Camp Townsend to Manhattan before heading to Jersey City and then, finally, for the South.

The spy story of this day was more sensational than most. Spanish civil engineer Romigno Sapatero Jimenez, 40, was arrested off Key West, on the steamer *Panama*, charged with carrying information about New York City's defenses to the Spanish. He was seized with charts of New York harbor.

8

THE BLOCKADE OF CUBA

WEDNESDAY, MAY 25: The location of Admiral Cervera's fleet, as portrayed in maps printed in newspapers, was some three or four miles from the entrance to the harbor or bay of Santiago de Cuba. The fleet was protected by mountains, the entrance to the bay by Morro Castle. Capt. Horatio S. Rubens of the Cuban Junta noted: "The approach to Santiago is very difficult now. It is through a channel naturally narrow, but made more so by the Spaniards, who have sunk blockhouses and obstructions and have planted mines liberally. Either the American or Spanish fleet outside and the insurgents could easily be held captive. With the American fleet outside and the insurgents in the rear, the position of the town and the Spanish fleet would soon become intolerable."

The Navy Department officially reported that the *Oregon* was safe, after traveling 13,000 miles in 65 days. She arrived in Juniper Inlet, Florida, and would set sail again for parts unidentified but certainly to take part in the war effort.

Thousands of soldiers waited to be sent to the Philippines or Cuba; yet McKinley issued a call for 75,000 more volunteers. Adjt. Gen. Corbin broke down the projected strength of the military force, which with the added 75,000 would total 278,500: Regular Army, 62,000; Volunteers from States (first call), 125,000; Cavalry Regiments at Large, 3,000; Engineers at Large, 3,500; and Ten Infantry Regiments, U.S. Volunteers immunes, 10,000. (Five of the ten immune regiments, it was revealed, would be of colored troops; and eight of the ten Colonels had already been named—all white. McKinley was being urged to name Negroes for the two remaining posts, and the logical choice for one was Maj. Charles Young. A First Lieutenant in the black 9th Cavalry battalion of Ohio, he was the only colored commander among the first volunteer army of 125,000, and the only colored graduate of West Point currently in the Army.)

The President's second call was very exciting to the men of the 7th Regiment who had refused to volunteer as individuals because they wanted the integrity of their regiment maintained and did not want to be split up after taking the oath of allegiance.

Having seen the government's preservation of the regiments at Camp Black and Camp Townsend, they were now anxious to volunteer. Running for reelection, Gov. Black was leaning to calling on them since they had many Republican supporters. "We are ready at all times to give up armory and organization for the good of the Nation," asserted 7th commander, Col. Appleton. "[I]f we [are called], we are ready."

Among other newsworthy notes, the arrival of Gen. Fitzhugh Lee in Tampa reawakened hopes for an early departure to Cuba. Lee, who would command the 7th Army Corps, was honored at an impromptu reception by officers, soldiers, Cuban refugees, and natives. Among those on his staff was the newly assigned Maj. Russell B. Harrison, son of former President Benjamin Harrison, who would serve as Inspector General.

The distinction of being the day's most colorful enlistee went to Cleveland's Eugene A. Van Waldek, 25, a Dutch Count by birth, who enlisted as a private in the infantry of the regular army. He brought 13 years of military training and experience, having attended military school and having served as Sergeant Major in the Dutch Army and First Lieutenant in the German. Why was he now attracted to American service? "Spain has done more wrong to my country than to the United States," he responded, "and I want to avenge my ancestors for the Thirty Years' War carried out against them by the Spaniards."

No one described it as an issue of freedom of the press, but an unnamed Philadelphia publishing house, denied access to photograph the League Island Navy Yard and Fort Mifflin for security reasons, urged a correspondent to get the pictures by any means. The publisher hired a tugboat, and the photographer stopped in front of the yard and took several views, which led the publisher to urge *all* its agents to get photos by similar means. The issue was referred to Rear Admiral Montgomery Sicard, president of the War Board, and Brig. Gen. John Wilson, Chief of Engineers, who recommended a criminal offense for photographing views of navy yards, fortifications, new ships, and other government structures serving a military use.

In the latest spy story, federal authorities disclosed that while searching Jimenez's effects, they found a cipher letter, which was the key to 59 charts of the Atlantic Coast, from Maine to Florida, with extensive detail of the Florida Keys, the Tortugas, the vicinity of Norfolk, and New York, Boston, and Providence Harbors.

THURSDAY, MAY 26: The long-awaited sea battle between the Sampson-Schley team and Cervera had not begun; however, Washington was certain—as confirmed by the Madrid correspondent of the *London Daily Mail*—that the American fleet was in front of Santiago de Cuba blockading the Spanish warships. The navy felt that the Spanish could not escape; there was no chance of rescue, and America had enough warships to take on any additional fleet sent to attack them. The navy's immediate goal remained breaking of cable communication between Cervera and Spain, which might be a worse blow than losing the battle to Sampson and Schley.

Sensing a quick victory, strategists and officials thought more about Cuba. American militarists were planning to destroy telegraphic communications when they landed in Cuba. However, if America won the war at this point—or very soon—what would they have? Dewey had not captured Manila; Sampson had not taken San Juan; no one had seized anything in Cuba. Our only declared goal was the liberation of Cuba. If Spain offered to end the war, they could invoke the doctrine of fait accompli, which would be upheld throughout Europe.

Troops were headed for the front. Isidore Weill of Milwaukee was among those of the 2nd Signal Company headed for Santiago. As the transport *La Grande Duchesse* moved away from the dock and the band of the 2nd Wisconsin Infantry played martial airs, crowds cheered. "Several excited officers," said Weill, "began firing their revolvers into the air. A number of us had climbed into the ship's rigging, and the bullets were grazing our faces until someone warned the officers to cease firing."

The men left at Tampa were not happy campers. Excessive heat and lack of water were causing abnormal discomforts. Gen. Shafter was looking to move some of his command to Jacksonville.

The 69th New York Regiment, en route to Chickamauga, was received in Lexington, Kentucky, as if they were conquering champions. They were cheered by 10,000. Reported the *New York Times*, "About 100 of the handsomest young women rushed into the coaches and pinned freshly cut flowers on the coats of the officers and men." The Entertainment Committee treated the officers to dinner at the Phoenix Hotel, after which the officers walked with their men to the Opera House for a sampling of Kentucky's finest old bourbon.

Meanwhile, back in Albany, the capital of the Empire State, Gov. Black was projecting himself as an ever-thinking politician. Election time was approaching, and when New York's second quota of volunteers was filled, the state would have 19,000 men in the field—95 percent of them voters. With a close election certain, neither party wanted to disfranchise those who were serving, so politicos expected Black to convene the legislature to pass a provision, similar to one in existence during the Civil War, allowing these men to vote wherever they might be in the country.

The men were well treated in Kentucky, but their pay was not grand. An agreement reached between state military authorities and the federal government gave the men the pay of U.S. Army officers, more than the pay allowed officers by the State. When computed, the total pay was $1.25 a day—from the time they were ordered to camp until they were mustered in. After the mustering, they had to settle for 52 cents a day.

Adjt. Gen. Corbin announced that 118,000 out of the original 125,000 men called for had been mustered; the remaining numbers would come in part from Iowa, still short about 1,000, and several southern states who had not finished mustering. But no sooner was the President's second call issued than Secretary Alger's desk was flooded with dispatches: "I have applications from all over the state," said Minnesota Gov. David M. Clough, "for permission to raise companies"; Iowa Gov. Leslie Shaw said, "[T]he second call will be responded to promptly. . . . [A] large number of companies have been organized in anticipation. . . . The new recruits will be mobilized at the State Fair Grounds in [Des Moines]" and California promised to be the first state to furnish a complete regiment under the new call.

Financier John Jacob Astor was delighted when President McKinley accepted his offer to equip a light battery at his own expense. The battery would be recruited under the direction of Lieut. Peyton C. March of the 5th U.S. Artillery. The Astor Battery Mountain Artillery would comprise 102 men plus officers, equipped with 12-pound

Hotchkiss rapid-fire cannon mounted on mules. When word of Astor's offer became public, applications were received from lawyers, civil engineers, wagonmakers, and students from Columbia, Harvard, and other elite institutions.

FRIDAY, MAY 27: Militarily, this day was uneventful; however, the invasion of Puerto Rico rose to the top of military priorities. Driven by the possibility of the war ending, with America having seized nothing, militarists viewed Puerto Rico as a more viable conquest than Cuba. To take Cuba, America would need a force of 50 to 75 thousand men; gaining Puerto Rico could be achieved with 25 thousand. Moreover, yellow fever and other climactic problems were not major concerns in Puerto Rico.

Thirty-four physicians—many who served in Cuba and South American countries during yellow fever and cholera epidemics—met to discuss tropical diseases at the Red Cross hospital in Manhattan. Their discussions—in Spanish—produced several recommendations: live in high altitudes; thoroughly ventilate and disinfect rooms before occupancy; eat vegetables, but fruit only sparingly; avoid a diet of greasy substances; use alcohol only if recommended by a physician; take saline laxative and acid drinks; wear light clothing, close to body; do not wear flannels; keep feet dry; beware of walking in the sun; thoroughly boil water; take one grain of quinine three times daily.

On a day in which America discussed plans for taking Puerto Rico, it was appropriate that it thought of extending its boundaries to Hawaii. Amendments were introduced into the Senate linking annexation to the War Revenue bill. Said the sponsor, U.S. Massachusetts Senator Henry Cabot Lodge, "Henceforth, the two measures must travel together. Both are equally important, and under the circumstances it would be foolhardy for us to forego our advantages in Hawaii." Proponents argued that McKinley was very much interested in annexing Hawaii at this point because it would be very difficult to hold the Philippines without controlling Hawaii. It was vital to have a stopping place for American ships on the way to Manila.

Spy intrigue fizzled out: A Spanish-looking individual entered the Jersey City Post Office to send a package addressed, "Sagasta, Madrid, Spain." Laughingly, the clerk responded, "Sorry, no packages or letters to Spain." Overhearing the conversation, another clerk rushed out of the Post Office, followed the man to 142 Sussex Street, then told the story at the local Police Headquarters. A detective went with the clerk to that address, where a girl opened the door and said a man of that description had come before and asked for James Jones. No such person resided there. The suspected spy was never traced again.

SATURDAY, MAY 28: Reconfirmation of the locations of the fleets of Commodore Schley and Admiral Cervera reached the Navy Department from the same source as last week, but today's news relieved anxieties. The Commodore was outside Santiago Harbor; his opposition inside the harbor. That being so, according to militarists, Spain could do little damage. All Schley needed was a small force to watch the entrance of the harbor and defeat the overmatched Spanish forces.

The navy also announced receipt of a dispatch from Rear Admiral Dewey, dated May 25. The blockade was still effective, he said, but the situation had worsened for the people, who could not "buy provisions, except rice." He also reported that Captain Charles Gridley of the *Olympia* was seriously ill and replaced by Commander Lamberton. The news surprised the navy because one officer had seen Gridley several months ago, and he seemed in perfect health.

For the first time in more than 30 years, an army rendezvousing in time of war passed in review before the President of the United States The setting was Camp Alger, where more than 12,000 troops were in line. The reviewing party also included Mrs. McKinley; Vice President Garret Hobart, Secretary of War Alger, and Secretary of Navy Long and their wives; Gen. Miles and his staff, including Capt. Abelgaard of the Norwegian Army and Maj. Carlarsco and Col. Carlos Hernandez of the Cuban Army; and a delegation of Congressmen and Senators. The two-hour review included, in order: the 1st New Jersey; 7th Ohio; 65th New York; 6th Illinois; 6th Massachusetts; 8th Ohio; 8th, 12th and 13th Pennsylvania; 159th Indiana; 6th Pennsylvania; and 4th Missouri Regiments. The 9th Ohio, a colored regiment, was detailed on advanced picket duty. Troops A and C, cavalry, did not take part. All agreed that the volunteers performed exceptionally well—except the 4th Missouri, which had no guns or uniforms.

But better things were in store for the soldiers. The Quartermaster's Department announced that as soon as possible every one of the 106 regiments of the volunteer army would be supplied with a new set of national and regimental colors, made of the finest quality of silk. The Post Office announced it would invoke a long-standing regulation, all but forgotten, so letters from those in the military—marked "soldier's letter," "sailor's letter," or "marine's letter" and signed with his name, designation of superior, and forwarded—could be sent without postage with post due collected on delivery. The Commissary of Supplies, located in St. Louis, announced a huge purchase of fancy groceries—a $50,000 order being shipped to Chattanooga—which would be sold to officers and men at cost price.

SUNDAY, MAY 29: Commodore Schley, himself, today confirmed the location of his forces and those of Admiral Cervera. The American squadron was off Santiago de Cuba; the Spanish Cape Verde fleet in the harbor. According to a naval official, "The Spanish fleet is bottled up. . . . [T]he cork is in the bottle." Trying to escape would bring the loss of many lives and destruction of ships, reasoned the navy, so Cervera might decide to blow up his own ships, which might hasten America's expeditionary force to Cuba.

Information about civilian conditions in Santiago was received from two Italians who had landed near Môle St. Nicolas on May 23. People were dying of starvation, especially the reconcentrados. The mood worsened when Cervera arrived without food supplies. The Spanish forces were not in high spirits, either, since the city had been deluged by rain and many of the troops had contracted yellow fever.

The weather brought depression of another sort to the men at Camp Black. The three regiments remaining at Hempstead Plains—the 1st, 22nd, and 47th—wondered where they would be sent. Probably they would be assigned to garrison duty in the New York harbor area. Gen. Frank, officer of the Department of the East, promised post commander Gen. Pennington that he would visit the camp to see if additional regiments could be organized under the President's second call.

The last Sunday in May, preceding Decoration Day—later to become Memorial Day—was a time for much reflection and patriotic comment from the pulpit. Father Daly, chaplain of the 69th New York Volunteers, now in Chattanooga, celebrated mass and holy communion, with other regiments from New York and many other states attending.

The First Mounted Veterans and the Veterans of the 9th Regiment attended as a group to hear the Rev. Madison C. Peters' sermon at Bloomingdale Reformed Church: "The Cuban war is waged upon the same principle . . . [as ours] against British authority in 1776, but *we* had suffered no despotism and endured no wrongs. . . . We declared that taxation and representation should go together. If the Cuban fight for liberty had found no echo in America, . . . the future would have been one of gloom and tyranny."

More than 600 veterans attended a memorial service for the Grand Army of the Republic, conducted by Father Elliott at the Church of St. Paul the Apostle. "No man is at peace when his country is at war, and if his affairs . . . prevent his going . . . he can at least give his active sympathy. . . . Every man must look upon his own country as right . . . to invoke victory upon our arms, and . . . at this memorial time to turn our attention to warlike matters."

At Plymouth Church in Manhattan, the Rev. Dr. Lyman Abbott's sermon "The Duty and Destiny of America" called the Catholic Church of Spain a persecuting church as contrasted with the "Catholic Church of America, which loves and stands for liberty."

On the spying front, armed search parties roamed Key West and environs for three Spaniards who were thought to have escaped to Cuba and one of the neighboring keys after trying to blow up the mortar battery near Fort Taylor. At the same time, government officials were eager to corner Arturo and Antonio Cuyas and Manuel Angulo, alleged Spanish spies known to the Cuban junta, who reported that Cuyas was providing Madrid with news of the activities of the insurgent representatives in New York.

MONDAY, MAY 30: At long last, the military invasion of Cuba had begun, or at least it appeared so. Troops in the Gulf ports began breaking camp and boarding transports. Some 25 ships stood ready to receive some 30,000 men. It was reported that the men would depart from Mobile and Tampa, with the transports converging at Key West. The belief that departure was near was strengthened by the order that troops at Chickamauga leave for Tampa. The safety of the troops would be ensured by convoys of warships provided by Admiral Sampson.

Four separate military expeditions would be launched to arrive at different points. Maj. Gen Miles, his family, and personal staff left Washington for Tampa, reenforcing belief that he would direct the movement of the troops and the imminent invasion of Cuba.

Cheers greeted the announcement at Camp Vorhees that the 2nd Regiment had been ordered to Chickamauga, under the command of Edwin W. Hine. The men considered Chickamauga the best of any of the camps to which New Jersey regiments had been sent.

The Navy Department received its first information from Commodore Schley about the Spanish warships. The *Cristobal Colón* and *Infanta Maria Teresa* had been identified. Other information was dispatched, "but nothing it was considered wise to publish."

Nothing was heard directly from Rear Admiral Sampson. However, women neighbors and friends of Mrs. Sampson bought her a silk flag and placed it in front of her house in Bloomfield, New Jersey, with a note that voiced "the general desire . . . to indicate publicly to Mrs. Sampson their personal sense of the signal services Admiral Sampson is rendering the country."

Decoration Day was a time of solemnity and patriotism. At Hempstead Plains, it was also a time of sadness and embarrassment when Corporal Herbert A. Crouch of Company M, 1st New York Volunteers—whose family was prominent in Kingston, New York, political circles and whose father was city Postmaster—died of heart failure, brought on by pneumonia, which followed a serious cold contracted on May 26 during the brutal storm of the past two days; and members of the 47th Regiment were notified that Sgt. Curtin of Company G, accused of gross neglect of duty in permitting a squad of men under his care to break open a railroad car containing stores for the Commissary Department, would be court-martialed in the next few days.

For the first time in Mobile, Alabama, history the general public participated in Decoration Day services at the National Cemetery. The speaker, Col. John H. Page of the 3rd Infantry, said to continued cheers: "Today in yonder growing camp, amid the pines of our sunny South, the new generation—the sons of veterans of the blue and the gray—stand side by side fight[ing] their country's battle, shoulder to shoulder."

At the Hollywood Cemetery in Virginia, Gov. J. Hoge Tyler gave an inspiring speech, invoking the courage of Civil War soldiers: "This is the first time since . . . these brave spirits were consigned [here] . . . that the cause for which they died could be properly viewed by . . . a reunited country. . . . We have assembled here today to . . . honor . . . [those] whose bodies lie sacredly guarded in this beautiful enclosure. I . . . could [not] lay a . . . more fragrant wreath upon their graves . . . than to say that, if living now, they would be marching at their country's call to avenge the death of our unsuspecting sailors in Havana Harbor and to bring . . . freedom to the island of Cuba."

In Washington, the principal ceremony was held in the center of the field of The Bivouac of the Dead, the great amphitheater of the National Cemetery of Arlington. Some 6,000 people were gathered, and on the platform sat President McKinley, Vice President Hobart, Secretaries Russell A. Alger and James Wilson, Treasury Secretary Lyman Gage, and an array of other government officials, Congressmen, and Senators. The orator of the day, Nebraska's Republican Senator John Thurston, stressed the element of unity and absence of sectionalism in the Spanish-American War and praised the heroism of Admiral Dewey at Manila.

Another large ceremony was held in the amphitheater close to the old mansion of Gen. Lee. McKinley sent a message to an assemblage at Gettysburg, where the principal orator was Assistant Secretary of the Interior Webster Davis. The President linked the patriotism of participants in the Civil War and the current conflict: "Whatever . . . its temporary problems, this liberty-loving Nation . . . never can be forgetful of the immortal heroes of the Civil War. . . . Our reunited fellow countrymen

. . . have an abiding respect and the most cordial esteem . . . [and] those who contended on this historic field . . . and their descendants . . . [muster] under the same flag."

Secretary Davis talked of the vanishing of sectionalism: "In the face of foreign insults, prejudice and hate can no longer endure among the people of the North and South than the snow can last when kissed by beams of the life-giving sun. . . . A third of a century since . . . Appomattox—another call for volunteers echoed throughout our land, and . . . side by side, sons of the men who wore the blue and gray march away . . . under the same starry flag [with] . . . the gray-haired Generals of the Union and Confederate armies."

TUESDAY, MAY 31: The Plant Line steamer *Florida* returned to Key West after dropping 400 men, with arms and ammunition, near Guantánamo to join the 10,000-man insurgent army of Gen. Calixto García. The Spanish troops offered no opposition to the landing and withdrew to Santiago, Holguín, and Manzanillo.

In Washington, there was a heightened air of expectancy in the various bureaus of the War and Navy Departments. Although no information was forthcoming, militarists pinpointed the precise spots of invasion as the eastern end of Cuba (the Province of Santiago) and Puerto Rico. Puerto Rico remained choice one.

No matter where the invasion forces went, they would be well prepared—in terms of mules. Deputy Quartermaster General, Col. G. C. Smith, was instructed by Washington to stop purchasing mules after Uncle Sam had shelled out $1,200,000 on 12,000 mules, all purchased in St. Louis.

American journalists were strongly advised to stay out of Cuba by Alexander Gollan, British Consul General at Havana, following the imprisonment of three British journalists.

WEDNESDAY, JUNE 1: America moved to strengthen its forces in the Philippines. The monitor *Monadnock*, now at San Francisco, would follow another monitor, the *Monterey*, to Manila. Added to the cruisers *Philadelphia* and *Charleston*, Admiral Dewey would have no problem against any force the Spanish threw against him.

The 15th Infantry at San Francisco, the only regiment remaining on the Pacific Coast, was ordered to mobilize to join Merritt's forces. At its peak, Gen. Merritt's force would be 20,000 strong.

Gen. Francis V. Greene, recent Colonel of the 71st New York Volunteers, was ordered to San Francisco from where he would travel to Manila accompanied by First Lieut. William B. Bates, also of the 71st.

For the first time since the outbreak of hostilities, Secretary Alger revealed a game plan for the war in Cuba. Detailed in a letter to the House of Representatives, Islip, New York–born Lieut. Col. William Ludlow, later Military Governor of Havana, revealed that the War Department would send 70,000 to Cuba. A first landing of 20,000 would cost approximately $305,000. The Department also for the first time spoke of landing troops in Puerto Rico. These recommendations would require appropriations of $3,107,000.

Despite announcements from the Quartermaster General's Department that supplies and equipment met the needs of the camps, loud complaints continued. A table from Camp Alger showed that only 50 percent of the men were ready for active service. Half of the troops in Richmond lacked uniforms and guns; some 1,500 needed shoes and underclothing. Camp Thomas grumbled about inadequate food and water supplies.

The Rough Riders arrived in Tampa after a four-day journey that New Mexico's Frank Brito called a "nightmare trip." Brito, an Indian who survived into his mid-90s as New Mexico's last Rough Rider, said, "We loaded 1,200 horses and a pack train of mules. . . . Those old wood-burners poured smoke and when we got . . . off we *all* looked like Indians" (Walker, 1949, 34).

Patriotic women were anxious to aid the sick and wounded in the fields and hospitals, Surgeon Gen. Sternberg revealed. To answer their offers, he composed a memorandum that monies sent to his office would be "expended for delicacies for the sick, such as canned soups, jellies, lemons, oranges. . . . Those who prefer may contribute canned soups, clam broth, orange marmalade, ginger ale, biscuits, water crackers, and similar articles in hermetically sealed cans for use on the hospital ship *Relief*."

THURSDAY, JUNE 2: No one was leaving for Cuba, but the War Department secured additional transports to carry 5,000 more troops for the land invasion. There were now 30 available vessels with a carrying capacity of over 30,000. The warships were the *Comanche* of the Clyde Line, the *Louisiana* and *Knickerbocker* of the Cromwell line, the *Specialist* and *Unionist* of a foreign line.

On a day when the administration awaited developments of a naval confrontation, the attention on Capitol Hill centered on the issue of Hawaiian annexation. Not all were behind annexation: Speaker of the House Thomas B. Reed insisted that the majority of Congressmen would battle to stave it off. The only gain, he felt, was for capitalists and speculators eager to seize on the island's products. One opponent said, "I do not believe the President will seize the islands upon any pretext. That would be assuming a grave responsibility. The President is not seeking responsibility in addition to those clearly imposed upon him."

9

THE SINKING OF THE *MERRIMAC* AND ESCALATION AGAINST SANTIAGO

FRIDAY, JUNE 3: On the Cuban scene today: A big question mark hung over the Associated Press report that the fortifications of Santiago de Cuba were bombarded by an American squadron. During the two-hour encounter, an American auxiliary cruiser, the *Merrimac*, supposedly trying to force passage into the harbor, got past Spain's first line of defenses, but not past the second. She was torpedoed about 500 feet up the channel and sank instantly, bow first. The Spaniards captured one officer, one engineer, and six sailors. While the city of Santiago marveled at the daring of the American vessel, the navy gave no credibility to the report.

Regarding the Philippines, the press criticized the U.S. delay in dispatching a second detachment to Manila from San Francisco. The War Department explained that proper clothing, canvas suits, had not arrived yet. More logically, Gen. Merritt wanted more time to train the raw volunteers before they were sent to the long and difficult expedition in the Philippines.

Impressive scenes were reported at Chickamauga and Tampa. Gen. Fred Grant—son of the late President and Civil War hero U. S. Grant—was in command of the 9,000-man 3rd Army Corps—consisting of the 14th and 8th New York, 1st Missouri, 1st Vermont, 3rd Tennessee, and 2nd Nebraska—being reviewed at Chickamauga by Gen. Breckinridge and Col. John Jacob Astor: "There is so much of the old Gen. Grant in the son," said Breckinridge, and on seeing the New York troops, Astor beamed they were, "the finest he had seen." However, realist Breckinridge knew they were not armed properly; when asked how America would do against a stronger power than Spain, he responded, "You can judge for yourself; not one-half of our troops are armed or uniformed properly."

No one criticized the Rough Riders at Tampa. Their arms were carbines and revolvers, and later they would be equipped with machetes. In his brown canvas uniform with yellow stripes, the New York Society chap looked no different from the North Dakota cowpuncher. The group, which included many half-blooded and full-blooded Indians, delighted the Tampa crowd even though they were recruited at the last moment and had received very little drilling. What counted was honor and dignity, according to Maj. Gen. Miles, whose order, dated May 30, was made public today: "Every officer . . . will . . . guard and preserve the health and welfare of those under his charge . . . labor diligently and zealously to perfect himself and his subordinates in military drill, instruction, and discipline, and . . . constantly endeavor, by precept and example, to maintain the highest character, to foster and stimulate that truly soldierly spirit and patriotic devotion to duty which must characterize an effective army."

But even to the Rough Riders, especially those from New Mexico who had endured spartan conditions in Santa Fe and San Antonio, "Tampa was," as Pvt. George Hamner said, "unparalleled chaos. . . . The weather was much hotter. . . . The mosquitoes . . . [were] thicker, and the food . . . usually rotten by the time it arrived."

Merritt's standards were clearly not met by two privates of the New Jersey Regiment of Volunteers, who were to be tried in the general court-martial for volunteers called together by the Department of the East. This was the first such judicial action since the Civil War. The order was signed by Gen. Royal T. Rank, commander of the Department of the East. The accused, stationed at the Sandy Hook mortar batteries, were left to guard the electrical firing apparatus and were found asleep at their posts. The punishment of this offense during wartime could be death or any other punishment the court-martial deemed proper.

SATURDAY, JUNE 4: The circle of heroes, Dewey, Sampson, and Schley, made way for a new naval idol—seemingly from nowhere. Born in Greensboro, Alabama, and living in Brooklyn, naval constructor Richmond Pearson Hobson was being compared to Lieut. Commander William Barker Cushing, who destroyed the Confederate ram *Albermarle*.

What had been denied by the Navy Department was now fact, confirmed by Admiral Sampson. In the words of the Associated Press, "[S]even gallant seamen took the collier *Merrimac* under the blazing Morro battery and anchored and sank her beneath a spiteful fire of musketry and heavy cannonading from the shore, and the wrecked hull of the sunken vessel effectually closes the entrance to the harbor, within which the Spanish squadron is hopelessly and helplessly locked." Along with Hobson were Daniel Montague, George Charette, J. S. Murphy, Oscar Diegman, John P. Phillips, and John Kelly—all noncommissioned officers or enlisted men.

Under continued Spanish shelling, a steam launch from the flagship *New York*, commanded by Cadet J. W. Powell, began searching for survivors in the early dawn hours, but all had been captured by the Spanish. "The *Merrimac*," reported Powell, "lay well across the channel, her masts showing that Lieut. Hobson had done his work well. . . . The channel is not as wide as the *Merrimac*'s length, and it is impossible for the Spaniards to raise or destroy the wreck under the guns of the American fleet."

Quite a feat! Admiral Cervera agreed, and "in recognition of their bravery," wired Sampson, the Spaniard offered to exchange the prisoners—all held at Morro Castle—for American-held prisoners in Atlanta. Cervera's chief of staff, Capt. Ovideo, was sent with provisions for the prisoners. So overcome was Cervera with the courage of the *Merrimac* men that he himself sent news of their exploit to Sampson.

The plan to block the entrance had been considered for several days, but the *Merrimac* was only ready on Friday, June 3. All details were carried out successfully except the escape, supposedly on rope, which was blown up or otherwise disposed.

The last American to see Hobson was Maj. J. C. Powell: "At 1:45 [p.m.] he came on deck and made a final inspection, giving his last instructions. . . . Hobson was as cool as a cucumber. At 2:30 o'clock I took the men who were not going . . . and started for the *Texas*, . . . but had to go back for one of the assistant engineers. . . . He said, 'Powell, watch the boat's crew when we pull out of the harbor. We will be cracks, rowing 30 strokes to the minute.'"

The Navy Department—and all of Washington—was buzzing about Hobson's heroism. Everyone was amazed because the strategy had not come from Washington.

The army would soon be on the move to Puerto Rico. The War Department announced that four transports had been ordered to Fernandina to receive troops from the camp of the 7th Army Corps at Jacksonville. The chartered vessels were the *Gate City* and *City of Macon* of the Ocean Steamship Company at Savannah and the *Louisiana* and *Comanche*, chartered from the Clyde and Cromwell Lines, respectively.

The rebel party in Puerto Rico was near revolt, according to a German newspaper correspondent, Emersohn, who was arrested on the island but escaped to the nearby Danish island of Santa Cruz. Emersohn said he went to Puerto Rico as aide to Lieut. Henry H. Whitney of the U.S. Secret Service. When America invaded the island, he indicated, the rebels would aid them in great numbers. Whitney validated the report of unhappiness. Volunteers and regulars were deserting the Spanish cause. Food was scarce, prices exorbitant, and many were sick. If America did not invade soon, he predicted, the people would rise up against Spain themselves.

SUNDAY, JUNE 5: From Haiti and other points came reports that a large force of American troops had landed and an attack on Santiago begun. The Americans expected a major battle between the Spaniards and the combined force of insurgents and Americans, with the fleet of Sampson and Schley having a major role.

Added details of Lieut. Hobson's action were forthcoming. He had rendered the armored cruisers *Maria Teresa*, *Cristobal Colón*, *Vizcaya*, and *Almirante Oquendo*, and two torpedo-boat destroyers, *Furor* and *Plutón*, useless to Spain. The plan had been his own; in fact, Sampson had consented only with great reluctance.

Hobson had told the press: "Forward, there will be a man on deck, and around his waist will be a line, the other end of the line being made fast to the bridge, where I shall stand. By that man's side will be an axe. When I stop the engines, I shall jerk this cord, and he will . . . cut the lashing . . . holding the forward anchor. He will then jump overboard and swim to the four-oared dinghy . . . tow[ed] astern . . . full of life buoys and . . . unsinkable. In it are rifles. It is to be held by two ropes. . . . The first man to reach her will . . . pull the dinghy out to starboard. The next to leave the ship are the rest of the crew. The Quartermaster at the wheel will not leave until after having put it hard apart and lashed it so. . . .

"Down below, the man at the reversing gear will stop the engines, scramble up on deck, and get over the side as quickly as possible. The man in the engine room will break open the sea connections . . . and will follow his leader into the water. This last step insures the sinking . . . whether the torpedoes work or not. By this time . . . six men will be in the dinghy and the *Merrimac* will have swung athwart the channel . . . then all that is left for me is to touch the button. . . . Nothing . . . will be able to raise her after that."

The obvious question was, "Do you expect to come out of this alive?" So interested in the precision of the details and the plan, he hardly considered life and death. "Ah! That is another thing," he responded.

The *London Daily Chronicle* wrote, "This incident gives fresh lustre to the renown of the American Navy," and the *London Daily News* wrote, "All English sailors will join . . . in admiration of this exploit under . . . point blank fire. . . . Whether the *Merrimac* was intended to be sunk or to clear a way through the mines cannot affect the praise due men who heroically volunteered to face almost certain death in the service of their country."

Life in Tampa had difficulties for the newly arrived Rough Riders. The rations were quite unsatisfactory; men who unloaded the meat wore gauze or handkerchiefs around their noses because of the odor, and most meat was so rotten that it was transferred directly from the freight cars to ditches dug especially for it. The fare was mainly hardtack, sow belly, corned beef, coffee when available, and what became known as "Alger's embalmed beef" in "honor" of the War Secretary and in "recognition" of the food's formaldehyde taste.

"There was no training in Tampa," said Private Frank Brito. "We were paid $15.16 a month and given a few quinine pills." There were, however, some great times in the "opium den" and the shooting gallery: "Five or six of us . . . went into this place and laid down on some cots. A Chinaman brought in a pipe about three feet long and some black stuff that looked like coal tar. He worked this black stuff into a ball and put it into the pipe and touched a candle flame to it while we puffed. I took about four puffs and that was enough. All of us were sick for a week."

"I went in [the shooting gallery] with Tom Darnell and some other troopers. . . . There were bales of cotton behind the moving targets to catch the .22 caliber bullets and the whole place was surrounded by chicken wire. We told the man in charge we would use our own six-shooters . . . and, when we all started shooting, it scared the hell out of everybody. . . . People started jumping over that chicken-wire fence. Somebody called the 10th Georgia Cavalry . . . but we took the pins off our hats, and nobody knew . . . we were in Teddy's outfit. Col. Roosevelt later found out about it, but by then it had all blown over" (Walker, 1949, 34).

One of the developing personalities among the Rough Riders was New York's Col. Hamilton Fish, known as Roosevelt's "executioner," who was called for whenever a private got "too fresh" and was told to "smash that fellow in the face." Undoubtedly the most identifiable personality in camp, except for Roosevelt himself, was the regiment mascot, a half-grown mountain lion from Prescott, Arizona.

The Tampa community was not fond of the soldiers. In fact, the soldiers were not paid in Tampa because the citizens did not want the 30,000-plus soldiers gallivanting in the streets with money in their pockets and tomfoolery on their minds.

New Yorkers in Tampa were not happy. They were not paid and lacked water, food, and other supplies. They were bitter toward Gov. Black for the conditions. Especially disgruntled were the men of the 69th. The following letter was received by a sister of one of the men: "Owing to the State failing to pay the troops, they only lack a leader to refuse to go to Cuba or elsewhere. . . . New Hampshire, a poorer state, not only has paid its troops, but is giving each man $7 a month . . . in addition to the United States pay. . . . It is said that Gov. Black is too busy . . . trying to . . . convene an extra session of the Legislature to allow the New York troops to vote at the next election. In consequence the boys figure that he has not the time to look after the interest of the State troops . . . [so they] swear by all that is sacred that their vote will go for a Socialist candidate in preference."

MONDAY, JUNE 6: The talk in Key West—as in most other places—was of America's newest hero. Adding his encomiums was Capt. Miller: "Lieut. Hobson's act was the bravest I ever saw or heard of. . . . Every officer and man in the fleet would have volunteered to go, but Hobson, being a naval constructor, was the man for the place. . . . When [the *Merrimac*] was in range of the other forts, every gun in the harbor was opened on her. . . . [O]n the *New York* . . . [our] hearts . . . faltered, for it seemed as if . . . no one on board could escape. The *Merrimac* anchored, the men jumped overboard, and . . . Cervera's officer could not find the language . . . to express his admiration for the bravery of the Americans. His courtesy, and the action of the forts in sparing the Americans struggling in the water, changed our opinion of the Spaniards and made us think the stories of their honor and chivalry not so far wrong."

Hobson and the others were prisoners at Santiago. The exchange with the Spaniards held prisoners at Fort McPherson, Georgia, would take no less than two weeks. Meanwhile Capitol Hill was searching for the appropriate honors for the *Merrimac* men, and the navy was uncertain how to promote Hobson since he was at the top of the list of assistant naval constructors and 18 officers of higher rank were above him in the corps.

Back at the camps, the men were getting antsy, waiting to depart while complaining of conditions. Maj. Gen. Oliver Howard visited a number of camps and reported, "The evils . . . are grossly exaggerated and rest on a flimsy foundation. Take . . . the complaint of the Vermont regiment . . . at Chickamauga. On the [same] day [they] . . . made a complaint about bad water or lack of it, they were told that by nightfall water pipes would be laid and complete. . . . Before taps had sounded, good, pure water was running through pipes in every company street."

Howard also checked on the men's spiritual welfare. To date the Army and Navy Christian Commission had erected a large tent on the camping ground of each regiment at Chickamauga, Tampa, Mobile, and New Orleans. A committee to maximize the resources of the Commission and Red Cross Society, chaired by Lucien C. Warner with headquarters at 3 West 29th Street, Manhattan, was set up.

Conditions at Chickamauga still elicited sympathy and calls for assistance from communities across the country. "Save the Soldiers: Help Needed for Nick Volunteers," pleaded an editorial in the *American Israelite* of Cincinnati. "To see the sick lying with flies crawling over them and typhoid fever patients lacking ice, baths, and other necessities is abominable," said the editorial. What was needed were mosquito bars, ice chests, fans, hospital gowns, nightshirts, pillows stuffed with cotton, hand-kerchiefs, pajamas of light materials, sponge baths for typhoid fever cases, and canned goods for the sick. Those seeking to earmark aid for the Ohio boys, the paper said, should contact the community groups or Mrs. Harry Wise of Chattanooga, President of the Ladies Auxiliary at Mitzpa Congregation, a member of the Citizens' Soldiers' Relief Committee, and, most important, a relative of the editor of the *American Israelite*.

Certainly the most disappointed man at Hempstead Plains was James L. Kernochan. Previously rejected for the Rough Riders regiment because the regiment was formed before his name was reached, today he was rejected for membership in the 1st Regiment, to fill a vacancy in Company M. Things looked good until his examination by the regimental surgeon. His right leg was an inch shorter than his left, a "deformity" caused by an injury he incurred cross-country riding. Kernochan was depressed by the rejection, so the surgeon encouraged him to apply directly to the War Department for assignment to special service.

TUESDAY, JUNE 7: There were reports of a major American victory, a cablegram from Admiral Sampson telling only a fraction of the story: "Bombarded forts at Santiago, 7:30 a.m. to 10 a.m. today, June 6. Silenced works quickly without injury of any kind, though within 2,000 yards." Although not mentioned, it was understood that the bombardment was either for the landing of troops or to cover the landing of marines and the small number of troops already there.

Further details emerged. Commodore Schley's line fired at short range. The *Brooklyn* and the *Texas* quickly devastated the shore batteries. As the larger ships took on the heavy batteries, the *Suwannee* and the *Vixen* closed with the small inshore battery facing them and knocked it out of the fight. The *Brooklyn* neared to 800 yards and, joined by the *Marblehead* and the *Texas*, the havoc wrought by its guns was more visible. Shortly, the woodwork of the Estrella fort was on fire and the battery was silenced. Moving eastward, the *New York* and the *New Orleans* overwhelmed the Cayo Smith battery and shelled the earthworks higher up. Firing ceased at 9.

The warships turned in to permit the use of their port batteries. What followed was a reverberating crash of thunder as the shells blasted the Spanish batteries. Fire broke out in the Catalona fort, and the guns there were silenced. The Spanish fleet continued the fight until 10, when Sampson raised the "cease fire" signal.

Having achieved such a decisive triumph, the navy once more raised the priority of a land invasion, circulating reports that forces had been shipped from Tampa, heading for Santiago, and more would follow. They would join with Sampson to capture the city, the garrison, the shipping, and the fleet of Cervera. The forces—a minimum of 20,000—would be directed by Gen. Shafter.

Following not long after would be a Puerto Rico expedition and then an invasion of Havana, after which, the arguments went, Spain would realize the futility of the war and evacuate Cuba.

Talk at Chickamauga was that the best-equipped regiments were headed for the front: the 2nd Nebraska, 1st Maine, 14th, 8th, and 9th New York. The men of the 14th received socks, soaps, towels, abdominal bandages, and many other needed items for the hospital corps from the Woman's Auxiliary of the National Guard of Brooklyn, via Mrs. Russell Waldron.

The Rough Riders in San Antonio received orders to sail for Cuba, but lack of transport space meant at least one New Mexico troop would remain in Texas. Col. Leonard Wood suggested Captains Curry and Luna flip a coin to decide on who would go and Luna won. Curry remained behind and was placed in charge of supply logistics.

It was made clear in San Antonio that proper preparations had not been made to receive the men. Inadequate food supply, quarters, and other facilities faced them. Temporary quarters had been set up at the fairgrounds, where they would receive their arms, horses, clothing, and food; but from one day to the next, the soldiers did not know who would receive what.

Supply distribution was far from scientific. The troops lined up single file and went into the Quartermaster's warehouse. A supply man looked at the trooper, guessed his size, called it out, and another soldier handed him a uniform. The same for shoes and hats: A supply man looked at the trooper's foot and gave him what he guessed was the proper size. If he was wrong, the Rough Rider was told to come back for an exchange, a process that could take up to three days.

Each soldier was allotted $56.30 a year for clothing. His barracks consisted of a half shelter, his feet sticking out from one end and his head from the other. One blanket was parceled out to each man. When the time for departure finally came, the excited Rough Riders were stunned to learn their ship would be delayed until Spanish raiders were flushed from the coast.

Meanwhile, on the west coast, Brig. Gen. Francis Greene, commander of the second Manila expedition, visited the camp of the 10th Pennsylvania Regiment in San Francisco. He announced that his flagship would be the *China* and his troops, besides the 1st Colorado Volunteers, would be the 10th Pennsylvania Volunteers, part of the 18th and 23rd U.S. Infantries, and either the 8th Utah or 3rd Utah Artillery. The troops were excited to be under Greene, who was decorated in Europe for bravery and praised for his writings.

The Administration reported Dewey's confidence that the defenses of Manila could easily be retained until the first troops arrived. Even with as few as 2,500 troops, he expected little resistance in seizing control of Manila. The government was finalizing plans for the governance of the islands and for developing a rapport between the natives and the Military Governor, Gen. Wesley Merritt.

America learned more about the now-almost-legendary battle of Manila from four men from Dewey's ships, who arrived in San Francisco on the *Belgic* from Hong Kong. Dr. Charles P. Kindleberger, a surgeon on the *Olympia* whose sea time had expired, spoke of the valor of the Spanish opponents, who remained at their guns until the last moment. During the first engagement the entire American fleet concentrated on Cervera's fleet. The badly injured Spanish ship turned around to put back, but the *Olympia* let loose an eight-inch shell that struck her stern and traveled almost her entire length to the engine room, destroying her machinery. The shell killed the captain and set the vessel on fire.

Then, two Spanish torpedo boats moved out to attack the U.S. fleet. A fusillade from the *Olympia* sent one to the bottom with all on board, and the other was riddled.

In a second fight, the *Baltimore* overwhelmed the fort at Cavite and, within a few minutes, a shell struck the ammunition and the fort blew up with a thunderous roar.

WEDNESDAY, JUNE 8: "Ceaseless activity" was a new motto for the administration concerning the war, and it *was* ceaseless activity, for the second consecutive day. Five ships of the American squadron bombarded the fortifications at Caimanera, on the Bay of Guantánamo, with $200,000 worth of ammunition. Many houses beyond the fortifications were demolished. The commander of the district issued orders to burn Caimanera before conceding it to Americans.

It had been erroneously reported that Captain John W. Philip, commander of the battleship *Texas*, was seriously injured by a shell during Monday's bombardment of Santiago. He was not injured at all; in fact, Sampson's official dispatch said there were no casualties.

Preparations of all kinds continued. Lieut. H. H. Whitney met with officials of the War Department, apparently to discuss an expedition to Puerto Rico. He had arrived on the steamer *Ardanrose* after observing the military strength and defenses of the island.

Suitable materials were found to clothe the troops for tropical weather. A contract for brown canvas uniforms went to Biwerman, Heidelberg & Co. of New York; another, for "drill" weave outfits, went to C. Kenyon & Co. of Brooklyn.

In case an emergency—such as sickness, lack of water, or unsanitary conditions—necessitated the abandonment of one or more of the existing volunteer camps, a board of officers was set up to find other camping sites in the South.

Col. D. A. Dickert formally applied to South Carolina Gov. Ellerbee for command of the next state regiment to be organized. Said to be among the first to volunteer for the Civil War—before reaching his seventeenth birthday he was Captain and at 18 he commanded the 3rd South Carolina Regiment—and last to leave the field, he was endorsed by the top military men in the state.

Former Mississippi Congressman John R. Lynch, now Paymaster of Volunteers, and Judson Lyons, Register of the Treasury, met with the President to urge him to seek colored volunteers. Lynch said thousands of colored men from the South—especially Georgia, South Carolina, and Mississippi—had volunteered their services to state authorities, and he asked the President to assign them to one or more of the immune regiments.

Lyons told the President that Georgia was already prepared to provide one or more colored immune regiments—Savannah had a colored troop of cavalry and the only thoroughly colored artillery company in the United States—and that South Carolina had also raised a regiment of colored troops, principally from Charleston, commanded by Col. Robinson. Mr. Lynch said that the President was agreeable to give colored troops the chance to show how "nobly" they could fight in a hot climate.

New York's 108th, 112th, 122nd, and 171st provisional regiments formed to replace those now in the field, were reviewed by Adjt. Gen. C. Whitney Tillinghast, Brig. Gen. Howard Carroll (chief of artillery), Maj. Burbank (U.S. Army), Col. Hilton (Assistant Inspector General), and Paymaster Gen. Healy. "I am both pleased and surprised," said Tillinghast after the inspection. "All . . . made a capital showing, especially the 171st. . . . [It] looks a little crude to a military man, but all that will be remedied as soon as the equipments are used."

At Chickamauga, the staff were so impressed with their men that they invited President McKinley and his cabinet to inspect the park on the Fourth of July. Company K of the 109th, on the other hand, gained notoriety when, for the first time in the history of New York City's National Guard, members would be tried by a court-martial for refusing to drill. The episode began when Maj. Solomon E. Japha, chief recruiting officer of the 109th, asked Bruno Kirschner and Emmanuel Barnett, two men in the 9th Regiment Armory, formerly members of Company K, why they were not drilling. A reasoned objector told the Major: "We are members of the 9th Regiment . . . willing to drill with them. We wanted to go out with them, but were turned down by the surgeons. Now, we don't propose to drill with an organization we . . . never joined. When the 9th comes back we will fall in and drill."

Not satisfied, the Major gave them one minute to make up their minds to obey or be court-martialed. The duo did not move. They would be tried under Paragraph 232 of the Military Code: disobedience of orders, disrespect to superiors, mutiny, desertion, and conduct prejudicial to good order and military discipline; a case that could have wide-ranging implications because hundreds of Guardsmen shared the sentiments— although not necessarily the stubborn courage—of the duo.

The hero story of this day had to do with the men of the *Merrimac*. The President announced that he directed Admiral Sampson to forward a detailed report on the heroism of Hobson and the other *Merrimac* men. Once he received it, McKinley would send a message to Congress for special honors.

Ironically, rumors were the family of America's newest hero almost found itself homeless. A report from Cincinnati said Hobson's homestead and birthplace at Greensborough, Alabama, still occupied by his mother, was heavily mortgaged and a popular subscription was begun to release it. Hearing this, the *Cincinnati Times Star* wired the editor of the city's newspaper for the facts. A note signed, "H. C. Benners, editor, *Beacon*" replied, "Your inquiry received. . . . There is a dispute as to the amount of the debt, but money is in hand to pay any amount due, and no aid is needed of any sort."

THURSDAY, JUNE 9: The blockade of Cuba—so effective to this point—may have lost its potency. Bulletins from Key West spoke of four Spanish warships that had supposedly run the blockade into Havana. An American tug that had joined the fleet off Havana reported sighting a battleship, two cruisers, and a torpedo boat, but naval officers were dubious about these reports. Sampson's previous report identified six Spanish *warships* in Santiago Harbor, and the British cruiser *Talbot*, which left Havana on June 7, just might have been one of the vessels sighted by the tug. If there were not four enemy boats, perhaps there were none.

In the meantime, Sampson officially declared that the bombardment of Santiago, designed to pave the way for an American land force, had accomplished its mission. He personally cited Ensign Palmer, who advanced within some 500 feet of the Spanish batteries at night and discovered the enemy remounting guns.

The Admiral's hopes for land troops were closer to fulfillment. Although the government was not anxious to reveal the exact time of departure, destination, or other information that might be helpful to the enemy, newspapers reported that the 5th Corps and Gen. Shafter were 24 hours removed from Tampa.

Hero Hobson and his men, however, were no closer to release. Sampson sent the *Vixen* to Santiago Harbor with a flag of truce and Spanish prisoners to exchange, but Cervera notified him he was powerless to decide. The decision rested with Gen. Blanco.

No news was received from Dewey in Manila. However, the Navy Department announced that three expeditions would be dispatched to the Philippines. The first comprised 2,000 men; 12,700 would go next; a third would follow to bring the total to 20,000.

With America gaining at every turn militarily, rumors abounded that Madrid was interested in peace. However, the American attitude, according to Spanish sources, did not help. Wrote the Madrid correspondent of the *London Times*: "The possibilities of peace continue to be discussed. . . . [T]hat negotiations might be opened at once . . . that the psychological moment has arrived, but . . . I am skeptical . . . [and] venture even to declare that . . . we have drifted away from rather than toward the goal. . . . The Spaniards naturally shrink from adopting a conciliatory attitude when . . . [their] expressions about . . . seeking some honorable solution of their international difficulty . . . excite the offensive and blustering tendencies of American journalism expressed in such headlines as 'Spain Crying for Peace,' and 'Spain's Abject Poverty.'"

The ironic story of a runaway played out with drama at the North Avenue railroad station in Plainfield, New Jersey. Frederic Caspar, Jr., who had run away from his Bayonne home a while ago because he did not get along with his father, Frederic Caspar, Sr., was wanted by the police. At 1:17 a.m., the train carrying Caspar south arrived in Plainfield. As Caspar rushed into the baggage room, he recognized the baggage master, Hansen. "Say, old man," said the soldier cheerily. "Do something for me, will you? Tell my father that I have enlisted and I am on my way South to go into camp."

When Hansen responded, "I can't, sir," the angered soldier asked, "And why not? You ought to be willing to do that much for a fellow." Hansen then told the soldier of Caspar Sr.'s death. "You don't mean to say that he is dead and I didn't even know it," said the startled son. "Well, tell mother then, will you?" and the fugitive ran across the platform and headed south.

In greater potential trouble was Capt. Madison C. Peters, chaplain of the 9th Regiment, who had devoted a Sunday sermon to the mistreatment of National Guard troops, telling his audience that authorities were delinquent in keeping back the soldiers' pay. When Guard Officers heard about the scheduled court-martial of the duo who refused to drill at the armories, some felt a chaplain should also not be above the law—that no officer, including the chaplain, can criticize a brother officer.

When interviewed at his home, the chaplain dared the army: "[As long as] they won't shoot me, . . . they can go ahead with a court-martial, if they choose. . . . I take back nothing. . . . I know of what went on . . . because I was there and saw the things of which I speak. The Governor and his Adjutant General knew . . . practically nothing because they were with the soldiers less time than they took to eat their lunch. . . .

When the wives and children of [soldiers] . . . are suffering the pangs of hunger . . . through official neglect or incompetence, then it is time to throw human dignity to the winds if it prevent truth from being known. . . .

"A court-martial is for the ascertainment of the truth. That is what I want to find out both as a taxpayer and Chaplain of a regiment . . . and if I find [the million-dollar appropriation] has been properly expended, I will make an apology from my pulpit."

In the greatest trouble were Edward Montesi and a Mr. Lorenzo Montesi, of Coffey Street in Brooklyn, was being held in close confinement in Castle Williams on Governors Island. Suspicious letters were alleged to have been found in his baggage, and he was being held under orders of the Secret Service Bureau of the Treasury Department. Fellow prisoners marveled at his dignity and composure: he was smoking a big pipe, wearing the same gray traveling suit and cap as he was arrested in, and could easily have been taken for a wealthy businessman on holiday.

Lorenzo, a Spanish mule-purchasing agent traveling over the northwestern tier of Arkansas, was inspecting animals near Fort Smith when a letter fell from his pocket, bearing a Buffalo, New York, postmark. Written in Spanish, it was said to contain instructions from Lieut. Garranza, the Spanish agent at Montreal, telling him from where to ship his mules to avoid detection by the American government and the number and kind to send to Puerto Rico, Cuba, and other Spanish possessions. Lorenzo, who had reportedly purchased several hundred mules in northwest Arkansas during the past few weeks and had sent them to Spanish points via New Orleans and Galveston, was never seen again and believed to have been lynched.

FRIDAY, JUNE 10: The physical health of the military rather than the military health of America alarmed military officials when the Mississippi Board of Health announced seven cases of yellow fever in McHenry. True, McHenry was far from any camp now occupied by the army of the South—namely Tampa, Chickamauga, Jacksonville, and Mobile—but what if the dreaded disease spread? Congressmen and Senators visited the War Department with inquiries, advice, and suggestions concerning the possibility of moving from the four Southern cities.

Having had personal experience with yellow fever, Louisiana U.S. Senator Caffrey told those who asked that there were all the indications of a perfect conflagration of the dreaded disease. He felt the germs had survived from last year, and this year's winter conditions made it likely the disease would rage violently soon.

Many were especially troubled about Chickamauga. It was 400 to 500 feet above sea level and years back had had a high number of cases. Surgeon Gen. Sternberg was not worried since Chickamauga was near Chattanooga, site of a health resort, where sick and wounded could be sent for convalescence.

Precautions were being taken, nevertheless. Dr. R. D. Geddings of the Marine Hospital Service, now stationed at Tampa, was ordered to leave for McHenry and take charge of Camp Fountainbleu, which was opened during last year's outbreak.

The men at Chickamauga had other concerns. It was a morning off for them all, and they spent their free moments visiting the city, Lookout Mountain, and the Ridge. One of the trains was so full that some soldiers went to the top of the coaches. About three miles from Chattanooga, telegraph wires crossed the track. C. H. Ames (3rd Illinois),

Thomas Barrett (14th New York), and Judd Sharp (16th Pennsylvania) were standing on top of a car when the train reached that point. Sharp was caught under the chin and around the neck by one of the wires and dragged off the car. He pulled with him Ames and Barrett, who had tried to catch him and prevent the fall. All three were expected to recover.

On a more pleasant note, Manager Frank Burt of the Casino in Toledo was told by Paul A. Albert, manager of the new opera house of Chattanooga, that he had closed a contract with the government to furnish an amusement park and theater for the soldiers at Chickamauga. On June 6, 400 workmen were sent to get the grounds ready, and by the next night the theater would be open.

Busy Chickamauga gave a hearty welcome to the 1st Kentucky, under the command of Col. John B. Castleman, which became the first regiment in the volunteer service to fill its quota under the President's second call.

Unpleasant news came from Tampa, where two colored members of the 10th Cavalry, John Young and James Johnson, were on trial before the Circuit Court in nearby Barlow. They were indicted for the murder of Joab Collins, killed in a fight while the soldiers were encamped at Lakeland. But the Sheriff experienced difficulty in obtaining witnesses. When he asked Gen. Shafter at Port Tampa for two witnesses, the General refused.

In an unprecedented move, two honorary members of New York's 7th Regiment were dropped from the roll of Company K at a boisterous meeting at the armory. Maj. George Rathbone Dyer and Capt. Newbold Morris, both of whom were now officers in the 12th Regiment at Chickamauga, had written to Company K of their displeasure that the 7th had denounced military authorities because they had not been called to serve and had passed a resolution to that effect the day before. Those in the armory censured the two, calling them "cowards," "traitors," "curs," "miserable traitors," and "worse than Spaniards!"

From the American fleet, no action was reported. However, the Navy Department issued a report from Admiral Sampson, dated June 8, which arrogated the idea of sinking the *Merrimac* to himself, not to Hobson: "As stated in a special telegram before coming here, I decided to make the harbor entrance secure against the . . . egress by Spanish ships by obstructing the narrow part of the entrance by sinking a collier at that point. Upon calling upon Mr. Hobson for . . . a sure method of sinking the ship, he manifested the most lively interest in the problem."

It was not military strategy, but Chinese physician Joseph F. Chan of Cleveland had a plan for helping America in its conquest of the Philippines. Dr. Chan proposed to enlist in the regular army or to receive an appointment as Surgeon. He would then ask for authority to enlist a party of about 200 Chinese in San Francisco to take to the Philippines as "missionaries." According to the good doctor, one-third of the 9 million Filipinos were Chinese, and while the Chinese were not taking part in the insurrection against Spain, they were strongly against Spanish rule. He added that the Chinese Filipinos knew little about the United States, so the Chinese-Americans were needed to sway their sympathies to America and possibly even organize them to fight the Spaniards. The Chinese Consul General in San Francisco knew nothing of Dr. Chan, but liked his proposal.

More information was released on alleged spy Edward Montesi. Reportedly worth about $200,000, mostly in real estate, he had been set to sail for Genoa with his wife and child. He owned the Waldo apartment house at the corner of Hamilton Avenue and Union Street and a house at Coffey Street, where he ran a small store.

A 1st Lieutenant of a volunteer regiment at Camp Alger, Virginia.
Source: Stan Cohen, *Images of the Spanish-American War: April–August, 1898—A Pictorial History* (Missoula, MT: Pictorial Histories Publishing Company, 1997). Courtesy of Stan Cohen.

At San Juan, the 16th U.S. Infantry under Spanish fire. *Source:* Stan Cohen, *Images of the Spanish-American War: April–August, 1898—A Pictorial History* (Missoula, MT: Pictorial Histories Publishing Company, 1997). Courtesy of Stan Cohen.

Richmond Pearson Hobson and his crew at the blowing up of the
Merrimac, June 3, 4 a.m. *Source*: Stan Cohen, *Images of the
Spanish-American War: April–August, 1898—A Pictorial History*
(Missoula, MT: Pictorial Histories Publishing Company, 1997).
Courtesy of Stan Cohen.

The 71st New York Volunteers in its heroic dash to the blockhouse on San Juan Hill, along with the 6th and 16th Regiments of U.S. Regular troops. *Source:* Stan Cohen, *Images of the Spanish-American War: April–August, 1898—A Pictorial History* (Missoula, MT: Pictorial Histories Publishing Company, 1997). Courtesy of Stan Cohen.

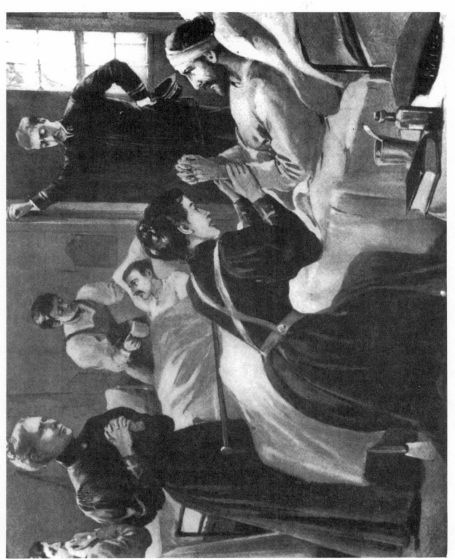

A scene of healing with wounded being treated by the Red Cross organized by Clara Barton. Courtesy of American Red Cross.

Frederic Remington's painting *Grimes Battery Going Up El Pozo Hill*. *Source:* Charles H. Brown, *The Correspondents' War* (New York: Charles Scribner's Sons, 1967).

The landing of American troops at Daiquirí, June 1898. *Source:* Charles H. Brown, *The Correspondents' War* (New York: Charles Scribner's Sons, 1967).

War heroes: Theodore Roosevelt (left), in command of the Rough Riders, and General Fitzhugh Lee (above), one of two former Confederate generals, had important roles in the Spanish-American War. *Source*: Stan Cohen, *Images of the Spanish-American War: April–August, 1898—A Pictorial History* (Missoula, MT: Pictorial Histories Publishing Company, 1997). Courtesy of Stan Cohen.

Honorable Discharge from the United States Navy.

This is to Certify that No. _Edgar G. Du Casse, Ship Wright_ late "TESTIMONIAL OF FIDELITY AND OBEDIENCE," is HONORABLY DISCHARGED from the U. STS. Pensacola and from the Naval Service of the United States, this _3rd_ day of _August_, _189_ at _Navy Yard, Pensacola, Fla._

No. ____ according to the provisions of Section 1573 of the Revised Statutes, if within three months from this date the said _Edgar G. Du Casse_ shall present this, his Honorable Discharge, at any United States Naval Rendezvous, and is found physically qualified, and shall reenlist for three years or longer, then he shall be entitled to _____ dating the said three months equal to that to which he would have been entitled had he been employed in actual service.

Upon reenlistment, and the surrender of this Discharge, should he so desire, he will receive a CONTINUOUS SERVICE CERTIFICATE, showing his service and honorable discharge, and shall receive an addition of one dollar _____ per month to the pay of this rating in which he enlists or to which he may be promoted.

_____ _____ _____

_____ _____ _Captain U. S.N._
Commanding U. STS. _Pensacola_

Rating best qualified to fill _Ship Wright, 1st Class_

10

THE INVASION OF GUANTÁNAMO

SATURDAY, JUNE 11: No improvement was evident in McHenry, where two new cases of yellow fever were diagnosed. While there was no panic, the town was quarantined. The Marine Hospital Service announced that a house-to-house inspection was being conducted on the line of the Gulf Port and Ship Island Railroad to make certain there were no cases outside of McHenry.

The invasion of Cuba had begun, reported the Associated Press. Capt. Clark and the battleship *Oregon* achieved the first successful landing of the war when 40 marines from the *Oregon* went ashore and occupied the left entrance of Guantánamo Bay. The *Panther* followed with nearly 600 marines under the command of Lieut. Col. R. W. Huntington, and within half an hour, they burned the buildings of the Spanish camp and set fire to the tiny village on the beach under the hilltop of Guantánamo.

The way was prepared by the *Marblehead, Dolphin, Vixen*, and two colliers, who had been off the entrance of the harbor for several days before sailing a mile into the channel and sending 50 shots at the fortifications on the left. In controlling the outer harbor of Guantánamo, Sampson now had possession of Cuba's terminus of the French cable to Haiti.

Meanwhile, Admiral Cervera and his fleet were still under the eyes of the squadrons of Sampson and Schley, who were off Santiago to ensure that the Spanish fleet did not escape. One top American naval officer observed, "Spain . . . has never sought a naval fight and never will. She has always dodged and is dodging now. Cervera . . . intended to dodge and he has succeeded. Spain will never send another fleet to these waters during the present war." Santiago was on famine rations, mainly because of the network Sampson and Schley had placed around the city; when Cervera arrived, the natives thought he had brought them food, but all he brought was ammunition and 700 more men to feed.

Unfortunately, the Americans were not very successful in finding out about the military conditions of the island, despite their daring expeditions. Some 6,000 Spanish soldiers, and 2,000 home guard troops still covered every roadway.

The voyage on the *Yucatán* was anything but idyllic for the New Mexican Rough Riders headed for Cuba. The men were herded on board "like cattle," with hardly any room to stand by day, not to speak of sleeping at night. There was inadequate food and water for what would be a two-week odyssey, and with the $13 in back wages they finally received, they men were compelled to buy extra food rations at highly inflated prices. Sgt. William Mattocks of Santa Fe reported that ship stewards charged 75 cents to $1 for pies; Sergeant Prentice told of the Rough Riders paying up to $5 a meal for scraps from the officers' mess. A creative Florida businessman rowed out to the *Yucatán* with a supply of pies for five cents each, but jubilant soldiers turned angry when reports of sour dough surfaced, and tossed pies and salesman overboard, hoping the sharks would have a better meal than they had had.

With the proper nourishment of soldiers a continuing concern of family and friends, the *Salt Lake City Desert Weekly* championed use of the California raisin: "It has many advantages and virtues. Dried fruit is bulky and awkward . . . [and] unfit to eat raw. Canned fruits take up too much room. . . . [But California's raisin] is both wholesome and low priced. A handful . . . now and then will keep the system in order, mitigate hunger, and impart strength. . . . [It] has remarkable properties, not unlike those of the date by which the Arab [is able] to ride and fight all day."

From physical health to spiritual health: The Army Christian Commission promised that, in effect, two large churches would go to Manila with the troops to be places of worship on Sundays and to offer weekday lectures, reading and writing rooms, and entertainment activities. There was also favorable government response, they reported, to their application to send laymen to Cuba and Puerto Rico as well. The number of tents offering religious materials and services at home had multiplied to 17 at Camp Alger and seven, with five to come, at Chickamauga, while Frank L. Smith in Jacksonville was awaiting shipment of tents, chairs, hymnbooks, writing materials, and the like. Itinerant ministers serviced the camps, among them the Rev. Dr. R. A. Torrey of Chicago and the Rev. Dr. H. M. Wharton of Baltimore.

An appeal to "patriotic young colored men" to enlist was made by John E. Lewis of the black 10th Cavalry in a letter published in the *Illinois Record* of Springfield: "It is time every patriotic young colored man should come to the front and defend its honor and show that we are true American citizens; that we can protect our homes and government."

However, his narrative of events in Lakeland, Florida, May 16–17, would have dissuaded most blacks from enlisting: "Some of our boys . . . went into a drug store [in Lakeland] and asked for . . . soda water. The druggist refused . . . stating [they should] . . . go where they sold black drinks. That did not suit the boys, and a few words were passed when Abe Collins . . . said: 'You *!* niggers . . . get out of here and that d— quick or I will kick you B*S*B*s out.' And he went into his barbershop . . . adjoining the drug store. Some of the boys saw him get the guns, and . . . never gave him a chance to use them. . . . [All] five shots fired . . . took effect."

Patriotism was obviously the most important reason for enlisting, but the exceptions were fascinating. One New York recruiting officer told of a man who enlisted because he wanted to escape from the temper of his wife, of whom he was in mortal terror.

Two days after his enlistment, he was met by fellow recruits around headquarters, teasing him that his wife had enlisted. Unruffled, he answered, "She isn't enlistin' at all. And you [can] bet if she gets into this regiment, it won't be as a private; she'll be the colonel."

SUNDAY, JUNE 12: A torturous 13-hour battle raged from 3 p.m. Saturday until 4 a.m. Sunday, June 10–11 between a battalion of marines and Spanish guerrillas at the entrance to the outer harbor of Guantánamo, the Associated Press reported.

The marines, led by Lieut. Col. Robert W. Huntington, had landed from the transport *Panther* on Friday, June 9. They were encamped on the hill, guarding the abandoned cable station at the entrance to the harbor. Four Americans were killed, one wounded, and the advance pickets under Lieuts. Neville and Shaw missing.

The number of Cubans in the battle was estimated from as few as 200 to as many as 1,000. Despite the casualties and brutal encounter, the marines were gratified to have finally taken on the enemy. They had sailed from New York the day war was declared and had been dormant in the *Panther* ever since. They had been sure the army of invasion would be in battle before them.

It was only a matter of hours before the 5th Corps of Gen. Shafter would link up with Sampson's men to reduce Santiago and capture the Spanish ships in the harbor. An expedition to Puerto Rico would follow, with volunteers from Jacksonville and Tampa forming part of the army of invasion. The state of readiness at Jacksonville, where Gen. Lee was in command, was excellent, with clothing for 7,500 men already delivered and the railroad facilities in excellent shape. However, the invasion of Puerto Rico could not proceed until Santiago had fallen and Shafter's men, nearly all regulars, could join forces with the volunteers.

The transports that carried the 5th Army Corps to Santiago would be used for the expedition in Puerto Rico, bolstered by seven more ships ordered to Fernandina: the *Gate City*, *City of Macon*, *Comanche*, *Knickerbocker*, *Louisiana*, *Catanta*, and *Arkadia*.

The War Department was mightily pleased with its own record, so Secretary Alger issued a massive report, meticulously prepared by the heads of the various departments, encompassing individual reports from the Quartermaster, the Commissary, Ordnance, Engineers, and Subsistence.

Since May 14, the report told readers, the Subsistence Department had loaded 12 solid miles of freight cars with provisions—29,125,945 rations for regular and volunteer troops, weighing 64,300,952 pounds or 32,150 tons. Prior to April 21, the department, anticipating conflict, built up a supply of small arms and cartridges, totalling 20 million of all kinds. Uncounted millions more had been procured since then. The manufacture and delivery of small-arm cartridges were approaching 700,000 daily.

The issuance of arms and equipment was somewhat complicated by uncertainty about what stores the individual regiments had on hand. Among items added since April 21: 1,000 small horses; 500 mules; 4,000 wagons; 425 ambulances; 17,052 single harnesses; 1,500 saddles and bridles; 3,100 halters; 1,755 artillery horses; 544 draught horses for siege trains; 106,382 blankets; 123,128 blouses; 25,739 canvas coats and trousers; 55,580 Canton flannel drawers; 123,905 summer drawers; 121,709 campaign hats; 23,950 canvas hats; 92,844 leggings; 104,287 ponchos; 130,785 flannel shirts; 192,656 leather shoes; 300,399 cotton stockings; 24,270 woolen stockings; 24,830 hammocks; 8,125 helmets; 3,820 mosquito bars; 2,000 headnets; 6,000 common tents; 141,562 shelter halves; 3,562 wall tents; and 1,350 conical tents.

The Engineer Corps, according to the report, had distinguished itself. In addition to a large number of permanent batteries, it had created temporary batteries at defenseless places, overhauled old armament at existing works, purchased submarine mines, maintained minefields, purchased siege material, pontoon materials, tools, and instruments. In progress was construction of 21 batteries, with 75 encampments for modern 8-, 10-, and 12-inch guns, and 47 emplacements for rapid-fire guns. Double shifts worked at many places. Already, 52 temporary emplacements of old-style armament and modern siege guns had been constructed at 15 localities; old-style armament had been overhauled for service at 10 permanent posts; and more than 400 miles of cable had been delivered and about 1,500 submarine mines placed in harbors—and these were being increased as material was delivered.

Said a pleased Secretary Alger: "We hope the general public will appreciate the vastness of the undertaking thrown upon the War Department . . . in the very brief space of time . . . since the declaration of war. We have produced and done it well."

Alger was pleased, but the New Mexican Rough Riders aboard the *Yucatán* still sailed on their unhappy ship, destined for Cuba. To divert their need for food and other provisions, some men turned to the Bible. Arthur Spencer of Albuquerque reported Scriptures "going the rounds . . . as though it was a fresh morning [news]paper." However, when Spencer finished his letter to home, the boys—rather than reading the Bible—"[had] made cigarettes [from the pages] of Revelation and St. Paul's Epistles. . . . [So Troop F was] now as nearly out of Bible as it [was] out of grub" (Melzer and Mingus 120).

MONDAY, JUNE 13: Names and biographies of the four men killed at Guantánamo were released. Their bodies were found, stripped of shoes, hats, and cartridge belts and horribly mutilated. The four were comrades in Company D of the 1st Battalion of Marines, commanded by Capt. William F. Spicer: Assistant Surgeon John Blair Gibbs of New York; Sgt. Charles H. Smith of Smallwood, Maryland; Private William Dunphy of Gloucester, Massachusetts; and Private James McColgan of Stoneham, Massachusetts.

The bodies of Privates McColgan and Dunphy were found, both shot in the head. The large cavities from the bullets indicated they were killed at close range. The number of Spanish losses was unknown, but the splashes of blood showed they were considerable.

Gibbs' cousin spoke about the doctor from his Wall Street insurance office: "A powerful sense of duty to his country urged Dr. Gibbs to go to the front. Fidelity to his own conception of duty was one of his most remarkable characteristics . . . only approached by . . . his taciturnity." Dr. Gibbs' father, Alfred Gibbs, was Major of the 7th Cavalry, a detachment of which was in battle with Gen. Custer and wiped out.

Before the engagement, however, Maj. Gibbs had died of illness.

In the battle with yellow fever, the Marine Department had good news: No new cases and no new foci (points of infection). Nine cases had been reported to date, so Camp Fontainebleu was put into operation, under government supervision, as the detention point for McHenry's fever victims and suspects.

The State Department cautioned those at Santiago about the year-round incidence of yellow fever, aggravated by the city's unsanitary conditions, for example, dead dogs and cats thrown into the gutters, remaining with the sewerage to pollute the atmosphere.

Newspapers were filled with editorials and cartoons about the issue of Hawaiian annexation, exclaiming it was being blocked by the Sugar Trust. According to the *Washington Star*, a vigorous proponent of annexation: "the President feels that to put off action on Hawaii . . . might prove a great blunder, and he will take no chances. . . . Until the matter of the Philippines is permanently settled, the Sandwich Islands . . . cannot be ignored. . . . There is no longer a question of the President's intention to seize the islands if Congress does not annex them."

TUESDAY, JUNE 14: Early in the morning Spanish guerrillas unexpectedly attacked the American rear and left flanks at Guantánamo Bay. Leaving their breakfast behind, the marines rushed to the trenches and opened fire. They were supported by the *Panther*, which fired six-pounders into the Spaniards.

After repelling the attack, Lieut. Col. Huntington decided to launch an aggressive assault against guerrillas. The marines went on an exhausting and grueling five-mile march up and down hillsides under the tropical sun; 25 Americans needed medical attention before reaching the battleground. The Americans routed the enemy and captured what had been a vital base for the Spaniards. Only one American was wounded, while two Cubans were killed and four wounded.

The 600 marines had spent weeks of inactivity on the decks of the *Panther* and were deficient in training and experience. Yet, according to the Associated Press, "When the story of the war . . . [is] told, there will be no part . . . more creditable to Americans than . . . the events of the week since the *Panther* disembarked her troops in Guantánamo Harbor. One American officer and five privates have been killed, but at least 100 Spanish deaths settled that score." They succeeded because they jumped into the guerrilla campaign "with the steady nerves and patient endurance of veterans of a dozen wars."

Correspondent Stephen Crane, author of the celebrated *Red Badge of Courage*, described the battle in "The Red Badge of Courage Was His Wigwag Flag," written for the June 30 issue of *World*: "The sky was speckless; the sun blazed as if it would melt the earth. Far away on one side were the white waters of Guantánamo Bay; on the other a vast expanse of blue sea. . . . The surrounding country was nothing but miles of gaunt, brown ridges."

The battle intensified: "[R]ifle locks were clicking incessantly, as if some giant loom were running wildly, and on the ground . . . came a dropping, dropping rain of rolling brass shells. . . . Two hundred yards down the hill there was a thicket . . . about an acre in extent, . . . its whole expanse . . . plain from the hills, . . . alive with the loud popping of the Mausers." The battle changed quickly to the Americans' favor as the Spaniards began fleeing the bullets. It was now "a most extraordinary game—of trapshooting—and coveys of guerrillas . . . in bunches of five or six . . . flew frantically up the opposite hillside."

Upon receiving a report from Admiral Sampson, the Navy Department posted the following: "Admiral Sampson . . . has been reinforced by several hundred Cubans and . . . our forces at Guantánamo are in a very satisfactory condition. The town of Aserradero has been occupied by the troops under Gen. Jesús Rabí. The men under Gen. García are cooperating with the American forces." Exactly what Calixto García's cooperation meant was uncertain, but if he himself had arrived from Bayamo, in the western part of Santiago Province, the joint forces of García and Rabí would make 5 to 6 thousand seasoned fighters, recently armed with Springfields.

On June 11, the Admiral sent Lieut. Victor Blue of the gunboat *Suwannee* on a mission to investigate whether Admiral Cervera was really in Santiago Harbor, and another war hero was born. South Carolina native Blue traveled on his dangerous 72-mile mission, going with guides to the hills overlooking the harbor and city. He clearly located four Spanish armored cruisers, two torpedo boat destroyers, and three small cruisers of gunboats. He delivered his report personally to Sampson on the deck of the flagship *New York*, also mentioning the continued fighting in the hills around Santiago between Cubans and Spaniards. "Bergee" Blue, as classmates and comrades called him, though no one can explain why, was one of the most popular men in the service. His report helped Sampson, who would now definitely bombard the weakened fortifications.

Meanwhile, the heroes of the *Merrimac* lingered in Castle Morro, unable to enjoy the promotions they were given by the Navy Department. Daniel Montague, master at arms, for example, was promoted to boatswain, and George Cheretta, gunner's mate, was promoted to gunner, each with a salary increase from $50 a month to $1,300 yearly. Hero Hobson's reward was not yet determined.

Earlier talk of the transports leaving Tampa for Cuba had been grossly misstated. They first left at noon on this date. The Navy Department said nothing about the misleading reports, only that 20,000 men left. It was a "magnificent spectacle," with troopships carrying the largest invading army ever sent such a distance, in the largest expedition ever organized by any country since the Crimean War. (At a special service in December 1898, Gen. Shafter placed the actual number at less than 17,000—all of the regular army plus the 71st New York, 2nd Massachusetts, and Col. Wood's regiment of Rough Riders. The ships, he said, were "crowded beyond their capacity [yet] . . . the men were [so] crazy to go . . . [they] would have stood on the deck as thick as possible. There was no suffering on board, and the trip was without storm.")

The four Negro regiments of the regular army were segregated into the most despicable quarters. Their berth was "under the water line," according to one black soldier, "in the dirtiest, closest, most sickening place imaginable." Their role in the Spanish-American War had not been fully appreciated. "Colored men are always forgotten in war," said John Mitchell, Jr. in 1898, quoted in Willard B. Gatewood's book *Smoked Yankees and the Struggle for Empire* (1977), "but are speedily remembered when defeat perches above our door." Sergeant Maj. Frank W. Pullen,

Jr., also cited in *Smoked Yankees*, said: "The Negro . . . was the first to move from the west; first at Camp Thomas, Chickamauga Park, Ga.; first in the jungle of Cuba; among the first to be killed in battle; first in the block-house at El Caney; and nearest to the enemy when he surrendered."

Col. Duffy of the 69th regiment spoke of the hardships at Chickamauga in a letter to Justice Morgan J. O'Brien of the Benevolent Friendly Sons of St. Patrick. He wrote that the men had been under his command seven weeks—three at Camp Black, four in the South—and had not been paid a penny. At Camp Black, they were given heavy winter underwear, which they then had to wear in the oppressive heat of Chickamauga. They were sick of pork and beans. Their shoes were worn out. They were not in any condition to fight. . . . The complaint was directed against New York State authorities. "For if the men had money," reasoned Duffy, "they could buy . . . little things that are now denied them and would be . . . willing to spend their own funds to vary . . . the camp rations, and to provide . . . suitable underclothing and shoes."

Duffy hoped the Benevolent Friendly Sons would come to the aid of the soldiers. They did. A circular went out asking for a donations, of not more than $10, to start a fund for the 69th.

WEDNESDAY, JUNE 15: The five-hour battle of June 14 on Cuzco Hill decisively gained control of Guantánamo Bay. More than 2,000 Spaniards were knocked out of the spot where they could cause the most trouble for the marine encampment. On June 15 the last defenses were destroyed by the *Texas*, *Marblehead*, and *Suwannee*.

The *Texas* opened fire first, about 1:45 p.m. The warships let loose devastating blows a short time later. Some 12-inch shells tore down the wall of the fort, throwing the bricks and mortar 30 feet into the air. The bombardment continued until 3:30, when the brick fort and earthworks at Caimanera, at the end of the railroad leading to Guantánamo, were totally demolished. According to a Spanish deserter, 2,000 starving natives were anxious to surrender but afraid of being shot.

Artist-correspondent Carlton T. Chapman noted the battle from the nearby *Kanapaha*: "The *Texas* opened fire . . . and her shots followed one after the other with great deliberation and accuracy. Cheers burst . . . from the men . . . as a shell . . . struck the fort, sending up a great cloud of yellow dust, followed by the tremendous roar of the big gun. The flash of the discharge and the effect of the exploding shell seemed to be instantaneous; . . . then comes the smoke . . . and the shock of explosion . . . ringing in your ears."

The 2nd Signal Company of Wisconsin had left in May, headed for Santiago. But their destination was countermanded at sea, and they were ordered to Puerto Rico to join Gen. Miles. Living conditions were horrid, recalled Isidore Weill: "Our food consisted of hard tack, mouldy canned cornbeef in storage for years and canned tomatoes in one half gallon cans, mostly swollen. I [gave] . . . fifty cents for a small piece of fresh meat and two slices of bread. The meat was so tainted . . . [I threw] it overboard. . . . In Puerto Rico they added sow belly, full of maggots. . . . We had to parboil it to kill them. Later, we received embalmed beef, [so] . . . Gen. Miles [filed charges and] . . . Commissary Gen. Eagan . . . was forced to leave the army."

The situation was improving for the 69th regiment. The Benevolent Friendly Sons of St. Patrick announced that its fund already had $2,000; Col. Duffy already received $1,000 in Tampa. While John D. Crimmins, the Treasurer of the society, was eager to help, he took the opportunity to attack the government's position and commend the *New York Times* for its editorial support at the same time: "While we [will] . . . do all we can for our boys in the field, there should be no occasion for calling on individuals for aid. It is a burning shame that the troops cannot get their pay from the State [because] . . . of a lot of incompetent men . . . in charge of the War Department. . . . I am heartily with [the *Times*] in its efforts to show up the incompetency that exists. The government is not . . . above criticism, and should feel grateful that its shortcomings are pointed out so that a remedy can be applied."

Although he did not provide an actual remedy for the yellow fever problem, New York merchant Nathan Straus, of Macy's and Abraham & Straus, did help out by presenting the expeditionary force with refrigerating plants. For this he received commendation from Commodore Schley.

THURSDAY, JUNE 16: The success of the marines over Gen. Pando's army boosted the confidence of the War Department in the inevitable triumph of the American land forces. The War Department categorized the Spanish fighting men into three groups: The guerrillas—mainly an outcast class of blacks, crafty in the woods and on trails, who could inflict atrocities on prisoners of war—were smallest in numbers but the most troublesome; the volunteers—Cubans who fought for Spain with devotion, but lacked military skills—were well equipped and numerous, especially in Havana; and the regulars—not well drilled or disciplined and without training to march long distances—were most numerous.

A crack group of collegians left the Baltimore and Ohio stations in Pennsylvania for the South. Among them were Yale University's John M. Longacre (crew and football), Granville D. Montgomery (also football and crew), and Hiram E. Dewing (crew, football and Cloister Club President); the University of Pennsylvania's John M. Reugenberg, Jr. (ex-captain, crew), Charles C. Bacon (track), and Miflin W. Huey (baseball); Harvard University's William E. Kent (crew and track); Lafayette College's Thomas A. Hickey (football and track) and John W. Logan (football, baseball, and track); and Cornell University's John M. Hedman (football and crew).

In the ongoing battle of the journalists the *American Hebrew* was angered when the *Atlanta Constitution*, in an article about attributing Jewish patriotism to their past persecution in Spain, wrote: "we do not review . . . [the old persecutions] for the purpose of explaining why the Jews . . . are so pronounced at present in their allegiance to the stars and stripes. We . . . know that they could plant themselves squarely underneath the flag of their ADOPTED land no matter what nation they may be called upon to face."

The *American Hebrew* editor was perturbed at the word "adopted": "[The editor] probably did not stop to think that a very large majority of Jewish-Americans are native born. . . . Surely to speak of our country as . . . 'adopted' . . . is an error . . . calculated to mislead the unthinking."

Meanwhile, the *American Israelite* focused again on calling for help for "[those] of our brave young volunteers who . . . left comfortable homes and . . . pleasures . . . to fight the battles of their country, [only to be] . . . stricken down by disease . . . suffering, perhaps dying, for want of comforts we could easily supply."

FRIDAY, JUNE 17: Were Lieut. Hobson and his fellow prisoners human shields in the mind of Admiral Cervera? Statements attributed to Admiral Sampson indicated that whenever the Americans bombarded Santiago, they avoided hitting Morro Castle, where the prisoners were confined. "If that report is true," said a naval officer, "it is creditable to Admiral Sampson's humanity, but it is not war. If Admiral Cervera has . . . American prisoners in a fort subject to bombardment . . . for the purpose of exposing them to the danger of . . . American shells, . . . [he] is inhuman, and . . . should . . . [be condemned by] all civilized people."

If this was the mind-set of Cervera, argued others, why not put each prisoner in a *separate* fort? "[T]his inhuman treatment of prisoners ought not to be possible, but Admiral Sampson ought to notify Admiral Cervera to take the prisoners to a place of security when another attempt at shelling is about to be made."

The scarcity of ships threatened to weaken operations in Santiago and the Philippines. Ships were needed for a third Philippine expedition and to take an expedition from Tampa to Santiago, to join those of Gen. Shafter's men who left a week earlier. Congress was reluctant to admit any more foreign vessels to American registry because that would give the ships trade privileges and contest American interests, but few American ships were adequate, and the owners were unwilling to charter, except at exorbitant prices.

Undaunted, Gen. Miles visited the War Department to announce that an additional 10 to 12 thousand men would be sent to Cuba, with heavy artillery and cavalry that could not be dispatched with Shafter's expedition of 15,000. The transportation facilities could not, however, accommodate the originally planned 25,000.

Taps at Tampa had just sounded and bands had played their good night, when 3,000 horses and mules broke from their corrals and rushed into the New York camp, near a break in the fence. The animals then stampeded through the District of Columbia camps of Gen. Carpenter's brigade. Shots directed at the animals only excited them more. Apparently no one was injured, but before they calmed down, the animals rushed through the brigade of three regiments and back again.

Had anyone been injured, it would have been too soon to have benefited from the following statement in *Medical News*, by Army Assistant Surgeon Dr. Henry I. Raymond: "[A]ll members of . . . regimental bands will [now] be instructed in hospital drill and as much of first aid . . . as is practicable [so] . . . all musicians will hereafter report to a medical officer . . . for one hour each day . . . until they are pronounced qualified. . . . This arrangement will add largely to the numerical force and efficiency of first-aid bearers upon the battlefield."

SATURDAY, JUNE 18: American forces were in almost total control of Guantánamo Bay, according to a report from the Associated Press. The American warships had resumed bombardment of the town on June 17 and, in the course of one and a half hours, targeted it with 75 shells. The damage was thought to be considerable. Spanish firing was now only occasional and totally ineffective. No Americans were killed.

Caimanera, four miles up the bay, was also under fire from American ships. Cuban scouts reported that the streets had been covered with straw and oil, every building in town was being readied for the torch, the Spanish gunboat was being prepared for the fire to deprive America of a prize, and the natives were preparing to flee for the hills. They had no food, were convinced of American victory, and had lost all faith in Spain's commitment to protect them. Even the Spanish forces, under the command of Gen. Perrejo, had not been adequately fed.

The President met at the White House with the Secretaries of Navy and War about the desirability of attacking ports in Spain. Affecting the decision was news of Spanish vessels under Gen. Camara sailing from Cadiz. Troopships were being exposed to predatory Spanish cruisers.

Perhaps he didn't speak for the majority, but New Hampshire's U.S. Senator thought America should even attempt the capture of the Queen Regent and King, if possible. In an editorial in the *Monitor*, he said: "Before the war we demanded . . . [only] peace and freedom for Cuba. . . . But when the war came we captured Manila . . . [soon] Puerto Rico and . . . we have made the Sandwich islands an outpost. . . . [We will] try to conquer everything in sight . . . the Canary Islands . . . Cadiz . . . Barcelona. . . . But Uncle Sam intends to capture everything Spain has . . . and to enter upon a new career, not of imperialism, but of legitimate republican influence and commerce in all the lands of the earth."

Stung by continued criticism from New York State troops in Camp Alger and Chickamauga, Gov. Frank Black intended to get a firsthand look. However, state business canceled that possibility. In his stead he sent Gen. Howard Carroll, along with Maj. Theodore L. Poole of Syracuse. Carroll defined his assignment "to make a minute inspection of men . . . officers . . . of food and equipment . . . [and] to report without fear or favor. In addition . . . I shall make confidential inquiries as to the condition of the families . . . and make a list . . . [to] be reported to the Woman's Patriotic Relief Association and . . . Soldiers' Relief Association, which have . . . funds for relieving distress."

Indeed, volunteers still had much to complain about. The new Yiddish-language daily, the *Jewish Forward*, ran a story from "a Jewish volunteer" identified only with the initials "D. P.," who told about the horrid life he endured. In articles headlined "Like Animals; That's the Way Volunteers Are Treated" and "Those Who Offer Their Lives for the Fatherland Are Dealt with Harmfully," D. P. wrote that the trip from Chicago to Tampa had been very unpleasant. "The animals of our transport were treated better than . . . [we who were] packed together like sardines, in second class accommodations. . . . At every door there was a guard to see that we didn't escape . . . [or] even . . . move from one car to another car to meet with comrades."

For three days, the men were so packed together they could "not move a limb." Finally, in Ocala, Florida, they were allowed to "crawl out from the cars," for a 15-minute rest. Later, they stood by a side track for three hours, under an oppressive sun. "We cursed the day that we were born such 'fools' to freewillingly bring upon ourselves such misery."

The food was awful—biscuits, zwieback, and old, stale swine meat. "Half the trip we had no ice, no water, suffocating . . . we arrived dead tired, broken, but still full of smiles. . . . I hope they will let us rest for two or three days . . . to find ourselves with renewed strength to survive forthcoming hardships."

SUNDAY, JUNE 19: The War Department announced that, until enough vessels were secured to carry the army to the Philippines, impressment would be the rule. *Newport*, the Pacific Mail Company's steamer, was impressed, becoming the company's sixth vessel in government service. Two more of their steamers were expected to be impressed when they returned from the Orient: the *Peru*, due June 24, and the *City of Rio de Janeiro*, July 5. When the *Alameda* returned from Australia and Honolulu on June 28, the Oceanic Steamship Company would lose that vessel, as well.

The folks in Ossining, New York—more notorious in the twentieth century for its maximum security prison, Sing Sing, than it was in 1898—were beaming over the doings of a local son, Harvard University student Howard Kipp, son of Mr. and Mrs. George W. Kipp, serving with on the auxiliary cruiser *Yankee* in Cuba. An avid letter writer, his most recent letter told of a Decoration Day accident on his ship: The men were having target practice when one of the guns did not go off. As the breech was opened to investigate, the charge suddenly exploded and the shell left the muzzle, but the remainder of the charge flew back, fatally injuring a gunner and costing another gunner his arm. Newspaper correspondents had not yet reported the death, but in case they eventually did, Kipp wanted to tell his parents that *their* son was alive and well.

11

ESCALATION OF THE LAND FORCES IN CUBA
THE ROUGH RIDERS AND BLACKS STAND OUT

MONDAY, JUNE 20: The American fleet had reason for rejoicing. Help had arrived when the 5th Army transports were sighted in early morning. Correspondent Chapman filed his report from the *Kanapaha*: "The day was perfect, a light breeze ruffling . . . the sea, the sky filled with brilliant clouds . . . and the fresh morning air . . . like the breath of summer on the New England coast. . . . Thousands of soldiers looked down from the decks, and at the blue hills they were coming to conquer. There were cheers and shouts and waving of hats . . . and presently the booming guns as the navy saluted the army, welcoming them right royally."

Other good news came from the Philippines. Manila had fallen, according to a report from a French correspondent in Madrid. "The success of the rebel forces," wrote the Hong Kong correspondent of the *London Daily Mail*, "has more than surpassed the expectations of those who favored the return to the Philippines. He has captured 3,000 Spanish troops, including 900 regulars. The latter include 11 officers of and above the rank of Lieutenant Colonel." The provinces of Batangas, Laguna, Cavite, Bulacan, Pampangu, Tarlace, and Pangasiman were in full rebellion against government control.

Meanwhile, two well-received troops were heartily welcomed at Camp Merritt in San Francisco. Although not well equipped, the 151 men of the 51st Iowa Regiment were a tough-looking group. They were preceded by the 101 men of New York's Astor Light Battery, who observers were certain would instantly become camp favorites: "The men . . . are by far the most handsome-appearing soldiers that have arrived in this city . . . thoroughly equipped, their outfit being the regulation U.S. artillery equipment."

Negotiations remained stalled for the freeing of Hobson and the other men of the *Merrimac*. Commodore John Watson cabled the War Department: "[Blanco] states Spanish Government refuses to exchange prisoners. The British Consul at Santiago . . . advised Washington to offer a ransom. . . . The Navy and War Departments agreed that the Spaniards realized . . . Hobson's [value and] . . . were looking for a better deal."

Washington was concerned over reports that the men were being mistreated. The Madrid correspondent of the *London Times* speculated: "Spain's refusal to exchange Lieut. Hobson and his companions . . . is easily explained . . . [since] they must have seen many things . . . naval and military authorities would gladly have information about."

An unexpected "benefit" followed the shooting of the white barber at Lakeland, Florida, wrote John E. Lewis of the black 10th Cavalry to the editor of the *Illinois Record*: "Since the shooting of Abe Collins, . . . there has been a marked change in the disposition of the people, and many believe that it was through the providence of God that he was killed. People who refuse[d] to sell to colored people . . . now ask you to their place of business and intimate . . . they are glad to have you."

Because black troops have served so well, Lewis also wrote, there is a need for competent black officers. "We have many . . . who are capable of commanding a troop. Sergeant James H. Alexander, James R. Gillespie, Sgt. Maj. Edward L. Baker, Pasco Conly." On a final note, Lewis applauded the comradeship of "the white Northern soldier . . . [whose] friendliness . . . is gratifying."

TUESDAY, JUNE 21: The American Navy cut the cable between Santiago and Kingston, the last link from Madrid to Cuba. Captain Blanco was now cut off from any communication with the outside world—except through the American-controlled Key West cable. America seized on the situation and brought the first American military station in Cuba, at Camp McCalla, Guantánamo Bay, into electrical communication.

To counter the stream of criticism about the condition of New York State volunteer troops in the field, Gen. Tillinghast made public unsolicited letters from Colonels of the 5th, 3rd, 1st, and 8th Regiments, claiming, in short, that in no other state's camp were the men better equipped or cared for. Col. T. H. Barbor, for example, reported: "[The 1st New York Volunteers] went into camp in very good condition. The uniforms were good and serviceable. The men had provided themselves with good shoes and the rifles were in good order. The State food was good and bountiful. The U.S. rations . . . ample, and the health of the regiment was excellent, barring the few cases of measles."

The new uniforms displayed in the New York windows of Heidelberg and Co. were not for New York soldiers, but for Cuba, Puerto Rico, and the Philippines. Thirty thousand (24,000 for the infantry, 4,000 for the cavalry, and 2,000 for the artillery) were being made, to be delivered to the army within 15 days. Fashioned after the English hunting jackets, the uniforms were made of brown duck, woven of a special yarn.

In Washington, opponents of Hawaiian annexation dominated Senate discussion. Wisconsin's Democratic Senator John Mitchell argued: "Our nation . . . was shorn of its judgment. The effort to establish our Government in the Far East and the adoption of a policy of imperialism was evidence of that. The seizure of Hawaii removes all doubt."

In Chicago, history was recorded with the appointment of John R. Marshall as the first Negro to serve as Colonel in the U.S. Army. He would command the colored 8th

Illinois Volunteer Regiment. Born a slave in Alexandria, Virginia, he had been employed for five years as a clerk in the Tax Redemption Department of the County Clerk's office in Chicago.

WEDNESDAY, JUNE 22: Six thousand trained American soldiers were encamped in the hills in and around Daiquirí; as soon as they could be carried in transports ashore, 10,000 additional troops would join their comrades. They were reinforced by 1,000 Cuban insurgents, were ensconced in dark thickets and ravines. Every road and mountain path was watched, from Santiago to Guantánamo. The Spaniards could not approach, even under cover of darkness.

The Associated Press offered this picturesque view: "At four o'clock this morning the Cuban coast was wrapped in a soft mist like . . . the dog days in Northern latitudes. Dull, leaden clouds lay on the Eastern horizon, and the color was reflected in the gray waters of the horizon. . . . Distant objects loomed dimly, but it was seen that . . . troopships that had been laying several miles . . . had drawn in toward shore."

Once arrived in Cuba, Gen. Shafter's army disembarked and settled in the direction of Santiago. At dark they bivouacked and strung out in a column covering three miles. The front rested at Demajayaho, the rear within a mile of the base at Daiquirí. The plan of attack remained muddled. Sampson thought his plan to attack the batteries at the harbor entrance was agreed on, but Shafter decided to attack the city itself, from the side and rear. Sampson related, in a later report to the Navy Department: "I do not know why a change of plan occurred unless . . . the troops . . . advanced themselves so far on the roads towards Santiago before any specific plan . . . had been decided . . . it was found inconvenient to divert them to other points."

Meanwhile, a historic meeting was happening at García's camp. As Richard Harding Davis described in his report for the *Herald*: "Gen. García, Gen. Shafter, and Admiral Sampson met for the first time . . . grouped together under a sun so hot that it burns the eyes, on a high cliff overlooking . . . a blue sea broken only by lines of white breakers on the shore, and . . . the slow moving hulls of thirty transports and thirty ships of war. The three commanders are seated on boxes under the palm leaf roof of an open hut. One . . . has a blueprint map on his knees and before they roll it up again, the attack on Santiago will be decided upon and her fate sealed."

Back home, Gen. Miles must have presented his case well because a battalion of troops and a regiment, headed by Gen. Guy V. Henry, left Camp Alger to reinforce the army of Gen. Shafter at Santiago. Miles had long felt that all energies should be directed to capture Santiago; Puerto Rico could come later. Three regiments would be sent from Camp Alger, and several thousand men were being assembled from Tampa. Ships were also being secured for transporting horses and heavy guns, and the War Department made certain a large amount of supplies were sent to the Cuban camps, including 1 million cartridges for the insurgents. Miles said, "It . . . required a month to work out, and it was eminently successful. Especially . . . the work performed by the Cuban forces . . . in the landing of our forces. The harassment of the enemy in the rear . . . is always most demoralizing, and it contributes no small amount in the fruition of the project. Their work [has] been well planned and finely carried out." When Gen. Miles later left for Santiago and then to Puerto Rico, he commanded the entire army, not just any one branch.

Sadly, it was a day of tragedy on the *Texas*. While shelling the batteries of Santiago, she was struck by a six-inch shell through her port side. The Associated Press announced one death, apprentice F. E. Blakely, and seven wounded: R. C. Engel, H. A. Lee, J. E. Lively, G. D. Mullin, J. E. Nelson, R. Russell, and J. Simonsen. The casualties took place during a three-hour exchange. The *Texas* was the only American vessel in the battle. A resident of Providence, Blakely was 18 and had enlisted five years earlier. His remains were buried at sea off Santiago.

THURSDAY, JUNE 23: A dispatch from Santiago reported insurgent Gen. García and 1,200 of his men in camp about 18 miles west of the city; 500 more were east of the city and about 4,000 to the north. García opposed the army of Gen. Luque, encamped on the road leading to the large garrison at Holguín. For Luque's command to reach Santiago, it would have to march 65 miles over a bad road, harassed by García's men—half-naked, mostly colored, well armed, and disciplined. Washington was pleased.

The blockade of Santiago Harbor was very much secure, the War Department insisted; Spanish newspaper stories that "the cruiser *Reina Cristina* escaped from Santiago" were ridiculous, the truth being that she was at the bottom of Manila Bay, sunk by Dewey. Looking at the records, continued the navy, the blockade has been the most successful ever known considering the extent of the blockaded territory.

Madrid next tried to keep up its spirits by reporting an outbreak of yellow fever among American troops in Santiago, and the Spanish military commander claimed that Gen. Linares was 12 battalions of infantry and several batteries of artillery strong. In addition, he claimed that all the strategic positions around the city were strongly occupied.

The day's most notable arrivals were Theodore Roosevelt and the Rough Riders—and their horses! Correspondent Morton Smith reported for the *Atlanta Journal* how Roosevelt supervised the unloading of the horses from the transport: "snorting like a bull, [he] split the air with one blasphemy after another. . . . Miserably, [the young crewmen] looked at the second horse. The disaster had inspired a caution bordering on paralysis. With the greatest care they banded the horse [and] hoisted it up. . . . Before each pull . . . opinions were exchanged and judgments rendered . . . if the animal did not collapse from the strain of sheer suspension it would . . . from starvation. Even when Roosevelt bellowed, 'Stop that g—d— animal torture!' the crew did not quicken their movements. . . . At last, lowered into receding water, the horse splashed safely ashore."

Meanwhile, Hobson and his companions were still in Castle Morro. Secretary Long wanted to reward Hobson appropriately, but did not want to do injustice to other meritorious, veteran officers. If he were to become, as ardent supporters wanted, Lieutenant Commander, he would have received a greater advancement than ever known in American naval history, gaining 344 numbers on the list and 20 years in time, becoming senior officer of the navy in about 15 years. Because of his youth, he would keep that place at least an unprecedented 20 years. Even Admiral Dewey, for his Manila heroics, gained only 10 numbers.

The American naval fleet expressed appreciation to associations throughout the country who had contributed money to the Surgeon General to purchase delicacies, especially for the sick and wounded. Surgeon Gen. M. H. Simons of the *Iowa* acknowledged: "If the ladies . . . could see how they are appreciated by the poor fellows who have had nothing of the kind for nearly two months . . . continuously aboard ship in a temperature between 80 and 90 . . . , they would understand . . . how refreshing the fruits are and how grateful all are for the angelic thoughtfulness."

FRIDAY, JUNE 24: In a bloody one-hour battle, fewer than 1,000 dismounted American cavalrymen—eight troops of the Rough Riders, four of the 1st C and four of the 10th Cavalry—routed 2,000 Spanish soldiers in a dense thicket overlooking Santiago. Thirteen Americans were dead and 50 wounded, with eight of the wounded expected to die.

In actuality, there were two simultaneous battles—one at the top of the plateau, under the immediate command of Col. Leonard Wood, and the other on the hillside several miles away, fought by the regulars under Gen. S.B.M. Young—both parties hitting the Spanish at the same time. Although the enemy had the advantage of numbers and position, the Americans forced them back and stormed the blockhouse around which they made their final stand, scattering them over the mountains. The Cubans under Gen. Castillo did not appear until the battle was practically over, and Young did not allow them to take part.

The *New York Evening World* told the story in gigantic headlines, "Troops March on Santiago; Spaniards Flee Like Sheep; Americans Fight Their Way to Juragua and Capture Town." Dateline: Playa Del Este, as sent "by special cable . . . from the dispatch boat *Simpson* off Aquadores": "The Spaniards are in full retreat . . . with Brigadier-Gen. Lawton, at the head of the American troops close behind. Gen. Linares is in command of the Spaniards, who abandoned . . . Juragua in such haste that they didn't have time to set fire to the place." Young and his men left Juragua at daybreak accompanied by three Hotchkiss guns. Their route was level and relatively easy.

The journey of the Rough Riders was much more difficult, carrying over 200 rounds of ammunition and heavy camp equipment over steep hills several hundred feet high. There was nearly 20 minutes of intense fire. As it subsided somewhat, Roosevelt, ordered his men back from the thicket into the trail. He barely escaped a bullet, which landed on a tree beside his head. During the cessation, small teams moved the wounded from the thicket to a more protected spot on the trail until they could be taken to the field hospital. Most of the American casualties were the result of their own wild shooting in the thicket; the Americans did their best fighting in open country.

Stephen Crane, in an article later to appear in the *New York World*, described the beginning of the battle: "[W]e came in touch with a few stragglers . . . down with heat, prone and breathing heavily . . . about four miles out, with no troops nearer than those by the road. I know nothing about war . . . but I have . . . [seen] brush fighting, and I want to say . . . these rough riders while marching through the woods shook me with terror as I have never before been shaken. . . .

"[T]he Spaniards have learned a great deal . . . and they are going to use against us the tactics which the Cubans have used so successfully against them. The marines at

Guantánamo have learned it. The Indian-fighting regulars know it anyhow, but this regiment of volunteers knew nothing but their own superb courage . . . babbling joyously, arguing, recounting, and laughing; making more noise than a train going through a tunnel."

Among those seriously injured was Edward Marshall, a journalist on the *New York Journal*. In *The Correspondents' War*, Charles H. Brown describes Marshall's dedication to his craft and patriotism (Brown 317–19). Marshall was out in the open, noting the reaction of men hit by bullets. He himself was hit, but his journalistic sense never left him: "I fell into the long grass, as much like a lump as had the other[s] . . . I had seen go down. . . . [N]o pain, no surprise. The tremendous shock so dulled my sensibilities that it did not occur to me . . . there was the least reason to be worried."

Realizing a bullet had shattered his spine, a surgeon asking if he wanted to write any letters home, said, "If you do you'd better . . . be quick!" When Marshall finished his third letter, the soldier who had taken the dictation fainted. "I . . . tried to help him," related Marshall, "[but] I couldn't move. For the first time I knew I was paralyzed."

Crane was led to Marshall and said: "[I]n hard luck, old man? . . . What can I do for you?"

"Well, you might file my dispatches," Marshall replied. "I don't mean . . . ahead of your own . . . just . . . if you find it handy."

Crane, 27, wrote: "No man could be so sublime . . . concerning the trade of journalism and not die. There was the solemnity of a funeral song in these . . . sentences about dispatches."

As the wounded were being taken to the hospital in Siboney, Marshall, among them, started singing to relieve his pain: "My country, 'tis of thee / Sweet land of liberty / Of thee I sing," and the chant was taken up by the other wounded. Marshall wrote during his later hospitalization, "The quivering, quavering chorus punctuated by groans and made spasmodic by pain, trembled up from that little group of wounded Americans in the midst of the Cuban solitude—the pluckiest, most heartfelt song that human beings ever sang."

After the day's end, Crane filed a simple, matter-of-fact story: "Roosevelt's Rough Riders . . . ambushed yesterday, advanced at daylight without any particular plan of action . . . talking volubly, when suddenly. . . . Fierce fire was poured into their ranks and there began a great fight in the thickets. Nothing . . . was visible to our men, who displayed much gallantry . . . their bearing was superb. . . . They suffered a heavy loss, however, due to the . . . wrong idea of how the Spanish bushwhack . . . a gallant blunder."

Most notable was the heroism of the black 10th Cavalry at Las Guásimas, between Siboney and Santiago. According to Theophilus Steward (*The Colored Regulars in the U.S. Army*), general agreement prevailed that the black soldiers distinguished themselves; however, not all claims were verified (38–59). Stories were advanced that if not for the black warriors, the Rough Riders of the 1st Volunteer Cavalry, who had arrived at Las Guásimas late, would have been wiped out in a Spanish ambush.

Black infantryman John R. Conn put his thoughts in a letter to his sister, Mrs. J. W. Cromwell of Washington, D.C.: "[T]he Rough Riders . . . [struck] the enemy in ambush about 500 yards east of the junction . . . receiving a volley that would have routed anybody but an American. The first regulars, hearing the 'music' . . . hurried forward to join in the dance, and awoke a hornet's nest of Spaniards . . . north of the party engaging the Rough Riders . . . more music than they could furnish dancers for. But . . . there is no account of either column giving an inch. They advanced sufficiently . . . holding their ground until the . . . poorly appreciated sons of Ham burst through the underbrush, delivering several volleys and yelling as only colored throats can."

The War Department announced that when the President's second call was completed, the volunteer army would include more Negro soldiers and officers than ever before in U.S. service. The figure would be between 8 and 10 thousand.

The seven companies of colored troops to be mustered in North Carolina, added to three already in service there, would make a 10-company regiment of more than 1,000 men. In Alabama, two battalions would be added to the one taken in under the first call, making a full colored regiment in that state. Virginia would muster two colored battalions under the second call.

Camp Alger already had a colored battalion from Ohio, and one of the Massachusetts regiments included some colored privates. In addition, the 7th, 8th, 9th, and 10th immune regiments would be made up of Negroes.

According to a report in the *New York Times*, "Army experts regard the officering of Negro regiments with Negroes as an experiment. . . . The Negro needs to be led well . . . to make a good fighter, and there is some doubt . . . [they] will follow one of their own race as well as they would a white officer." The War Department announced an experiment for North Carolina's black regiments: All officers would be colored, including a colonel who would be the only one of that rank in the army. In Alabama, the officers would be white. In the colored immune regiments, the Colonel, other field officers, and the Captain would be white, and the Lieutenants and lesser officers would be colored. Would the combination work?

Lieut. Blue received a letter from Secretary Long about his heroism on the *Suwannee*: "The department takes much pleasure in highly commending you . . . and feels sure that your action will prove to be an example for your brother officers . . . and a most favorable augury for your future career."

President McKinley commended Lieut. Frank H. Newcomb—who commanded the *Hudson* when it ran into the fire of the Spanish batteries to secure the *Winslow* (at the time Ensign Bagley was killed and Lieut. Bernadou wounded)—and recommended he be awarded a gold medal, his officers silver medals, and his crew bronze medals; and the President also asked that Capt. Daniel B. Hodgston, a veteran of many years with the revenue cutters, which has no retirement system, and commander of the cutter *Hugh McCulloch* in the battle of Manila Bay, be commended by Congress and placed on the permanent orders list with full pay.

SATURDAY, JUNE 25: The Navy Department drew few callers today; it was the War Department that was besieged from the moment it opened. The air of romance had moved from Dewey, Sampson, and Schley to Roosevelt and the Rough Riders. "What was new?" the Department was asked.

What they knew at this point came from dispatches filed by such correspondents as Stephen Crane, George Bronson Rea, and John P. Dunning. The Associated Press story summarizes the battle of Las Guásimas in its lead paragraph: "That it did not end in the slaughter of all the Americans engaged was not due to any miscalculation . . . [by] the Spaniards, for as perfect an ambuscade was prepared as ever . . . and Lieut. Col. Roosevelt and his men walked squarely into it. For an hour and a half they held their ground under a perfect storm of bullets . . . then Col. Wood to the right and Lieut. Col. Roosevelt to the left led a charge which turned the tide . . . and sent the enemy flying."

Maj. Gen. Joseph Wheeler reported 22 Americans dead and 70–80 wounded, with 39 Spaniards found dead, and their actual casualty count expected to be much higher than that of the Americans. He wrote, "In the two hours' fighting, . . . enough deeds of heroism were done to fill a volume. One of the . . . wounded, was lying squarely between the lines of fire. Surgeon Church hurried to his side, and with bullets pelting all around him . . . dressed the man's wound . . . and walked unconcernedly back . . . returning with two men and a litter. . . . Another soldier . . . [concealed] behind a tree, gave up his place to a wounded companion, and a moment or two later was himself wounded."

Among those killed from Rough Riders' Troop L was its Captain Allyn Capron. The Associated Press told of his last moments: "Sgt. Bell stood by [Capron's] side . . . when the latter was mortally hit. [Capron] . . . never flinched. 'Give me your gun a minute,' he said . . . and kneeling down . . . fired two shots in quick succession. At each a Spaniard was seen to fall. [As Capron prepared to take another shot, his revolver fell from his hand and he tumbled to the ground. 'Don't mind me, boys,' he cried, 'go on and fight.'] Bell, [who] in the meantime had seized a dead comrade's gun . . . knelt beside his Captain and fired steadily. . . . Capt. Capron . . . [conveyed] parting messages to his wife and father and bade the Sergeant good-bye in a cheerful voice."

The casualty New Yorkers read about most was the Rough Riders' "executioner," Sgt. Hamilton Fish, Jr. He was the grandson of his namesake, who was Secretary of State under President Grant and had conducted the negotiations with Spain that prevented war in 1873. His great grandfather, Col. Nicholas Fish, served in the American Revolutionary War, at age 17. Young Fish was born in Berlin in 1874, where his father, Nicholas Fish, was Secretary of the German Legation.

Fish died fighting alongside Capt. Capron, whom he greatly respected. As he died, at the rim of the firing line, the Spaniards attempted to capture his body and nearly got it. The Associated Press filled in details: "He was near the head of the column as it turned . . . into range of the Spanish ambuscade. He shot one Spaniard . . . a bullet struck his breast [and] he sank at the foot of a tree. . . . Capt. Capron stood over him, shooting, and others rallied around him. . . . The ground . . . was thick with empty shells where Fish lay. He lived 20 minutes. He gave a . . . lady's hunting-case watch . . . to a messmate as a last souvenir." Like the other Rough Riders, he was buried in the field of action, at a service by Chaplain Brown.

His parents, who lived at 53 Irving Place, Manhattan, had waited anxiously for news. After being informed of his son's fate, Nicholas Fish said his son's last letter, from Tampa, told of the camp discomforts—without complaint—and of his yearning to go to the front. "In all of his letters," said the father, "Hamilton spoke only in terms of praise of his officers . . . particularly . . . Capt. Allyn K. Capron. . . . Our son . . .

never knew fear. So eager was he to reach . . . action that when he . . . [learned] his own troop, in which he held the rank of Sergeant, was not to go . . . first . . . he resigned his rank and . . . as a private in another troop . . . [went] aboard the transport *Yucatán*. He was . . . soon afterward . . . promoted [back] to Sergeant."

Mr. Fish proudly showed the media a letter from Roosevelt, dated June 6: "Hamilton has done excellently. He has been promoted to Sergeant and no man . . . has done his duty better or been more useful in his position."

Mrs. Fish told how she had written her relative, Alfred T. Brice, Treasurer of Riggs Bank in Washington, D.C., to send young Fish funds so that he could be more comfortable in camp. The youngster said no. "He could not be persuaded to take [even] a rubber blanket until . . . old army officers had assured him that such precautions might enable him to preserve his efficiency as a soldier."

Shafter sent the War Department a cablegram: "I am well satisfied with the progress . . . being made. The disembarkation is slow, but, considering [the circumstances] . . . the men have done well. I only await . . . sufficient supplies to begin the movement to Santiago." (Later, in his address in December 1898, he recalled the speed in landing at Siboney and Daiquirí: "We were no more than two days in getting the whole force ashore. I knew that in . . . a few weeks at the utmost . . . my men would . . . be liable, almost sure to be stricken with yellow fever . . . and I determined to drive the campaign with the utmost speed.")

Lieut. Joyce of the regular army informed Gen. Miles about the number and location of the Spanish troops: 12,000 in Santiago; 10,000 in Holguín; and 15,000 in Manzanillo. Maj. Gen. Brooke ordered the movement of 15 more regiments from Chickamauga to Cuba. The 1st Division and two brigades of the 2nd Division of the 1st Corps were ordered to be immediately prepared and equipped for active field service.

It was Manila that was on the minds of the crowd cheering the troops assigned to the *Colón*: Four companies of the 23rd Infantry and two of the 18th Infantry, both of the regular army, and Battery A of the Utah Volunteer Artillery, commanded by a recently promoted Major, Richard W. Young, grandson of Brigham Young. The crowd tossed kisses and fruit to the departing soldiers. Wrote the *San Francisco Chronicle*, "[T]he oranges flew so fast as to suggest a bombardment. Scores . . . were not caught and flew into the water."

Loaded down with men and stores, the *Zelandia* awaited its orders to sail for the Philippines. On board were the 10th Pennsylvania Volunteers and part of Battery B of the Utah Artillery. One of the Utah men, observed the *Desert News*, was Color-Sergeant Harry Palmer, a Civil War veteran and journalist who was "buoyantly proud of being once more sent to the front."

To give the Americans an added advantage, Capt. E. L. Zalinski, U.S. Army retired, reputed for his work with the dynamite gun, was developing a field mortar-howitzer which, he argued, had the special advantages of delivering a vertical file that could not be guarded against by field entrenchment, could be concentrated within a smaller space than is possible for ordinary file artillery, and was very light, so that it could be transported on a narrow one-horse cart.

SUNDAY, JUNE 26: Four soldiers of Col. Torrey's Rough Riders regiment and a porter were killed in a rail accident near Tupelo, Mississippi, about 3:40 in the afternoon. Fifteen others were injured, among them Col. Torrey. Part of the regiment was carried in two sections of the train, en route from Wyoming to Jacksonville via the Kansas City, Memphis, and Birmingham Railroad. The first section stopped to take water and had whistled to start on when the second section rounded a sharp curve in the track, slamming into the first section and completely demolishing it.

MONDAY, JUNE 27: A great battle was imminent, militarists predicted. The Spanish and American advance posts were virtually eyeball to eyeball. The American advance force rested on the stream of Rio Gaumo, four and a half miles west of Santiago. The outposts, two companies of the 7th Infantry, occupied positions at right angles to the road, guarding the crossing a mile and a half beyond Sabanilla where the 1st, 4th, and 17th Regiments camped. Behind them, toward Juragua, were the 8th, 22nd, 2nd Massachusetts, 10th Cavalries, the Rough Riders, and a blending of other regiments.

Some 3,000 Cuban insurgents led by Gen. Calixto García arrived in Juragua from the mountains west of Santiago. They now totalled 5,000 in the vicinity of Juragua, most of them armed with modern rifles and plenty of ammunition. About 800 Cubans were camped around Sabanilla.

Gen. Shafter was expected to relocate his headquarters from Daiquirí to Juragua. Only the 3rd and 9th Cavalry remained at Daiquirí; all other regiments were removed to Santiago. The last supplies of forage and ammunition were landing at Juragua; the last of the four light batteries of artillery would be there shortly.

Col. Wood wired Gen. Shafter the details about the battle of Las Guásimas: "getting along very comfortably . . . climate much better than we expected. Also, the country . . . rough and full of undergrowth, is rather picturesque. . . .

"We commenced our advance from our first landing place on the 23rd, and that night Gen. Young and I . . . had a long talk about taking the very strong Spanish position about five miles up the road to Santiago. He . . . would make a feint on their front, while I was to . . . detour by trail under a couple of Cuban guides and take them in flank . . . to get them out of their very strong position . . . in the wildest and toughest part of the trail. . . .

"I located the Spanish outpost and . . . when in position fired. . . . Shortly after . . . I could hear Young on the right . . . in the valley. The fight . . . over two hours . . . was hot at close range. The Spanish used the volley . . . while my men fired as individuals.

"[I]nstead of 1,000 men we had struck . . . several thousand. However, . . . we drove them steadily . . . and finally threw them into flight. . . . [R]eports coming out of Santiago report a great many dead and wounded . . . also that the garrison were expecting an assault that night; [and] that the defeated troops reported that they had fought the *entire* American army . . . but, compelled by greatly superior numbers, had retreated. . . . My men conducted themselves splendidly and behaved like veterans."

Also filing a report was Captain Charles G. Ayers, who, in a communiqué to Brig. Gen. Samuel B. M. Young, wrote: "[O]n the 24th Instant two commissioned officers and fifty-three enlisted men of Troop E, 10th Cavalry, went into action . . . against the regular Spanish infantry [and] . . . pursuant to their instructions they held their positions one hour and a quarter without firing a shot, for fear of firing upon their own men. Their coolness and fine discipline were superb. . . . [I] call attention to Second Lieut. George Vidmer, 10th Cavalry, and Privates Burr Neal, W. R. Nelson, Augustus Walby, and A. C. White, who under heavy fire [helped me carry] Maj. Bell, 1st Cavalry, to a place of safety, he being shot through the leg."

Critical to the success of the Americans would be Shafter's ability to unite and maximize the strength of his forces. According to the War Department, 22,000 Spanish regulars—10,000 in one column and 12,000 in another—were marching toward Santiago under Gen. Pando, considered the best fighter and strategist in the Spanish Army. Could García prevent them from entering Santiago, or would they meet the 15,000 Spanish fighters already inside Santiago before Shafter's additional troops reached him? If Pando did join all his forces, could the American attacking force succeed against 37,000 enemy soldiers, entrenched and supported by the four cruisers of Cervera's fleet?

Meanwhile, according to the Madrid correspondent of the *London Times*, Gen. Blanco sent a large body of troops toward Guantánamo to resist the anticipated advance by the Americans from that point.

In another piece of strategy, the Navy Department announced: "Commodore [John C.] Watson sails today in the *Newark* to join Sampson . . . [to] take under his command an armored squadron with cruisers and proceed at once off the Spanish coast." The squadron was set to harass the enemy and inflict damage upon commerce and fortified places, capture prizes they might encounter, and engage their warships in combat if the situation arose. In addition to the *Newark*, the squadron included the battleships *Oregon* and *Iowa*; auxiliary cruisers *Yankee*, *Yosemite*, and *Dixie*; the colliers *Scindia*, *Abarenda*, and *Alexander*.

On the home front, two men of the 7th Illinois were tried at a court-martial at Camp Alger: Lieut. C. C. Ames, for going to Columbus, Ohio, without leave, on charges of absence without leave, disobedience, and conduct unbecoming an officer; and Private Hodges, who was captured in Philadelphia after leaving camp while acting as a Major's orderly. The court findings would be reported to the War Department and a final decision made public by the Judge Advocate General of the Army.

The men at Camp Thomas at Chickamauga had heartier news. Their checks finally came—$8.76 for every soldier who had volunteered on May 2, covering the portion of the State pay advanced by New York, the remainder to be paid by the Federal government next payday. The men slipped out of camp en route to Lytle, and when roll was called, some 30 men were not there to respond. Understanding officers let the men off with a $2 fine.

The *New York World* sent the men a large quantity of canned goods, but the quality was poor from the start, and after being opened and left standing in open tin cans, the food was totally unfit. Assistant Surgeon Capt. Chalmers found food in all stages of fermentation in the tents. Henceforward, no canned food would be accepted into the camp.

Another camp surgeon, Division Surgeon Maj. Ward was married to a Miss Clark in New York. Chaplain Dr. Terry performed the ceremony at the Lookout Inn, where the honeymooners would remain for 10 days to two weeks. The Major would then return to the 12th Regiment and his wife would stay in Chattanooga as long as he remained in Chickamauga.

TUESDAY, JUNE 28: "All is progressing well," read the War Department in a dispatch from Gen. Shafter, dateline Siboney, via Playa del Este. "We occupied today an advance position abandoned by the enemy yesterday on the Sevilla and Santiago Road, west of the San Juan River, within three miles of Santiago, and from which it can be plainly seen."

The War Department announced that the American Army was now at the fork in the road. One branch led to Santiago and the other to Morro Castle, at the entrance to the harbor. Shafter had been reinforced by 1,300 men from the *Yale*; another brigade would reach him tomorrow. Additional reinforcements would come from the several thousand who sailed from Tampa today.

Further information stated that Gen. Jacob Kent's division—formed of the brigades of Col. Hamilton Hawkins, Col. Edward Pearson, and a Col. Worth—had joined the division of Civil War hero Gen. Henry W. Lawton. Together with the cavalry division of Gen. Joe Wheeler and four batteries of light artillery, they would now be strung out in the rear of Lawton's division.

The *Yale* brought the brigade of Brig. Gen. John C. Bates, an officer in the battle of Gettysburg, along with the 33rd Michigan Regiment and a battalion of the 34th Michigan Regiment. They would be stationed at either Juragua or Sabouty.

The soldiers were facing unheard of war difficulties, said the department. "For the first time in civilized war," one belligerent was using barbed wire as a defensive tactic. Each regiment was now provided with wire cutters and assigned to cut down those fences so that troops could advance.

Maj. Gen. Adna Romanza Chaffee and his staff were busy reconnoitering the road near Morro Castle, some seven miles from Gen. Lawton's headquarters. The staffs of Lawton and Chaffee were dealing with two forts of importance within the Spanish lines: Punta Blanca, at the southern end of the bay, and Santa Ursula, at the southeast corner; another fort was on the road to El Caney. Some 450 men were present in each fortification. Stretching around the city were nine barbed-wire fences 50 yards apart. Just inside of these were lines of rifle pits. About two miles beyond the American outposts was a line of entrenchments, stretching from the northern extremity of the city to Morro Castle.

Most journalists gloried in the deeds of the Rough Riders, who could do no wrong. However, strong exception was taken in a letter to the *New York Times* by a writer identified as "Veteran of the Civil War." He pointed to the 22 dead, 78 wounded, and 15 missing in the battle of Las Guásimas: "This loss was partially owing to the incompetency of the commanding officers, as brave men as ever lived, but bravery does not qualify a man for command. . . . The talk of an ambush is ridiculous. An advance in an enemy's country should be made with scouts in advance of the column and on both flanks. With this . . . precaution, an ambush would be impossible, . . . we would not now have to mourn the loss of so many valuable lives."

WEDNESDAY, JUNE 29: It was a day of intensive preparation for Gen. Shafter. He was fully aware that never in the opening campaign of a war had volunteers been entrusted to fight on equal terms with regulars. With his staff he carefully studied the maps. The time was near, he reasoned, that the Spaniards must fight him to avoid his entering Santiago or retreat to the country and abandon the city to the Americans.

With little food to sustain them, Linares and his men were not in a position to move. If they did, they would be forced to fight in a situation where they would not enjoy the advantages they had in Santiago. His choice might come down to surrender or die. "If they cannot resist us behind fortifications," said Shafter, "they will not be a match for us in the open."

Washington expected to hear of a quick knockout and the taking of Santiago. When Adjt. Gen. Corbin was asked, "What of Pando and his reinforcements?" he answered quickly, "We expect to take the city." Asked "Will then Shafter take the city before Pando with his reinforcements comes up?" he said, "We think he will." The War Secretary, trying to hide his concern since his son was actively employed at the front, spoke of the difficulties but predicted a victory.

After his meetings, Gen. Shafter went with a small escort to El Caney, a small town five miles northeast of Santiago. The best information had El Caney with only 300 Spanish troops, a change from previous reports that the Spaniards had fled there from Daiquirí and Juragua.

In the meantime, the Navy Department vehemently discredited reports from Kingston, Jamaica, that the *Brooklyn* had been sunk by a Spanish shell, taking down Commodore Schley and 24 seamen. The Spanish Consul claimed that Spaniards in Kingston were drinking champagne and ecstatic, having supposedly laid an extensive mine that would blow up half the American army when they entered Santiago. Secretary Long was convinced that if there had been trouble at sea, Admiral Dewey would have wired quickly.

Hobson was still not free but was able to cable his father, Judge Hobson: "My health continues good. Feel no uneasiness about me."

In Manila, the American fleet awaited the *Newport*, carrying Maj. Gen. Merritt and his staff along with Companies H and K of the 3rd U.S. Artillery and the Astor Light Battery. The ship had orders to hasten to Honolulu, take on fresh supplies, and proceed to Manila. A sizable delegation came to bid farewell, especially to the Astor Battery.

Tidbits from the Newberry, South Carolina, *Observer*: American generals were very popular in American households, as evidenced by the report that an Alabama woman who named her twins Fitzhugh Lee and Joseph Wheeler was outdone by a Pennsylvania woman, who named her triplets, Sampson, Schley, and Dewey, the latter being a girl; and the war ironically brought tranquility to some homes, as indicated by a letter from an 11-year-old boy, who wrote: "My Pa has gone to fight the Spaniards, and they ain't been no row at home since he left. Ma says peace was declared when he left. An Pa . . . said he thanks God for war, as now he'll have a holiday; and he said he hopes the war'll last 10 years and end so far from home that he can't get back, and when Ma read that she said, Amen. . . . But I guess if Pa was killed, she'd put on mourning and make out like she was sorry. Men is curious, but women is curiouser, and neither one knowes more'n they orter."

12

THE BATTLES OF EL CANEY
AND SAN JUAN HEIGHTS

THURSDAY, JUNE 30: On the eve of battle Americans were edging closer to the fated city of El Caney. From a narrow ridge in the Santiago Valley, the 5th Division of Gen. Lawton could look down on the attractive town. A picturebook scene, but this was war, and the once-charming country hotel, Dugure House, was now home for the Spanish barracks, with a corporal's guard of soldiers.

On the northern side of the valley stood a broad plateau, reachable by road, on which control of Santiago was dependent. With artillery, Americans could command El Caney and force the Spaniards to leave. The battle was not expected to be serious since the Spanish forces were concentrated in Santiago.

The American troops were very close to Santiago. Gen. A. W. Greely announced that a telegraph and telephone station had been set up within two miles of it. They were practically within rifle shot, and reports amusedly came in that Spain had put Red Cross flags on many of the buildings. At least seven were counted, on the city's largest and most prominent buildings. Obviously, the Spanish were hoping to spare them from devastation.

Americans were not flying flags. On the eve of the big battle, they were trying out a comparatively new device in warfare—a big balloon. As a means of surveying Santiago and the surrounding country, Gen. Greely sent a complete balloon train with Gen. Shafter's expedition. Of the latest make, the balloon contained when inflated 17,000 cubic feet of gas.

Confidence reigned. In the words of the *New York Times*, "For all that has been done and all there remains to do in the first Cuban campaign, there is at the White House and the War Department all the confidence in the commanding General that his warmest admirer could desire."

Back in Washington, widely respected journalist Edward Marshall was the object of queries and good wishes after his being wounded in the battle of Quasinas. Dispatches about his condition were contradictory, so Secretary Alger cabled Shafter, who responded, from Playa del Este: "Marshall reported better. *Olivette* should be kept here. About forty men will be sent back by first opportunity to Key West."

At the Presidio in California, Salt Lake City's Private Brattain was tried by court-martial of the 3rd Brigade for sleeping at his post. His defense successfully maintained that as a victim of lead rheumatism, which brought on spells of drowsiness, he was overcome with sleep during one such period. He was given an honorable discharge because of physical disability.

FRIDAY, JULY 1: The great battle began at 10:30 a.m. near Santiago. Anxieties were relieved somewhat in Washington when Gen. Corbin received this early report from Gen. Shafter, dateline "Camp, Near Savilla": "Action now going on. The firing only light and desultory. Began on the right near Caney by Lawton's Division. He will move on that northeast part of the town of Santiago. Will keep you continually advised of progress."

Less than 150 men each were assigned to San Juan Hill and Kettle Hill, two rises on San Juan Heights, the latter of which was so named when soldiers found a large sugarcane kettle at its top, with bullets from the heights ringing of it.

The Rough Riders and the 9th Cavalry, a black regiment, stormed up Kettle Hill and cleared the hill of the enemy. At the same time Gen. Henry Lawton's infantry assaulted the Spaniards at El Caney. The battle was not easy, and casualties mounted on both sides. After five hours, Gen. Shafter ordered Lawton to stop the assault and proceed to below the San Juan Heights. Lawton resisted and convinced Shafter to let him complete the battle.

Finally, at 4 p.m., Lawton's men had beaten the Spaniards, with help from the brigades of Miles and Bates. Had the battle ended earlier, the men would have been available for the assault on San Juan Heights, but the victory at El Caney was important because it cut off the water supply from Santiago.

To control the eastern approach to Santiago, the Americans needed to capture the San Juan Heights. The divisions of Gen. Lawton and Gen. Jacob Kent were positioned to attack San Juan Hill. Well-aimed fire hit them from the top of the ridge, but they charged to take the heights. Gen. Shafter described the action: "After completing their formation, under a destructive fire, and advancing a short distance, both divisions found in their front a wide bottom in which had been placed a barbed-wire entanglement, and beyond which there was a high hill, along the crest of which the enemy was strongly posed."

Correspondent Caspar Whitney has given a masterful description of the battle setting so that the reader is prepared to better understand the three days of fighting: "[T]he road on which the troops were . . . runs westerly past El Pozo hill (one and a half miles out), and crosses water four miles to the San Juan [Heights] blockhouse and ridge. At the last crossing, two creeks, one from the north and one from the eastward join to form . . . forks . . . which . . . become the San Juan River, which runs south to the sea. To the right of the forks, several hundred yards from the road and almost shut out of view by the thick brush . . . is a small rounded hill, an outpost of observation . . . [which] on its east side . . . commands all the country east and south. The road goes on past the forks for 3–400 yards, with dense brush on both sides, and then suddenly leads into an open meadowland, which is 300 yards across . . . in front of and under the . . . blockhouse hill, but narrows to north and south as it runs under . . . ridge. Northeast of San Juan [Heights] about three and one-half miles is El Caney, and three miles almost due south of El Caney is El Pozo. The country between these points is a densely brushed basin, with three roads bearing east and west, and one north and south."

The planned attack was to begin against the heights of San Juan ridge, where the Spaniards were firmly planted, with an artillery bombardment of El Pozo.

The engagement at El Caney continued until sundown. The attack was by land and by sea. One correspondent reported, "It has been a terrible day. . . . [T]he soldiers fought through it and performed . . . [with] valor and endurance. . . . From sunrise until sunset, with only an occasional short intermission, they had to face an enemy strongly entrenched, hidden behind an underbrush so dense it could not be pierced by the eye and scarcely even by a bullet and this enemy trained in exactly that sort of fighting and armed with one of the most effective of magazine rifles. . . .

"We . . . [planned to run] the Spaniards out of El Caney, while a small part of our troops should make a demonstration against Santiago, and another . . . a feint in front of Aguadores, [but] we had to struggle hard for every inch of ground in El Caney the demonstration against Santiago developed into a pitched battle and the feint beyond El Pozo toward Aguadores developed into a scene of carnage."

The Spaniards were valiant fighters, well led, as if defending Madrid rather than an insignificant Cuban town. The artillery was faulted for not having a more major role in the battle. "A few mountain guns or some Gatlings would have given us an easy and swift victory," continued the correspondent. The few artillerists involved were highly commendable: "This is especially true of guns Nos. 3 and 4, handled by Lieut. Hamilton. Gunner Neff of No. 4 did magnificent work. He found the range of 2,350 yards and put every shell just where he ordered. But, despite these instances of good and effective work, the artillery contributed hardly anything toward a victory which cost us dearly, and was hardly necessary to our success at Santiago."

Lawton and his men advanced and seized Cabona, a Santiago suburb. The *Vesuvius* used her dynamite guns with devastating effect. The American fleet bombarded Morro Castle and the other forts at the entrance of the harbor. The War Department received a dispatch at 10 p.m. from Shafter, datelined Siboney: "We have carried their outworks, and now in possession of them. There is about three-quarters of a mile of open between my lines and the city. By morning troops will be entrenched and considerable augmentation of forces will be there. Gen. Lawton's division and Gen. Bates' brigade will be in line and in front of Santiago during the night. [But] I regret . . . our casualties will be above 400, . . . not many killed." (In a brief dispatch about American casualties, the Associated Press reported, "One man had both arms shot off and was wounded in the hip, but was laughing.")

Gen. Corbin admitted that numbers of losses could not be determined precisely at this point. "[T]he loss of an army in an engagement . . . where the battle line extended over several miles, will be much heavier than is indicated by the first results. It is . . . impossible . . . where the battle has raged all day . . . to ascertain with definiteness the loss sustained." Some estimated 500 wounded and killed. Evaluating the day's success, Gen. Corbin noted that despite the difficulties of training the troops for battle and the discomforts the men faced in the camps, "There is every reason why we should win. Our army is the best physically, the best-equipped, the best clothed and shod, and the most intelligent that ever undertook to defeat a foe."

McKinley was so pleased with the results from the first day that he was silently predicting that Monday, July 4, at the latest, could be celebrated as the end of the war. July 4 could also be the day that there would be news of the first expedition landing in Manila under Gen. Anderson. Military authorities were predicting that the Spaniards would begin retreating from Santiago tomorrow and the Americans would not only seize Santiago but also 12,000 enemies in retreat.

The men of three black units were applauded for taking part in the assault: upon the Spanish entrenchments atop San Juan Heights. The 24th Infantry took part in Kent's charge on the blockhouse and the 9th and 10th Cavalries helped assault Kettle Hill and the movement to the extension of San Juan Hill. The valor of the black soldiers had previously earned them Spanish praise as "Smoked Yankees" or "Negretter Soldadas." Now, American correspondent Richard Harding Davis recognized that in the battle of San Juan Hill, "Negro soldiers established themselves as fighting men." The campaign brought 26 Certificates of Merit for black soldiers.

"We officers of the 10th Cavalry could have taken our black heroes in our arms," said Lieut. John J. Pershing, called "Black Jack" because of his assignment with the 10th Cavalry. "They had again fought their way into our affections, as they here had fought their way into the hearts of the American people."

To contemporary scholars, such as Booker T. Washington, the courage and fighting skills of blacks should have been no surprise. They had fought in some 100 battles in the Civil War and in all the Indian wars in the West, since 1866. In *A New Negro for a New Century*, he writes that no one should have been amazed to see these soldiers "emerging on the top of El Caney and San Juan Hill, in a mad surge, singing as they mowed down the enemy, 'There'll Be a Hot Time in the Old Town Tonight.'" So why the incredulity? Answers Washington, "There is a deep-seated disposition among the white Americans to discredit the Afro-Americans, however worthily they acquit themselves, in war or peace" (Washington 37).

Military journals will never record battle heroics of Sherwood Anderson, but it was a day of private glory and fantasy when the Ohio volunteer was promoted to Corporal. "Ha," he exulted. "Was not Napoleon once called the 'little Corsican corporal?'" Later, in *A Story Teller's Story*, he wrote: "[M]y fancy played with the notion of becoming a great general. Why might not Napoleon in his boyhood have been just . . . [like] myself? I had read . . . he had an inclination to be a scribbler. I fancied the army . . . hemmed in on all sides. . . . No one could think what to do and so I (Corporal Anderson) was sent for . . . [as in] the French revolutionists . . . when young Napoleon appeared and with a 'whiff of grapeshot' took the destinies of a nation in his hand. . . . In fancy also I could be a great and cruel conqueror. . . . I sat up . . . outside the tent where my comrades were sleeping and in the darkness gave quick and accurate orders" (279–80).

The biggest battle of the war notwithstanding, Gen. Carroll and Maj. Poole, as representatives of New York State Gov. Black, issued a statement about the condition of their state's troops in three southern camps. For three weeks they visited Camp Alger and the camps at Chickamauga and Tampa. Neither agreed to be interviewed about their findings, but both were sharply critical of the allegations that the New York boys had suffered and endured unfair hardships. Their statement called such reports "bitter falsehoods." The New York volunteers, in fact, were "the finest in the land." In each camp, added Gen. Carroll, "the New York troops compared favorably with the volunteers."

Sadly, the bitterness between enemies again reached down to youngsters. Thirteen-year-old Nellie Connelly of Newark filed charges of assault and battery against Mrs. Manuel Suárez, a Spanish woman, and her six-year-old son, Amata, also of Newark. According to the charges, Nellie had waved an American flag in Amata's face in response to his marching up and down the street near his home wearing the Spanish colors. Amata became incensed and allegedly struck the girl with a beanbag and threw a piece of glass at her, which did not cut her. The case would be heard on July 2 by Judge Lambert in the Second Criminal Court.

SATURDAY, JULY 2: An editorial in the morning's *New York Journal* proclaimed, "Seventy million people in the United States went to bed . . . knowing . . . American guns were thundering at the gates of Santiago. . . . American men were fighting and dying in the . . . fetid thickets of Cuba that a new nation might be born and the cause of human liberty make yet another forward stride."

As the day began, El Caney was firmly in the control of the United States, but could they hold San Juan heights? Washington had read cheerful reports of battle gains the first day, but the day passed without news from Shafter. The White House was deeply concerned. When the papers reported unpleasant news about day two, Secretary Alger told questioners, "Although the department had no information to such effect, the press dispatches announced Gen. Shafter's serious illness; that Gen. Wheeler, next in command was sick, and unable to perform his duties; and that yellow fever had appeared among the troops at Siboney."

In actuality, Gen. Corbin received a note from Shafter at 4 a.m., about the severe underestimate of American casualties, dateline Siboney: "I fear I have underestimated . . . casualties. A large and thoroughly equipped hospital ship should be sent . . . at once. . . . The Chief Surgeon . . . [needs] forty more medical officers. The ship must bring a launch and boat for conveying the wounded."

Within two hours, orders were sent to the hospital ship *Relief* at New York to leave immediately for Santiago. Most cases of sicknesses and wounds would be treated in the regimental and division hospitals; *Relief* would be primarily utilized to bring back to the United States such cases that required treatment in America.

Nonofficial sources estimated the casualties of the first day at nearly 1,000—one-fourth killed, including many officers. In some companies every officer was killed. Shafter told a war correspondent that American soldiers took 2,000 prisoners, and Spanish casualties were at least double that number.

Among the Americans killed was Jacob Wibusky, a Russian Jew from New York who enlisted under the name of Jacob Berlin. He was but 16, and, according to *Jews in the Wars*, he was the first victim in the skirmish.

Among those wounded in action was Samuel Goldberg of New Mexico, a private with Troop A of the Rough Riders, who had received the affectionate nickname "Porkchop" among his comrades.

Samuel Greenberg of Prescott, Arizona, also a private in Troop A, survived and became the most celebrated Jew in the Rough Riders. One of 14 Jewish Rough Riders, his fighting abilities—outside of his troop among his own men—were included in a list cited by Roosevelt after the war: "One of the best colonels among the regular regiments who fought beside me was a Jew. One of the commanders of the ship which blockaded the coast so well was a Jew. In my own regiment, I promoted five men from the ranks for valor and good conduct in battle. It happened by pure accident (for I knew nothing of the faith of any one of them) and these included two Protestants, two Catholics, and one Jew [Greenberg]." His gallantry at San Juan and El Caney led Col. Roosevelt to promote him to Second Lieutenant. These sentiments certainly influenced Roosevelt to accept honorary membership in the Hebrew Veterans of War with Spain.

Associated Press reports highlighted the heroism of American troops in advancing against the enemy's outer works, fighting over two and a half miles of strongly fortified country that was defended with unexpected stubbornness by the enemy. During a break in the action, the 21st Infantry sang "The Star-Spangled Banner," joined by the wounded.

Shafter was aided by the American fleet. Admiral Sampson bombarded the fortifications of the harbor for two hours. Morro Castle was heavily hit, and the eastern, western, and Punta Gorda batteries were devastated in many places. The fleet suffered no casualties. Shafter had turned to Sampson, cabling the naval hero on July 2: "[T]errible fight yesterday. . . . I urge that you make effort immediately to force the entrance [to Santiago Harbor] to avoid future losses among my men, which are already very heavy. You can now operate with less loss of life than I can." Sampson informed Shafter it was "impossible to force entrance until we can clear channel of mines—a work of some time after efforts are taken by your troops." Sampson could not force his way into the harbor. Instead, the Spanish fleet sailed out to meet the blockading fleet of America.

The Utah Packers hardly sound like a group of soldiers. However, they were an unheralded, courageous contingent of soldiers entrusted with transporting supplies and munitions of war. Because Cuba was lacking in wagon roads and trails, supplies had to be transported to the interior on the backs of mules. Packing was a fine art for which the War Department turned to the mountain communities of the West. Those trained packers from Utah who passed the examination had to tie "cargo" on an animal's back, with a "hitch" rope to form a diamond within which the pack or cargo was securely fastened for the journey.

The assignment was filled with danger: fire of the enemy on the battle lines and sharpshooters along the trails. "We never got more than two hours' rest at any one time," said one packer, "generally none at all." Packer Joseph Lee related one incident: "On July 2nd I thought for a minute my time had come. I was on the trail with ammunition at 12 o'clock at night . . . about seven miles from camp . . . riding behind the train. . . . I heard a shot . . . felt the bullet go through my hat and did my best to dismount. It was good and dark. As I raised my right leg, another bullet struck the saddle, just under my leg, and broke the mule's back. As I struck the ground . . . the man in front of me [fell] from his mule. . . . [H]is mule stopped and I grabbed it. [The man] was not very large and I managed to mount his mule with him in my arms. It was but . . . a second, and we made our escape through a shower of bullets."

SUNDAY, JULY 3: An impatient Secretary Alger wired Shafter at 1 a.m., "We are awaiting with intense anxiety tidings of yesterday." Another cable was sent off to Shafter at 11 a.m.: "I waited with the President until four o'clock this morning. . . . Not a word was received, nor has there been up to this hour, 11 a.m., except an account of the battle of Friday, upon which I congratulate you most heartily. I wish hereafter that you interrupt all messages . . . being sent to the Associated Press and others, and make report at the close of each day, or during the day if there is anything of special importance to us."

Shafter finally responded at noon. American troops were having difficulty capturing Santiago, although it had been blockaded by the navy and encircled by land. "We have the town well invested on the north and east but with a very thin line," wired Shafter. "[W]e find it of such a character and the defenses so strong it will be impossible to carry . . . with . . . present force.

"Our losses up to date will aggregate a thousand, but list has not yet been made. But little sickness outside of exhaustion from intense heat and exertion of [Friday's] battle . . . and the almost constant fire which is kept up on the trenches. . . .

"Gen. Wheeler is seriously ill and will probably have to go to the rear today. Gen. Young also very ill, confined in his bed. Gen. Hawkins slightly wounded in foot during sortie enemy made last night, which was handsomely repulsed.

"The behavior of the troops was magnificent.

"Gen. García reported he holds the railroad from Santiago to San Luis, and has burned a bridge and removed some rails; . . . Gen. Pando has arrived at Palma, and . . . the French Consul, with about 400 French citizens, came into his line yesterday from Santiago, have directed him to treat them with every courtesy possible."

That was Shafter's first official communication in 36 hours. Certainly, the President and Secretary Alger were unhappy with the situation. Nevertheless, they agreed to let Shafter devise his own strategy. "Of course," they told him, "you can judge the situation better than we can. . . . If, however, you can hold your present position, especially San Juan heights, the effect upon the country would be much better than falling back."

With all their disappointment, the White House recognized that the troops had fought determinedly inch by inch, under a torturous sun, through a thick tropical vegetation, slowly beating back the opposition, taking position after position. Therefore, Alger's message to Shafter was laudatory: "The President directs me to say that you have the gratitude and thanks of the Nation for the brilliant and effective work of your noble army on Friday, July 1. The steady valor and heroism . . . thrill the American people with pride. The country mourns the brave men who fell in battle. They have added new names to the roll of heroes."

Perhaps additional men would make the difference, said Gen. Miles at a later White House conference. If necessary, 5,000 men could be rushed to Santiago. At present,

Shafter commanded a 23,000-man combined American and Cuban force. The Spaniards had 32,000 men. However, some 10,000 were now at Holguín.

Lists of casualties, often appended with biographies, appeared in the American press. Among the wounded was Lieut. Col. John H. Patterson, born in New York, and appointed a First Lieutenant of the 11th Infantry on May 14, 1861. His heroism in the battle of Chapel House, Virginia, in 1864 led to his being breveted Captain. In 1895 he was promoted to Lieutenant Colonel and transferred to the 22nd infantry, with whom he served in Cuba.

Shocking, detailed scenes of battle were presented in a July 3 letter from Private Walter Ober of the 6th U.S. Cavalry to his brother, Phil, in Hartford, Connecticut. The letter appeared later in the *Hartford Times*: "I am still alive. On the 1st we opened the battle, and were at it from 6:15 a.m. until 6:45 p.m. Phil, it was horrible. The enemy . . . entrenched on the hills, and we were in the open and fought inch by inch to their rifle pits, although shell, shrapnel, and Mauser bullets were flying. Our Captain . . . was shot through the arm. A good friend of mine—Jim Wilson— . . . was shot through the breast and died shortly after the battle. Our regiment lost over 12 percent in killed and wounded. Our colored boys, the 9th . . . fought nobly and were about the first to gain the rifle pits.

"The final charge was glorious. The bugles gave the signal and about 9,000 American soldiers, with yells and cheers, started. The Dons stood it for awhile, but nothing could stop that steady line of blue. A Lieutenant right at my side was shot through the heart, and . . . as I saw him leap in the air and fall dead, such a feeling came over me . . . I was hardly able to go ahead and even now I hear his death cry in my ears.

"The heights were gained and the results of our deadly fire . . . visible. The dead and wounded were thick all around. . . . Our Gatlings had literally mowed them down. One officer lay . . . with the side of his head blown off and his gold lace stained with life blood.

"We had the position taken by about 1 p.m., now to hold only with one brigade and a cavalry division against unnumbered Spaniards. Up the hill they came. . . . A perfect hail of lead met them—carbines, rifles, and Gatling guns. As I worked the magazine of my carbon, my heart turned sick with horror. Men, horses, and every living thing fell, and the enemy fell back . . . about 1,200 yards nearer the city . . . and we had a chance to rest. But with nothing to eat since 4 a.m., we were weak.

"After dark, instead of sleep, we had to dig entrenchments nearer the enemy. We . . . then manned the works and have kept up a fight ever since.

"I think the Dons are getting their fill of Yankee lead. Our little Lieutenant is . . . as cool as ice and with a long head. Our loss in troops was slight on account of [this]. . . . A foreign officer remarked that the taking of this ridge was one of the bravest and best fought battles in history . . . nothing but American grit and courage won the day. The volunteers fight nobly, but got excited and shot their men in front. The 71st New York accidentally killed one of their own. . . . They don't know 'Cease firing' when the bugle sounds it."

13

Sampson's Gift . . . Cervera's Fleet

MONDAY, JULY 4: Independence Day—celebration of freedom and celebration of one of America's great military victories. President McKinley received the following message from Sampson about the exploits of Sunday: "The fleet under my command offers . . . as a Fourth of July present the whole of Cervera's fleet. It attempted to escape at 9:30 this morning [July 3]. At 2 the last ship, the *Cristobal Colón*, had run ashore 75 miles west of Santiago and hauled down her colors. The *Infanta Maria Teresa*, *Oquendo*, and *Vizcaya* were forced ashore, burned, and blown up within 20 miles of Santiago."

Sunday's events were recreated by correspondent George Graham in Charles H. Brown's *The Correspondents' War* (1967). Schley was "relaxing" on the *Brooklyn*. A little after 9:30 word was received that *Iowa* had fired the first shot. Then *Texas* opened with a shot, as Captain Francis A. Cook shouted to the Quartermaster, "The enemy is escaping. Full speed ahead" (378). Cervera's flagship *Infanta Maria Teresa* came out from behind the shore battery, cleared the harbor, fired her forward battery, and started to the west. Next, into the open sea rushed *Teresa*, *Colón*, *Oquendo*, and *Vizcaya*. Rushing out to meet them were the *Brooklyn*, *Oregon*, *Iowa*, *Texas*, and *Indiana*.

Correspondent Henry B. Chamberlin wrote: "Four great battleships began to rain a terrible tonnage of twelve- and thirteen-inch shells, the eight-inch ammunition of the *Brooklyn* shrieked and wailed . . . as it flew on its awful course of destruction. . . . [T]he starboard side of . . . Schley's flagship was a continuous line of flame as secondary batteries and rapid-fire guns spit their murderous contents with such . . . rapidity that the heavy smoke from the . . . broadsides seemed to burn up in the . . . fire as though it was the [fire's] purpose to consume the smoke [so it would] . . . not interfere with the precision of aim" (Brown 377–79).

The *Brooklyn* came almost side to side with *Maria Teresa*, followed by *Vizcaya*, *Oquendo*, and *Colón*. "It was at this time," wrote Graham, "that the frightful work being accomplished . . . by the American squadron could be appreciated. [They were one] . . . pall of smoke . . . from out of which shot blasting flames . . . [licking] the ends of steel projectiles, as they sped on their journey" (Brown 381).

Close to 10:30 the *Oquendo* caught on fire. Then, a shell from the *Texas* followed by a volley from the *Brooklyn* slammed into *Maria Teresa*, which headed back for the beach in flames. A few minutes later the *Oquendo* made its way for the shore. The *Oregon* and *Brooklyn* pounded away; the *Oquendo* went down at 11:05.

Correspondent George E. Graham reported: "As the men started to cheer, Captain Philip admonished, 'Don't cheer, boys! Those poor devils are dying'" (Brown 385). *Brooklyn* and *Oregon* next pursued the *Cristobal Colón*, considered the finest Spanish ship. The *Vizcaya* was run ashore at Aserraderos, destroyed, and on fire. The *Colón* sped close ashore, still chased by the *Brooklyn*, the *Oregon*, and, further back, the *Texas*. They neared Cape Cruz about 12:30 p.m. Schley commanded the *Oregon* to fire her guns. Ten minutes later the *Brooklyn* followed. At 1:15 the Spanish ensign was lowered and the ship ran ashore.

Schley hoisted the signal for the *New York* and the *Texas* in the rear: "A glorious victory has been achieved. Details later." The cable to America was delayed for seven hours because the *Vixen* crew mistook an Austrian flag for a Spanish flag. The cable was sent at 2 a.m. on July 4.

Typical of the newspapers' patriotic exultation, the *New York Morning Journal* shouted in its headlines: "Cervera's Fleet Smashed; Shafter Demands Santiago; It Is a Glorious Fourth." In its editorial it addressed the question being debated everywhere: "Who was *the* hero?" Since Sampson was seven miles away from Santiago Harbor when Cervera came out and Schley was there from beginning to end: "Moreover, it was Schley who originally bottled up Cervera in Santiago Harbor. He ran the Spaniards to earth, kept guard over them until Sampson joined him, and now has exterminated them as a fighting force. Schley is as much the hero of Santiago as Dewey is at Manila."

Historians would long debate Sampson's role in the battle. Did he actually steam away in the heat of the battle? Many felt he had a series of mild strokes causing him to suffer moments of catatonia and aphasia and that naval doctors prescribed sea duty as a means of mental rehabilitation. In fact, a December 1995 *Naval History* article, entitled "The Trouble with Admiral Sampson," linked Sampson with Vladimir Lenin and Woodrow Wilson as a trio who, incapacitated by strokes, spent their last months unable to speak and seemingly demented (Natsky and Beach 8–16).

The joy of the military was articulated in a cable from Gen. Shafter, dateline July 4, Playa del Este: "When the news of the disaster to the Spanish fleet reached the front . . . during the truce, the . . . band [members] that had managed to keep instruments on the line, played 'The Star-Spangled Banner' and 'There'll Be a Hot Time in the Old Town Tonight,' men cheering from one end of the line to the other. Officers and men, without even shelter tents, have been soaking for five days in the afternoon rains, but all are happy."

Having annihilated the Spanish Navy, Shafter demanded the surrender of Santiago at noon; in response the foreign Consuls made a joint representation that women and children have until noon, Tuesday, July 5, to leave town before the bombardment would begin. Spanish Commander José Toral refused to surrender, but Shafter still agreed to the postponement. "It is my duty to say to you," responded Toral, "that this city will not surrender and that I will inform the foreign Consuls . . . of your message."

According to Sampson, Americans casualties were two injured and one killed; 1,300 Spaniards were taken prisoner, including Admiral Cervera. The American killed was Yeoman George H. Ellis of the flagship *Brooklyn*. Ellis, 27, of Peoria, Illinois, and residing in Hills Head, New York, had a little more than a year of naval service. His only cruise was his last; his death was captured in all its poignancy by Graham: "Plainly distinguishable from the hum and buzz of the Spanish shells . . . flying over us . . . [was] a dull, sickening thud, and the warm blood and brains splattering in our faces and on our clothes gave warning of a fatality even before the smoke cleared. When we could see, there lay Ellis' body curled in an inanimate heap on the deck, the head having . . . [been] carried away by the impact of a large shell."

The *Jewish Veteran* of April 1938, however, maintains that Edward Gratz, chief master-at-arms on the *Oregon*, was also killed during the battle, along with First Lieut. Frank Lyon.

Dewey, who was a full Commodore when his heroism became legendary at Manila, was now a Rear Admiral. During the engagement with Cervera, Sampson was a Captain, acting as Admiral; his promotion to Commodore was sent to the Senate today. The *New York Times* argued for his promotion to Rear Admiral. Comparing the exploits of Dewey and Sampson, the paper observed: "In dash and daring, and in the very isolation of his attack on the Spaniards in Manila Bay, . . . Dewey's was the more brilliant performance. . . . [But in] its effects on the war and in the size and character of the vessels engaged, Sampson's achievement is taken to be the greater."

Mrs. Sampson was joyous: "No words can express the joy and relief I feel . . . the first really happy day I have had in six months. While I always . . . knew our fleet would be victorious . . . and had every confidence in my husband, . . . still I constantly feared that . . . my husband's life would be in danger. He was . . . of course, but he has come through safely and so have his men. . . . Yesterday, . . . my husband . . . a Captain, in reality, . . . became entitled to the rank of Commodore. How well he seems to have celebrated it." Joining in the celebration were the residents of Palmyra, New York, his birthplace. A salute of 100 guns was fired, with a display of fireworks, and bonfires were lit in many parts of the city.

The talk was of Dewey, Sampson, and Schley, but Hobson was not forgotten. All hoped he would be freed with the surrender of Santiago or as a straight exchange for Cervera. But an exchange of a Spanish Admiral for a Naval Constructor? Proponents argued that Cervera had acted nobly when he captured Hobson and the other *Merrimac* men.

With the Spanish Navy destroyed, the fall of Santiago imminent, once more thoughts turned to the invasion of Puerto Rico. The transports used for Santiago would be available for the next expedition—some 30,000 men.

But the immediate attention was still Santiago. A report in the *New York Times* pinpointed the problem: "[The battle of Santiago] . . . was not finished . . . merely interrupted . . . to give the Spaniards an opportunity to surrender . . . [which] the enemy has not . . . embrace[d]. . . . [H]e has hardened his heart . . . resolved to fight to the last ditch. . . . [T]he Spaniard is quite capable . . . of dying in the last ditch if he does not suddenly take to flight and scamper over the hills . . . and disappear in the tangled thickets.

"We have given [them] . . . an opportunity . . . to get their non-combatants out . . . and to get reinforcements in. About 3,000 women and children . . . are [already] seeking refuge within our lines at El Caney. We have not food enough to support [them] long, and . . . to support our own forces so far from home.

"The problem will be doubled if we have to look after 30,000 persons from Santiago. . . . It would be more humane to kill the Spaniards and lose several thousand of our own forces than . . . to starve the Spaniards and decimate our army by fever and other diseases . . . far more deadly than the Mauser rifle."

TUESDAY, JULY 5: One ship of the Spanish squadron, the *Reina Mercedes*, had escaped destruction because she had not come out with the other ships. Today, after midnight, she came out—whether to escape or to be sunk to block the entrance à la the *Merrimac*, is not clear—however, once spotted, she became entangled in a 15-minute battle with the *Texas*, *Massachusetts*, and *Indiana*. The only shell returned by *Mercedes* landed in the forward deck of the *Indiana*. No one was injured. The *Mercedes* sank, her bow resting on the base of the beach under El Morro. It was later revealed that she did not participate in the July 3 battle because of defective machinery.

The War Department reached an agreement with the Merritt & Chapman Wrecking Company to salvage as much as possible from the Spanish wrecks. *Cristobal Colón*, the best ship in their navy, perhaps could be gotten off the rocks in its entirety. But time was critical. A violent tropical cyclone was raging on the Spanish coast and the ships could be destroyed if it reached Cuba before the wreckers.

Following the attack the population began emptying from Santiago. Stephen Crane observed the exodus: "One saw in this great assemblage the true horror of war. The sick, the lame, the halt and the blind were there. Women and men, tottering on the verge of death, plodded doggedly onward. Beyond were our lines and safety."

Gen. Shafter sent a message saying, "[Santiago] . . . is in a terrible condition as to food. The people are starving. Rice is practically the only staple . . . they have." The crops in the vicinity were depleted; a few mangoes were all that remained.

As for the Americans, Shafter said, "The men are in good spirits and remarkably well. All the wounded . . . doing singularly well." No one had died of yellow fever; no cases of blood poisoning had been reported; said a medic of the Hospital corps, "There is not a moan or a murmur among the whole 700."

However, two officers had died on July 4: Dr. Danforth, Assistant Surgeon of the 9th Cavalry, who was gunned down by a Spanish sharpshooter while treating the wounded of Company C, 6th Infantry, and Lieut. Putnam of the 6th Infantry. Their wounds indicated that the enemy was not only using explosive bullets, but also brass-covered bullets with the ends filed. They inflicted ghastly wounds, ripping the flesh like barbed wire.

Reinforcements were forthcoming. Col. Wood's Rough Riders would welcome 100 more men, coming by way of Savannah, more than half described as six footers and daring riders. The 1st and 2nd Volunteer Brigades of the 1st Corps, led by Gen. James H. Wilson, would leave Chickamauga for Santiago by way of Charleston.

A *New York World* article, headlined "71st Men Heroes Every One; How New Yorkers Charged in Face of an Awful Fire and Bayoneted the Enemy," reported: "Undying glory has been won by the 71st . . . in the terrible struggle at Santiago. When it marches again through the streets of the city, after the Dons have been beaten and the peace won, its ranks will be thin and gapped, but its muster roll will be a roll of heroes. Side by side with the regulars, . . . the young New Yorkers . . . fought with a steadiness and cool daring unsurpassed by the soldiers of any nation. . . .

"San Juan . . . was the key to the Spanish position . . . the strongest outpost the enemy had. A fort of San Juan Heights commanded the foreground. . . . It was against this that the 71st was sent . . . to form the center of the attacking column. With [them] were the [6th] and 16th regulars. . . . [They] swept up the hill . . . went over the breastworks, capturing a stand of colors, several prisoners, and the Spanish wounded. Forts, blockhouses, and earthworks were taken and Old Glory was flung in the breeze . . . after the most desperate land fighting . . . up to that point. Everywhere praises were heard for the 71st."

The local casualties were 13 wounded and 4 killed. The four were Edward Holland, Private, of the Bronx, who gave up a "lucrative" job as an electrician to join the National Guard; F. W. Schofield, Private, of Manhattan; Lewis B. Sinner, Private, of Chester, New Jersey, prominent in Y.M.C.A. affairs; and George Trumen, Corporal, of Manhattan, a member of the regiment for two years and among the first to enlist in the regular army.

WEDNESDAY, JULY 6: No war bulletins were received on this date. Instead, President McKinley issued a proclamation: "At this time, when to the . . . remembrance of an unprecedented success . . . in the Bay of Manila . . . are added the . . . glorious achievements . . . at Santiago de Cuba. . . . It is fitting we should pause . . . and give devout praise to God, who holdeth the nation in the hollow of His hands and . . . has thus far . . . led our brave soldiers and seamen to victory.

"I therefore ask the people . . . upon next assembling for Divine worship in their respective places of meeting, to offer thanksgiving to Almighty God. . . . With the . . . thanks let there be mingled . . . prayers that our gallant sons may be shielded from harm . . . and be spared the scourge of suffering and disease while they are striving to uphold their country's honor; and . . . let the Nation's heart be stilled . . . at the thought of the noble men who have perished . . . and be filled with compassion . . . for all those who suffer bereavement, or endure sickness, wounds, and bonds by reason of awful struggle.

"And, above all, let us pray . . . that He, the Dispenser of all good, may speedily remove from us the . . . afflictions of war and bring to our . . . land the blessings of restored peace and to . . . the domain now ravaged . . . security and tranquility."

Americans were already grateful. Their hero was free. Hobson was exchanged for prisoners captured by American forces, at a tree between American and Spanish lines, two-thirds of a mile beyond the entrenchment occupied by Wood's Rough Riders, near Gen. Wheeler's headquarters.

The American prisoners left the Reina Mercedes Hospital, on the outskirts of Santiago, where they had been confined at 2:45 that afternoon. Under the charge of Spanish staff officer Maj. Irles, they were conducted to the exchange on foot, not blindfolded.

In charge of the Spanish prisoners were Lieut. John D. Miley and Col. John Jacob Astor, accompanied by interpreter Maestro. The 17 prisoners were taken through the American lines mounted and blindfolded. Three were Lieutenants, the rest noncommissioned Officers and Privates. The three Lieutenants—Aurolius (a German belonging to the 29th Regiment who was captured at El Caney), Amelio Voles (also captured at El Caney), and Adolfo Aries (of one of the most aristocratic military organizations of the Spanish army, the First Provisional Regiment of Barcelona)—were returned in exchange for Hobson.

The men of the *Merrimac* were first received by Gen. Wheeler and then escorted through the American lines by Captain French Chadwick of the *New York*. As they passed through the lines, soldiers threw all dignity to the winds, scrambling out of entrenchments, knocking over tents and paraphernalia to catch a glimpse of their heroes, and cheering wildly upon seeing them. It was the heroics of the navy on July 3 that made the freedom of the *Merrimac* heroes possible, yet, as correspondent Harding Davis wrote: "The men who had made it possible for . . . [Hobson] to . . . breathe free air again had waited for his coming for many hours, crouched . . . along the high banks of the narrow trail. . . . As brave men, they honored a brave man; and this sun-tanned, dirty, half-starved, fever-racked mob . . . danced about the educated, clever engineer as though the moment was his, and forgot that at the risk of their lives they had set him free, that the ground he rode over had been splashed with their blood" (Brown 396–97).

Writer Crane, who thought the homage had a touch of the comic, wrote: "The soldiers lay on the ground waiting for Hobson and his friends. Finally: 'Here they come!' Then . . . [they] did a strange thing. They arose en masse and came to 'Attention.' . . . They slowly lifted every weatherbeaten hat and drooped it until it touched the knee. Then . . . a magnificent silence, broken only by the measured hoofbeats . . . as [the *Merrimac* men] rode through the gap. . . . Then, suddenly, the whole scene went to rubbish. . . . Hobson was bowing right and left like . . . [the French military and political leader] Boulanger" (Brown 397).

When Hobson and his companions were finally received by Gen. Shafter, Hobson declined to be interviewed about the *Merrimac* incident, pending his report to Admiral Sampson. However, he told the large group of correspondents of his experiences as a Prisoner of War and of his personal regard for Cervera: "During the first four days . . . we were confined to Morro Castle, and . . . these were extremely uncomfortable and disagreeable days. The Spaniards did not exactly ill-treat us, but it took them some time to recover from the shock caused by . . . our Yankee 'impudence' in trying to block their harbor. As a rule, . . . [those] who came in contact with us were gruff in speech and sullen in manner. There were many threatening glances. . . .

"For Admiral Cervera, I have nothing but the highest admiration. . . . His act in informing Admiral Sampson of our safety . . . [was] that of a kindhearted, generous man and chivalrous officer. I expressed . . . my sincere thanks and the thanks of my men. . . . He repeatedly spoke to me of his admiration of what he called one of the most daring acts in naval history."

A cable from Siboney quoted more of Hobson's comments: "When Lieut. Hobson rode into Siboney . . . he was at once recognized and was welcomed with cheers. Wounded men . . . crowded around him to shake his hand, declaring . . . their admiration and breaking frequently into hurrahs. 'Don't men,' he said. . . . 'Any of you would have done the same thing.'

"'Did they treat you well?' the wounded soldiers inquired. . . .

"'Rather roughly at first,' . . . [he] answered, 'as they treat all their prisoners, but I protested that it was shameful, and then they gave me a good room and a chance to exercise and food, such as they had. You have taught them respect you lads, and you have damaged them considerably in spirit.'" (Hobson's confinement in Morro Castle is fully detailed in his book *The Sinking of the Merrimac* [80–130].)

Not all had the happy ending of those of the *Merrimac*. One of the war's victims had a foreboding of his tragedy. On June 26, Mrs. F. Beatty of 206 S. 8th Street in Brooklyn, received a letter from her tenant Charles D. Holland of the 71st Regiment, brother of John P. Holland, inventor of the submarine torpedo. An agent with the Metropolitan Life Insurance Company who enlisted with the 71st at the first call, he had paid one year's premium on a $1,000 policy on his life to his employer. In the letter he said he had a presentiment that he would be killed and asked Mrs. Beatty to dispose of his belongings if that happened. Word came the next week that he was killed at Santiago. He was an active member of Brooklyn's Iroquois Club, which asked to secure his body from Cuba.

Another member of the 71st, Oscar W. Hochstadter of Company F, predicted a difficult time in Cuba, but thankfully survived the battle of El Caney. In a letter dated June 25, to his father, Oscar Hochstadter, an attorney at 324 Broadway, Manhattan, he wrote: "Before me lies the harbor and one transport with about 1,000 Cubans . . . to guide me through the woods. . . . I had my first taste of . . . the front yesterday . . . in the fight on . . . those darned hills about eight miles' walk up. . . . Teddy's Rough Riders brought what they got on themselves. . . . [T]hey did too much. We were the reserves. . . . Lots of the men were knocked out by the heat, but . . . I was not. . . . You can't imagine . . . how I live. . . . This is war, and . . . by the time this reaches you, the battle of Santiago, will have been fought, and only God knows with what result. I don't want to worry you, but we will have a hot time. With my faith still in God, I . . . hope to come home safe and sound. . . .

"The heat is fierce, but in the morning . . . it is freezing cold. The . . . fog is very thick. . . . Was detailed last night to carry wounded. It was pitiable, their suffering. . . .

"The land here is picturesque to those . . . not fighting, but the Spanish devils are hidden in every nook and corner. I learned . . . we have gained many miles on them and forced their retreat. . . . 'Damn them, they won't come out' is the cry. I hope our guns will bring them out and . . . end this war."

It took courage to be out on the front lines, but it was hard to be at home, keeping the faith like Mr. Hochstadter and his wife. An unsigned poem in the *Baltimore Times*, titled "The Brave at Home," was dedicated to "the sweethearts and the wives." Eight stanzas long, it begins:

We do not send them all away—
Our bravest and our best—
When the battle cry is sounding
And the eagle leaves its nest;
There are brave battalions marching
And the heroes face the war
Of the guns that belch their lightning
In the thunderstorm of war.

But the brave hearts, true hearts,
The hearts that wait at home
For the news that tells of battle
On the field or on the foam,
Are the hearts that beat with courage
And the hearts whose hoping thrives,
O, the little lips of loving
And the sweethearts and the wives.

THURSDAY, JULY 7: The glow still not worn off of his release, Hobson granted the Associated Press an interview about the battle: "[I]t was owing to the splendid discipline of the men that we were not killed, as the shells rained over us, and minutes became hours of suspense. The men's mouths grew parched; but we must lie there till daylight, I told them. Now and again one of the men . . . his face glued to the desk, and wondering whether the next shell would not come our way, would say, 'Hadn't we better drop off now, Sir?' But I said, 'wait till daylight.'

"It would have been impossible to get the catamaran anywhere but on to the shore, where two soldiers stood shooting, and I hoped that by daylight we might be . . . saved. The . . . *Merrimac* kept sinking. I wanted to go forward and see the damage. . . . One man said that if I rose it would draw all the fire on the rest. So I lay motionless. . . . The fire of the soldiers, the batteries and the *Vizcaya* was awful. When the water came up to the *Merrimac*'s decks, the catamaran floated amid the wreckage, . . . still made fast to the moon, and we caught hold of the edges and clung on, our heads only being above water. . . .

"A Spanish launch came toward the *Merrimac*. We agreed to capture her and run [but] . . . the Spaniards saw us and . . . jumped up and pointed their rifles at our heads. . . . 'Is there any officer . . . to receive a surrender . . . ?' I shouted. An old man leaned out . . . and waved his hand. It was Admiral Cervera. The marines lowered their rifles, and we were helped into the launch."

Greensborough, Alabama, closed down to mark the freedom of its favorite son. Judge James M. Hobson, the father, received the news at 10 a.m. and immediately told his wife. Businesses were suspended and people conferred how best to honor young Hobson.

The voice of American Jewry, the *American Israelite*, celebrated America's victories in the war, with echoes from the Bible, in "The Miracle and the Revelation of the Fin de Siècle": "It is the most astounding miracle of our age . . . the first repetition in history of the Israelites passing the Red Sea, and the extinction of the pursuing host of Egyptians . . . the miracle of the Fin de Siècle. Right in the first conflict . . . Spain lost the Philippine Islands [and] Santiago . . . is at the point of losing Puerto Rico, and the whole of Cuba . . . and none but God Almighty can release it from our grasp. . . .

"The world's opinion about the American volunteer soldier is radically changed, for . . . at sea [and] . . . on land . . . one short battle . . . sufficed to rout and capture the Spanish army defending [Santiago], . . . an army of veterans crushed . . . by an army of volunteers. . . . [T]he same miracle that was wrought . . . when Joshua with his liberated slaves and unskilled laborers slew . . . the warlike and hardened sons of the wilderness. . . . The free man is always a better soldier than the trained and drilled slave. . . .

"In the present situation this . . . enlightened nation of America has . . . take[n] up the cudgels of war in the cause of liberty and justice. . . . We Jews must . . . realize the righteousness and piety of such an action. We above all, . . . from our own sad history, sympathize with afflicted, suffering humanity. . . . The very thought of the present crisis cannot but recall . . . the death cries of the . . . inquisition . . . the agonies and groans of . . . martyred Jews . . . shrieks of anguish . . . and the last words of prayer that escaped from the pallid lips of . . . the thousands upon thousands of Jews, Spain's most loyal and trusted citizens. . . .

"I do not hesitate to say that were Spain . . . wiped off the face of the earth, it would . . . not be able to atone for the blood which it has shed during the last 400 years."

Abraham Goldfeden, best known for his popular Yiddish song, "Rushenkes und Mandelen" (Raisins and Almonds), wrote "To War," identified by him as a "heroic poem dedicated to all Jewish volunteers in the Spanish-American War of 1898," for use in assemblies and synagogues. It begins with the blowing of the Shofar "from near and far," calling upon all who have a "Jewish feeling" to assemble and gather in the synagogue to hear the priestly blessing. It continues:

> Raise one hand upon another hand
> For your children, who are to do their service
> For the Lord, for their brothers, for their free land.
> Open the ark! Let them be influenced
> By the holy flag of the Lord of Hosts—

It tells the assembled they can take pride . . . they are following in the tradition of their heroic ancestors, the Maccabees:

> Now their descendants, freewillingly, joyfully, without fear
> Are able to advance without anxiety or hardship . . .
> As a legacy is their pride and courage
> Transferred in flesh and blood.—
> Show your brothers, the Americans
> That their law is but "liberty,"
> To fight for freedom, for foreigners, the Cubans,
> You have also learned in schools . . .
> Thousands of unhappy black slaves . . .
> Who freed them from their bondage?

You were also oppressed by Slavic tyrants! . . .
How do you now feel with Uncle Sam?!
Pay them back now freewillingly your tribute
With golden devotion, with life, with blood.—
Show sons of Zion that you can overcome the nations
That mistreat humanity; . . .
The despot sees . . .
That it is unpleasant to always be the Satan— . . .
He will see that not with a leather whip
Does one squeeze out patriotic blood.

Serving behind the scenes so far, Maj. Gen. Miles became a newsmaker when he left Washington tonight, as General commanding the army, to take charge of the American forces in Santiago. He had wanted to go for some time, but differences of opinion between Miles and the War Secretary had prevented this.

The Major General issued a detailed order to the Army in Cuba requiring abstinence from intoxicating beverages, because: "[I]n a hot climate abstinence from the use of intoxicating drink is essential to continued health and efficiency. . . . In this most important hour of the Nation's history, it is due the Government from all those in its service that they should not only render the[ir] most earnest efforts . . . but their physical and intellectual force should be given . . . uncontaminated by any indulgences that shall dim, stultify, weaken, or impair their faculties and strength in any particular."

Another newsmaker was the 13th Regiment, National Guard, which was disbanded and mustered out at Camp Black for refusing to go into camp as one body; when ordered to meet at the Flatbush section of the Long Island railroad station on May 2, only a small number of the 384 men showed up. Adjt. Gen. Tillinghast announced that the men would be attached to the 22nd Regiment of the National Guard and form one of its battalions.

While the destruction of Cervera's fleet only promised promotions for a select few, all the officers and men were guaranteed a sum of about $250,000 in bounty money, according to the law. To date seven Spanish ships were destroyed at Santiago, totalling 2,500 men, at $100 a head. According to the rules, Admiral Sampson's share would be about $12,000; Commodore Schley would be granted one-fiftieth of the amount given to his vessels.

FRIDAY, JULY 8: Gen. Miles was headed for Santiago, but chances were by the time he arrived, the battle would be on and perhaps over. Although thousands of noncombatants continued to leave the city, Toral refused Shafter's demand for unconditional surrender, and Shafter was preparing to resume operations. The siege guns that had been landed at Daiquirí were now in position to command the Spanish lines and the city. They were prepared to advance under the protection of the largest guns taken out from Tampa.

Shafter sent the War Department a statement of the casualties in his army, by division and brigade; casualties of the army under Wheeler's command were not yet reported. The hospital at Siboney had treated 1,052 wounded, with 200 still there; in Lawton's division (8th, 22nd, 16th, 4th, 25th, 7th, 12th, and 17th U.S. Infantry

Regiments and 2nd Massachusetts Volunteer Infantry)—4 officers and 74 men killed, 14 officers and 317 men wounded, and 1 man missing; in Kent's division (16th, 6th, 2nd, 10th, 21st, 9th, 13th, and 24th U.S. Infantry Regiments and the 71st New York Volunteers)—12 officers and 87 men killed, 36 officers and 662 men wounded, and 62 men missing; in Bates' brigade (2nd Brigade of Kent's Division, 2nd, 10th, and 21st U.S. Infantry Regiments)—4 men killed, 2 officers and 26 men wounded, and 5 men missing; in the Signal Corps—1 man killed and 1 man wounded. The totals were 182 killed, 748 wounded, and 68 missing.

With the release of Hobson, attention diverted to other important Prisoners of War. Admiral Cervera was reverently called by Americans the "old warrior," his treatment towards the *Merrimac* crew receiving praise. One proposal was to release him on parole or confine him to the Naval Academy reservation at Annapolis, where all other captured Spanish naval officers would remain. Rius Rivera, a Major General in the Cuban Army, was in charge of the Cuban troops in Pinar del Rio when captured in 1897. The Cubans sought to exchange Rius Rivera for Spanish prisoners, telling America his release would be most valuable in a Puerto Rican campaign since he was born there and very familiar with the country.

H. B. Bivins, a graduate of the Hampton Institute and decorated member of the black 10th Cavalry, described his experiences in the battle of San Juan Hill in a letter later published in the *Southern Workman*: "I was 60 hours under heavy fire; four of our gunners were wounded. I got hit myself, was sighting my hotchkiss gun. I was stunned . . . but soon forgot that I was hit. I was recommended . . . for bravery in action. . . .

"I need not tell you how my regiment fought. Bravery was displayed by all of the colored regiments. The officers and reporters of other powers said they had heard of the colored man's fighting qualities, but did not think they could do such work as they had witnessed in the 60 hours' battle." His postscript shows a touch of pain: "Sorry to tell you I have killed more than 100 Spaniards; some . . . with a carbine."

SATURDAY, JULY 9: Gen. Toral offered to surrender, but he insisted that it be "with honor," meaning that his troops be permitted to march away under arms and with colors. If not, the Spaniards would fight to the bitter end. Shafter said no. The surrender must be unconditional; but he would extend the deadline one more day. He felt that to allow Toral and his troops to make their way unhindered into the interior would have enabled them to reinforce the Havana garrison by thousands of trained soldiers.

McKinley hoped Santiago would fall without the need of additional American bloodshed. He said that Spain should be encouraged to surrender although he gave Shafter the "OK" to propose his own terms. In case Spain did not surrender, Shafter had everything ready for attack, including the dynamite gun, which was now in better working order than in the beginning of July. It was predicted that its charges, consisting of 20 pounds of guncotton and gelatine, would wreak havoc in the Spanish trenches. The gun had been so placed that it would be able to enfilade several of the Spanish lines.

The *Iowa* had been struck twice by Spanish shells during the engagement of July 3.

One shell exploded, but the other was unbedded, unexploded near the water line of the ship, so it would be necessary to keep the *Iowa* from accompanying the Eastern squadron to the coast of Spain. Either the *Massachusetts* or the *Indiana* would be substituted to accompany the Squadron, under its commander in chief, John Watson.

Obviously, the damage of the *Iowa* in no way was comparable to the ruins of the Spanish fleet, which littered the Cuban coast. Reported the Associated Press, "The scenes of desolation, ruin, horror, and death . . . [baffle] description." Speaking of the *Infanta Maria Teresa* and the *Almirante Oquendo*, the story continues: "Their boilers, engines, bunkers, and magazines have been blown into masses of twisted, melted iron. The deck beams are twisted, side armor plates weighing tons have been wrenched off, the protective decks only stand in places, and there are many evidences . . . of where the shots of the *Brooklyn* and *Oregon* landed. The decks are strewed with officers' uniforms, provisions, and some small arms, and pieces of yellow brasswork and gold and silver coin, melted by the intense heat."

When the news of American casualties reached New York, reports said that Woodbury Kane of the Rough Riders, a prominent member of New York society, was severely wounded. The notice drew so much attention that Clara Barton of the National Red Cross Society looked into the matter: "I have just seen Roosevelt. Woodbury Kane is . . . an officer in the trenches and . . . jim dandy."

However, not all the men in Cuba were so fit. While no statistics had been released, the climactic conditions in Cuba were bringing severe problems of yellow fever and other illnesses. The Associated Press carried a story from a correspondent in Siboney: "Some idea may be formed of the rapid inroad of disease when I say an officer has just told me that in one company of his regiment . . . eight men were sent to the hospital yesterday. More will go today and tomorrow. His men . . . have been sleeping, marching, working, and fighting in the same underclothing, unwashed and unaired, for 14 days. On the day of the battle of El Caney they had breakfast and marched almost continuously until the evening of the following day before they had another meal. Only the tension of fighting kept their muscles and sinews taut and their hearts stout. . . . Is it strange that . . . there is sickness and death? . . .

"It is sickening to write of . . . but the vultures still hover above dead soldiers rotting in the wilderness. . . . [I]t is not possible to discover all the bodies . . . in this tangled and matted jungle. I heard a soldier say . . . he and some companions . . . three days ago came upon a man who had been wounded on . . . the 2nd. He was . . . half-crazed . . . and thought it was still the day he had been hit. . . . He had lain in the woods four days.

"Disease is beginning to prey upon the little groups of noncombatants also. A number of the correspondents, probably 20, have had to . . . return home. Some, . . . after a day or two of the experience of this climate and the hardships of campaigning here. . . . Of about 100 correspondents who started . . . about 25 have had to yield to sickness or fatigue. Sickness has also [hit] . . . men in civil work connected with the army. . . .

"What does tell on us are the rain and the hot sun. Lying in wet clothing on a wet soil, and then marching through the broiling sun from 10 a.m. to 4 p.m. is filling our hospitals now, and will soon be filling graves. . . . With our resources it should not have been necessary for a single soldier to sleep in wet clothing on the reeking ground . . . or for men to fight and march without abundant and proper food or live in unwashed and unaired clothes for two weeks."

Nevertheless, Americans had much to be thankful for, said the President, and in keeping with his proclamation, services in synagogues today and churches tomorrow were planning thanksgiving services. The Rev. Dr. Stephen S. Wise of the Madison Avenue Synagogue changed his plans to go out of town upon hearing the President's call. In addition to the prayer read regularly since the beginning of the war, Rabbi Wise would open the ark and read the President's proclamation, offer a special prayer, deliver a sermon on the war, and call for fitting hymns of thanksgiving. At Temple Beth-El on 5th Avenue and 66th Street, the Rev. Dr. Herrmann Silverman said he would lead a special prayer, prepared by the Rev. Dr. Kohler, with responses by the congregation.

In St. Patrick's Cathedral, as well as other Roman Catholic churches, liturgical prayers of thanksgiving would be offered after each of the masses on Sunday, and prayers would be offered for those who died in battle. At Plymouth Church in Brooklyn, a thanksgiving service would be held Sunday, at which the Rev. Horace Porter would preside. The congregation would be addressed by Gen. C. T. Christensen.

One loud dissent emerged after the President's call. The Hudson Turn Verein of Jersey City Heights, primarily a Socialist group, denounced the proclamation and said that no one had to thank God. It was American heroism and arms that were responsible. Not all members agreed, and some left before the following was adopted: "Resolved, that we call attention of all free and liberal thinking Americans to the . . . Proclamation of the President, . . . wherein he enjoins this Nation to give thanks to the Almighty . . . as at variance with the spirit and progress of our age. Resolved, that we ascribe the victories won by our army and navy to their superior condition, and we are fully aware that throughout history battles and war have always been won by superior military force."

14

BOMBARDMENT AND CAPITULATION OF SANTIAGO

SUNDAY, JULY 10: When Gen. Toral rejected surrender, Shafter finalized arrangements for the naval bombardment of Santiago. He asked Sampson to start firing at 4 a.m., saying, "It would be very disastrous for the morale of my men to have . . . shells fall near them, . . . [so] it would be better at first to put your shots in the western part of the city near the bay." The *Brooklyn* and *Indiana* fired a few eight-inch shells but accomplished nothing.

Shafter alerted the War Department: "[R]eceived a letter from Gen. Toral declining unconditional surrender. Bombardment by army and navy will begin as near 4 p.m. . . . as possible."

The firing was confirmed in a later dispatch: "Enemy opened fire . . . with light guns, which were soon silenced by ours. Very little musket fire, and the enemy kept entirely in their entrenchments. Three men slightly wounded.

"Will have considerable force tomorrow, enough to completely block all the roads on the northwest. . . .

"Gen. García reports that the enemy evacuated a little town . . . Descantinos, about three miles from Santiago and near the bay."

The War Department reasoned that since the bombardment started so late, Shafter's force was probably not ready. Said Gen. Corbin, "I should say that the firing today was but the preliminary to the more serious business of tomorrow." Prebombardment telegrams indicated that Shafter was pleased with the condition of the American lines and that the lines were impregnable and precluded any Spanish sortie.

The auxiliary cruiser *St. Louis* arrived in Portsmouth, New Hampshire, with 746 Spanish prisoners, including 54 officers. Ill for the past three days, Admiral Cervera was confined to his cabin; he said he was treated most kindly on the ship although he was depressed over the loss of his fleet. The commander of the *Vizcaya*, Capt. Antonio Eulate, was also quite sick, wounded in the head during the battle of Santiago.

Observance of the President's proclamation continued. Archbishop Ireland devoted his sermon to America's victories and paid tribute to the President: "The chieftain of America prays for peace. Magnanimous McKinley, worthy chieftain . . . courted peace before the war. . . . War coming . . . he waged it with vigor, with skill."

Springfield, Ohio, minister Dr. E. A. Steiner of the First Congregational Church, a naturalized Austrian citizen, visited Madrid and reported: "The hatred of America is intense. . . . [P]igs are decorated with American flags and tortured as they pass through the streets. One was nearly killed by my side, and the brute who did it didn't know that the genuine Yankee was so near. The people there are helpless, most of them clamoring for peace."

MONDAY, JULY 11: The bombardment continued, starting at 9:30 a.m. and continuing until 1. The cruiser *Newark* first opened fire into Santiago with her eight-inch guns. The *New York*, *Indiana*, and *Brooklyn* joined in the firing at five-minute intervals. But the city was four and a half miles away, hidden by a range of hills 250 feet high at its lowest part. The shelling did little damage.

Reporting for the *Chicago Record*, Kenneth F. Harris observed: "At five-minute intervals the American guns and mortars have been sending their missiles crashing into the enemy trenches . . . in a perfunctory sort of way—a . . . gentle cuffing . . . to assure him that we retain our position on top, rather than . . . to inflict mortal damage." Firing from Santiago was equally of little value. "The Spanish were not terrified into silence, but their return fire was weak and ill-directed."

Gen. Miles arrived on the *Yale* off Santiago Bay, a little after noon. He had two goals: land his troops to the west of the harbor entrance and launch a direct assault with joint forces from the 5th Army Corps. But even though little damage had been done to Santiago—with the notable exception of a prominent church in the center of the city—a flag of truce was seen before Shafter and Miles could initiate a land attack. Upon his arrival Miles had met with Sampson and Shafter, and he reportedly leaned toward accepting Toral's terms for peace.

With the capitulation of Santiago, no major battles loomed. After a long wait, Carl Sandburg and his comrades of Company C, 6th Infantry Regiment of the Illinois Volunteers boarded the freighter *Rita*, with Guantánamo Bay its destination. The men slept on the upper deck. One man said, "This tub rolls like a raw egg in a glass of whiskey." To pass the time away, Sandburg read the day's best-seller, *Called Back*, by Hugh Conway.

TUESDAY, JULY 12: Guns were silent as terms for a possible peace settlement were brought up by diplomats, but no formal overtures from Spain or any other quarter had been made. The supposed conditions were labeled a "feeler" on Madrid's part.

The Americans' terms were also not official, merely "conjecture" of their demands: Spain's evacuation of Cuba and Puerto Rico; $240 million war indemnity; retention of the Philippines until the indemnity is paid.

Correspondent John Fox, Jr., wrote of the "feelers" put forward by Gen. Toral: "In the beginning he declined any and all terms of surrender; then an unconditional surrender; then he was willing to march out with the full honors of war, bearing his arms, with his flag flying, and the American soldier doing it homage, to march into another province . . . ready to fight us again some day. Now he was considering any terms that did not involve humiliation to Spanish honor and Spanish pride."

The Navy Department wanted to keep it out of the media, but the controversy over who should get the credit for the naval victory over Cervera's fleet embroiled Sampson and Schley. The Bureau of Navigation, which selected Sampson, as Commander of the North Atlantic station, favored the Admiral. Most naval officers were on Schley's side. Secretary Long had received personal letters on the dispute from both Sampson and Schley but refused to make them public.

In practical terms, if Sampson were to be promoted first, he had to be cited by Congress before he could be advanced more than one place, and it could only happen if an officer above him retired. This would keep Schley two numbers above him unless Congress were to alter their relative standing in the register.

WEDNESDAY, JULY 13: An impatient Shafter gave Toral an ultimatum. Shafter sent a dispatch to Adjt. Corbin, telling him that during his one and a half hour meeting with Toral he had set down the conditions. "I think it made a strong impression on him," said Shafter, "and I hope for his surrender; if he refuses, I will open on him at 12 noon tomorrow with every gun I have, and will have the assistance of the navy, who are ready to bombard the city with thirteen-inch shells."

However, the government was more flexible. In a dispatch to Secretary Alger, Gen. Miles said the administration had offered to send the Spanish forces back to Spain. Their removal would not interfere with U.S. operations in Cuba.

Four men of the 71st New York Volunteer Infantry were among six wounded soldiers who arrived in New York on the Savannah Line steamer *Kansas City*. All were Privates wounded during the battle that raged about El Caney and San Juan Hill on July 1–2.

James E. Keller of Company M, who lived at 511 Third Avenue, Manhattan, and worked at Colgate & Co., was first off the boat. He was met by his four brothers. Wounded in the first day's battle by a shot in his right hand, he had been reported dead. His family had been notified and mourned for him. Happily, they found out he had been confused with James *J.* Keller of Company K.

Of the six heroes, J. D. Hoekstra of the 1st U.S. Cavalry had the most painful and serious wounds. A Mauser bullet shot its way directly through his neck. Fortunately no vital organ was touched. Hoekstra, who lived at 147 East 15th Street, was not greeted by anyone because "I want to surprise my mom," testified to the barbarity of the Cubans. His division took 110 prisoners; one captured before the battle was turned over to the Cubans. "They immediately cut his head off," he related. "Their excuse . . . that they had no food for him, and he was in the way. . . . I myself saw a Cuban slash a wounded Spaniard to death."

Another group of wounded and sick arrived at Fort Monroe in Newport News, Virginia, aboard the *Washington*. They included 20 wounded officers and 200 wounded and sick privates, most of whom fought under Gen. Shafter. The loudest cheers from thousands of onlookers were for a colored trooper who had received nine Mauser bullets in his body. His stretcher was borne by four white men.

Some returnees spoke of Spanish barbarity in firing on American field hospitals in

Cuba. Major Nancrede, Chief Surgeon of the 3rd Division of the 2nd Army Corps, said, "I saw Spanish soldiers fire on litters being borne to the rear. They were instantly killed. The Spanish artillery delighted to drop shells into our hospitals. Several surgeons were killed while dressing . . . wounds. The Red Cross flag seems . . . a target for Spanish gunners."

A Staff Surgeon in the Royal Swedish Navy, Carl Rudberg took an active part in caring for the sick and wounded on the battlefield around Santiago. He returned temporarily to Washington to meet with Surgeon Gen. George M. Sternberg. "I have only the highest praise," he said, "for the way in which the Americans took care of its wounded."

Not all health care involved pleasant decisions. To prevent spread of diseases, Maj. Legardo of the Hospital Corps ordered the burning of buildings near the hospital camp around Santiago. "These buildings were dirty and unhealthful," he said, "and they had to be destroyed. We also had to burn houses along the trail to the front, blockhouses and dwellings."

While Santiago was ready to capitulate, the war was far from over. From Omaha, William Jennings Bryan cabled Gen. Corbin that his regiment was mustered into service. The 3rd Nebraska Volunteers would be attached to the corps of Gen. Fitzhugh Lee.

THURSDAY, JULY 14: "Thursday came," wrote correspondent John Fox, Jr., "and . . . the Spaniard had come down from his high horse. He would stack his arms, march out, evacuate the province, surrender all [20,000] troops . . . and in return we should feed them and carry them back to Spain. The sunny air . . . was rent with cheers. The sickest man in one regiment sprang from his blanket and led . . . a foot race for the trenches . . . to join in the hallelujahs" (Brown 399).

The surrender of Santiago was official after 2:00 p.m. The news reached the White House in a dispatch from a signal service official at Playa del Este to Gen. Greely. Earlier in the day, Gen. Shafter sent a dispatch to Gen. Corbin saying: "Have just returned from interview with Gen. Toral. He agrees to surrender upon the basis of being returned to Spain. This proposition embraces all of Eastern Cuba, from Asseradero, on the south, to Sagua on the north, via Palma. . . . Commissioners meet . . . at 2:30 to . . . arrange the terms."

After attending a meeting convened by Gen. Shafter to discuss terms with Gen. Toral, Gen. Miles sent this dispatch to Secretary Alger, prior to the official dispatch: "Gen. Toral formally surrendered the . . . troops and division of Santiago—on the . . . understanding that . . . [they] shall be returned to Spain. Gen. Shafter will appoint Commissioners to draw up . . . arrangements for carrying out the terms. . . . This is very gratifying and Gen. Shafter and . . . his command are entitled to great credit for . . . overcoming the . . . insuperable obstacles which they encountered."

The surrender ended a 10-day period of on and off negotiations which ceased July 10–11, when American batteries and warships hammered the enemy's position. That period enabled American troops to almost fully surround Santiago. Light batteries were posted to exact greater damage. Arrangements were made for a landing at Cabañas, west of the Harbor. Gen Lawton's division planned to fall on the enemy's left flank under the cover of artillery fire. In short, Toral realized he had no alternative but to surrender.

Speaking to a correspondent of the Associated Press, Shafter noted America's doggedness and Spain's stubbornness: "It has been a hard campaign, one of the hardest I ever saw. The difficulties . . . were very great. . . . The character of the country and the roads made it . . . almost impossible to advance in the face of the enemy. The transportation problem was hard, but all the difficulties have been . . . surmounted. Our troops have behaved gallantly . . . and I am proud to have commanded them. During all the hardships . . . they have shown tradition and spirit. They deserve to conquer.

"The resistance of the enemy has been exceedingly stubborn. Gen. Toral . . . a foeman worthy of any man's steel. . . . [He] has shrewdly played for time, always declining to surrender unconditionally and falling back . . . upon the statement that he was . . . powerless to agree . . . without the sanctions of his superiors . . . [and] that personally, he thought it useless to hold out. . . . But he and his garrison . . . would die if necessary, obeying orders."

Admiral Sampson was amazed at the surrender. He was certain that there would be further bloodshed before a truce was reached. He told the media that full terms of the capitulation would not be made public at this time.

But the army and navy were *keenly* interested in the details of the surrender. How large was the Spanish force? How many pieces of artillery? How many Mausers and other pieces of ammunition? What was the character and number of pieces mounted at harbor entrance? How much damage did the navy inflict?

The surrendered territory totalled about 5,000 square miles. H. J. Allen of Kansas City told Secretary Alger: "The country was so wild and rocky that it had almost no camping ground for any sizable body of troops. There is not a point in that part of the country suitable as a base of operations for the army."

Secretary Alger was indeed pleased with the surrender. He was even more heartened that his son, Frederick Moulton Alger, was alive and well. Young Alger had been appointed by McKinley as an Assistant Adjutant General with the rank of Captain. According to the *New York Times*: "It is no part of the proper duty of an Adjutant General . . . to handle a rifle, nor [are] such officers commonly found in the front at the time of an action." What of his future? Continued the *Times*: "As Capt. Alger is near the top of the list of . . . Captains, it is . . . expected that, with . . . a little influence, the Secretary of War, . . . may be prevailed on to make him a Major."

With the capture of Santiago, President McKinley now ordered sending the first "immune" regiments to Santiago. The 1st Volunteer Infantry from Texas, commanded by Col. Charles J. Riche, left from Galveston, and the 2nd, commanded by Col. Duncan N. Hood, left from New Orleans. The troops would also be a good test for the effectiveness of the volunteer army in general.

Originally to be formed with men who had either had yellow fever or a "constitutional immunity," once they began setting up their "immune" regiments, the Colonels looked for the best soldiers even if they had no proof of immunity. But little concern about yellow fever was voiced by Gen. García's Surgeon, Col. Vallente: "There is no great danger . . . along the southern coast. The fever district is along the

Cauto River Valley, where Pando and his 4,000 Spaniards are. The fever along the coast during the rainy season is a mere malarial fever, easily prevented by the use of quinine."

Americans were also confident they could control yellow fever because of the improved methods of treatment developed by the U.S. Marine Hospital Service. So far, there had been no signs of contagious disease among Sampson's fleet or among the marines at Guantánamo. Present in Santiago was Dr. John Guitera, University of Pennsylvania, an acclaimed of yellow fever expert.

The *New York World* was applauded for its on the spot coverage of the surrender—the plaudits self-congratulatory! "*Evening World* First as It Always Is," said the headlines, scoring "the biggest beat since the war began." The news was in the *World* office at 2:26 and two minutes later the paper was out on the streets: "No other paper in the city had received the news and it was 20 minutes later before the 'Yallowest Yet' heard of the surrender. The *Evening World* has added another to its long list of war beats and has again demonstrated the fact that it is first in war, first in peace, and first in newsgathering."

New Yorkers were delighted with the surrender. Guests at the Fifth Avenue Hotel were grateful there were no further casualties. One guest was former President Benjamin Harrison, whom a reporter solicited for his comment: "It is indeed a great event. Our soldiers and particularly our volunteer soldiers are a source of great pride. . . . They fought with a dash, vim, and élan worthy of veterans. And the heroic patriotism they displayed . . . is also a source of great gratification to every American citizen.

"It is . . . different . . . fighting on land from . . . on the sea. Not . . . to detract from . . . our sailors. At sea after a battle the ship is washed down and the sailors don their white, natty uniforms, and the officers go down to the cabin in well-appointed tables. On land the soldiers lie in trenches, exposed to . . . climatic changes, [very] often drenched to the skin and . . . compelled to wait a long time for something to eat. It is wonderful how well our soldiers have done in the tropics. . . . [T]hey have so far more than exceeded the anticipations of their countrymen."

The word was received at the Army Building with proper military analysis. Said Depot Quartermaster, Col. Kimball, "We have great reason to thank God. . . . Every mother . . . who has a boy . . . about Santiago should rejoice. The news . . . means the end of the war. . . . that our army will be free from yellow fever and will be able to proceed to Puerto Rico."

Visitors to Brooklyn's Brighton Beach race track had more important concerns that afternoon than war, until the blackboard posted, "Santiago Has Surrendered!" All bets were on hold, the band struck up "The Star-Spangled Banner," and all remained at attention, bareheaded until the music ended. The band began to march, and everyone followed, including the bookmakers. The biggest winners, however, were the bars, who doled out champagne in much greater quantities than recorded on any previous holiday.

FRIDAY, JULY 15: The Spanish army surrendered at Santiago. The commissioners making the arrangements were Gen. Joe Wheeler, Brig. Gen. Henry W. Lawton, and

Lieut. John D. Miley for the United States and British Vice Consul Robert Mason, Gen. Escarajao, and Lt. Col. Ventura Fontán for Spain. But what were the arrangements? For 18 hours the President heard nothing from Gens. Shafter or Miles, and he became impatient. Finally, in the middle of the day, cables arrived from Shafter and Miles. Negotiations were still in progress about final details. While not seen as a stumbling block, it seemed the Spaniards insisted on not being humiliated, which meant they wanted to retain their arms as they returned to Spain.

Another, although lesser, problem was the transporting of the troops back to Spain. America had many transports, but they would be needed for the Puerto Rico expedition. A proposed solution would be for America to secure vessels, and Spain would be held accountable in the indemnity arrangement.

Although the issue at hand was Santiago, a full end to the war was being aired in Spain. According to the Madrid correspondent of the *London Times*: "The feeling for peace is growing daily, especially in commercial circles. The Chamber of Commerce has received telegrams . . . from Cadiz, Vigo, and other towns. It must not be . . . however, . . . peace at any price . . . [but] with honor and without great territorial sacrifices. . . . Inordinate demands might . . . arouse the warlike spirit of the people [and] . . . the Government would be compelled to swim with the current, regardless of the consequences."

As Santiago capitulated, one of the heroes of the battle returned. Gen. William Worth of the 13th Regiment returned to his home in New York, at Governors Island, badly wounded in the charge at San Juan Hill. Upon the hero's return, President McKinley promoted him to Brigadier General.

He was pale and worn. His right arm was broken, and he had two gunshot wounds on his chest. He was accompanied by his wife and mother and orderly John Keller, also wounded, a Private in Company B. Reluctant to be interviewed, the General deferred all questions to Keller, who gave this narrative about the battle to the *New York Times*: "The fight at San Juan was a hard one. . . . The hill . . . is about 500 yards long, and it rises . . . about 45 degrees. The Spaniards occupied the top . . . and were strongly entrenched . . . protected by wire fences [like those] . . . seen around a Long Island farm. Each . . . was made of innumerable strands of wire . . . packed so closely together that it was impossible to put one's finger in between. . . . These fences had to be cut. . . .

"The brunt of the work fell on the 13th, and the way our men were mowed down was disheartening. . . . We advanced quickly to the first wire fence, firing rapidly as we went, and . . . cut the wires. Col. [Charles] Wickoff [commander of the 22nd Infantry] was . . . mortally wounded. Gen. Worth quickly went to his aid, but [Wickoff] waved him away, whereupon Gen. Worth took command . . . and led his own regiment up the hill. . . . The men were wonderfully inspired by [Gen. Worth] . . . and the way they worked was wonderful. . . . Our men were [still being] mowed down by the Spanish fire, but we gave them better than they gave us and . . . [were able to take] the heights. . . .

"I saw the General shot. He was leading the 13th, and in the thickest of the fight . . . was struck in the chest. . . . The bullet plowed through the fleshy part . . . then striking a bone, was deflected into his right arm above the elbow, causing a compound fracture. . . . Gen. Worth did not fall, but his sword dropped out of his right hand. He stopped . . . picked up his sword with his left hand, and waving it above his head, shouted to his men again, and all pushed forward . . . maddened at the sight of their commanding officer being wounded. . . . Gen. Worth kept on . . . for a few minutes and then fell. . . . He still shouted his commands . . . until he was . . . wounded in the chest by another bullet."

Another account of the battle was detailed in a letter made public on this day from Sgt. B. S. Long of the 71st Regiment to his employer, Caleb V. Smith, manager of Browning, King & Co. in Brooklyn: "I am wounded . . . shot through the right thigh . . . and am now at the hospital . . . awaiting transportation to the General Hospital at Fort McPherson. . . . We arrived here half-starved, as on June 30 we received our last rations consisting of hardtack, salt pork, . . . sugar, . . . tomatoes . . . rationed out one can to eight men. . . . [R]oast beef . . . a two-pound can . . . for three men for three days. . . . [C]offee . . . about one handful. These rations were for three days. . . .

"[A]t 3:30 a.m. we marched up the San Juan Hill, and by 5:30 . . . the battle had commenced. We dropped everything . . . except our haversacks . . . filled with ammunition, and our canteens . . . worth about $10 a drink. The sun was fierce, and heat prostrations were numerous. . . . At noon the firing ceased. . . . At 1:30 it commenced again . . . and under a heavy fire we silently advanced. . . . The bullets whistled like a hailstorm. Shells burst all around us, and . . . I thought we were repulsed; men dropped on all sides. . . . Officers were shot at their posts. A great many had been killed or wounded. . . . [We] became scattered, but . . . never stopped firing.

"It was now a soldiers' fight. . . . The 6th, 16th, and 71st were all mixed up together. We heard . . . 'Yankee Doodle.' It gave us new life. We took up the song and made a dash up the hill. . . . That dash goes down in history. In the face of a blinding, whistling storm of fire and bullets up we went. . . . The Spaniards lost their heads. The Blockhouse was ours. . . . [D]own came the Spanish flag, and up went the . . . Stars and Stripes. Just then I was shot. . . . I saw our flag floating grandly over the scene, where so many . . . lads lay dead and dying. Thank God . . . my life is spared; but those ten hours were hell. . . .

"Right over the hills lay Santiago. . . . it was all the commanding officer could do to keep from going right in. . . . Victory was written on every man's face—black and white. . . . [W]ith nothing to eat and . . . a burning thirst, they did not know when to stop. . . . The American flag floated on every hill. . . .

"Spanish sharpshooters were all along the road up in the trees, and to get back to the hospital was almost as dangerous as being on the firing line. . . . I saw men . . . on stretchers cruelly murdered by the . . . sharpshooters . . . and how we escaped is still another mystery. . . . We finally reached the . . . field hospital. My wound was dressed, and the Spaniards then commenced firing on the Red Cross flag. . . .

"We are getting fed now, but we passed through a long siege of starvation. We, the wounded, have lost everything we had. We have no clothes, except shirt, pants, and shoes. We are a bad-looking lot of American[s] but true as steel to the cause."

It would be of little use to soldier Long, but the Red Cross Society of America, Auxiliary No. 12, sponsored an evening of entertainment at the Manhattan Beach Hotel in Brooklyn. The leading performers were soloist Helen Gilmore, a Pittsburgh soprano, Raymond Moore, and Katie Davis. The goal: to raise money to purchase field hospitals.

Hospitals might be needed quickly, for cases of yellow fever. Prior reports had been encouraging, confirmed by a dispatch today from Surgeon Greenleaf, dateline Siboney: "Only 23 new cases . . . and three deaths reported within the past twenty-four hours. Type of disease mild. Camp sites, wherever practicable, have taken rigorous sanitary precautions to prevent the spread of the disease." But a number of medical and government officials said privately said that 23 new cases "so near to the beginning of an outbreak seemed by no means reassuring."

Sampson and Schley were in the headlines about military glory; but in New York State, the name Theodore Roosevelt was being boomed as Republic candidate for Governor. Said one district leader, "Col. Roosevelt is [currently] without question the most prominent Republican in the State . . . a war candidate who would be invincible. His popularity extends through the country districts, and is [even] greater there than here in the city."

The anxieties for loved ones back home were told and retold in many stories. However, the case of the Dickinson family of Brooklyn had a special poignancy. Benjamin Dickinson, 72, was a painter by trade. His wife was crippled. His son, John B., was also a painter, but having lost his position, enlisted and joined Company M, 47th Regiment, stationed at Fort Adams, Rhode Island. Since the son had received only one month's pay and had to use it to purchase clothes, he had no money to help out his parents or his eight-year-old daughter. His efforts to get a discharge had failed. The resourceful senior Dickinson took out the following ad in a Brooklyn newspaper: "WANTED—SITUATION—BY A COMPETENT man, aged 72 . . . a practical painter by trade . . . in dire need of work on account of son joining army and leaving me in destitute circumstances. BENJAMIN DICKINSON, 1016 Herkimer St."

SATURDAY, JULY 16: The Spanish Army surrendered—finally—on American terms. The White House learned of the surrender 9:00 in the evening, in a message from Gen. Shafter to Gen. Corbin: "The surrender has been definitely settled. The city will be turned over tomorrow morning, and the troops will be marched out as prisoners of war. The Spanish colors will be hauled down at 9 o'clock and the American flag hoisted."

The formal surrender was made earlier in the day in a letter to Gen. Shafter from Gen. Toral. The text was somewhat mystifying, perhaps due to a mangling of the translation: "I am now authorized by my Government to capitulate. I have the honor to so apprise you and requesting that you designate hour and place where my representatives shall appear to compare with those of your excellency to effect the articles of capitulation on the basis of what has been agreed upon to this date in due time.

"I wish to manifest my desire to know the resolutions of the United States Government respecting the return of army so as to note on the capitulations; also, the great courtesy of your great Graces and return for their great generosity and impulse for the Spanish soldiers, and allow them to return to the Peninsula with the honors the American Army to them, the honor to acknowledge as dutifully descended."

"The articles of capitulation" allowed "officers to retain their side arms and officers and men to retain their personal property. . . . All Spanish forces known as volunteers, Moirilizadves, and guerrillas who wish to remain in Cuba may do so under parole during the present war."

Confusion reigned because the American Commissioners had agreed to allow Spanish soldiers "to return to Spain with the arms they have so bravely defended," but Washington had put an end to that possibility, in an earlier statement by Secretary Alger: "The situation is just this. The Spaniards at Santiago are prepared to surrender, but they want to carry their arms. We have determined to grant no such concession, except the generosity of this Government to transport them to Spain."

According to American officials, the delay in effectuating the capitulation could be attributed to the difficulty in securing the surrender of the outlying garrisons without the go-ahead from Madrid.

In the continuing discussion of a comprehensive peace treaty, most government officials were certain McKinley would not strip Spain of all her colonial possessions. He would be content, they reasoned, with Spain's admission of Cuban independence; America's acquiring Puerto Rico; setting up a protectorate over the Philippines; and payment of an indemnity by Spain.

With the capitulation of Santiago, the Army issued a casualty report for the three weeks it had been in Cuba. The casualties totalled 1,914 officers and men killed, wounded, and missing. The killed numbered 246, of whom 21 were officers; wounded, 1,584, of whom 98 were officers; no officers were among the 84 missing. Of the wounded only 68 died. Col. Pope, Surgeon-in-Chief, noted that the fatalities were "remarkably small considering the large number of wounded."

One of those who died, but not in the battlefield, was Eben J. Brewer, a victim of yellow fever. He had been in charge of all U.S. postal arrangements in Cuba. A journalist and attorney, Mr. Brewer served during the Civil War as a volunteer nurse at the army hospital in Washington.

The death of Lieut. John J. Blandin in Baltimore brought the roots of the Spanish-American War back to the foreground. Lieut. Blandin was the officer on deck the night the *Maine* was blown up in Havana Harbor. His death was caused by meningitis, brought on by the shock he received when the *Maine* was destroyed. After the incident, he was given a post at the U.S. Hydrographic Office in Baltimore, with hope it would bring him mental stability. But he never was the same. "He seemed utterly unable to dismiss from his mind the horrors of the fatal night," said his friends.

SUNDAY, JULY 17: The American flag waved in triumph over the Governor's palace at Santiago. "The ceremony of hoisting the Stars and Stripes," wrote the *New York Times*, "was worth all the blood and treasure it cost. . . . 10,000 people witnessed the . . . scene that will live forever in the minds of . . . the Americans present."

A little after 9 a.m., Gen. Shafter, the American division and brigade commanders and their staffs were escorted by a troop of cavalry, joined by Gen. Toral and his staff. Trumpeters saluted their presence. The American General returned the Spanish General's sword, after it had been handed to the American commander. The ceremony was witnessed by American troops who lined up at the trenches. The townspeople, primarily women and noncombatants, lined the roofs to see the proceedings.

As the chimes of the old Catholic Cathedral struck 12, the 9th Infantry and 6th Cavalry presented arms. Capt. McKittrick hoisted the Stars and Stripes. After the 6th Cavalry band played "Rally Round the Flag, Boys," Gen. Chambers McKibben called for a round of applause for Gen. Shafter. As the men cheered, the band played "Stars and Stripes Forever." Next, a light battery fired a salute of twenty-one guns. A congratulatory message from the President was read to each regiment.

After the ceremony Shafter returned to the American lines. The city was left to municipal authorities under the control of the Military Governor, Gen. Chambers McKibben, known for his heroism in the Civil War Battle of North Anna River.

The War Department posted a bulletin from Shafter, received at 5:15 p.m., detailing the day's events: "I have the honor to announce that the American flag has been this instant, 12 o'clock noon, hoisted over the house of the City Government in the City of Santiago. An immense concourse of people present. . . . Perfect order is being maintained by municipal government. Distress is very great, but little sickness in town. Scarcely any yellow fever. [A] small gunboat and about 200 seamen left by Cervera have surrendered to me."

Actually, the White House had received an earlier message from Shafter, at about 11 a.m., as McKinley was preparing to go to church. Secretary Alger expressed gratitude that the Santiago campaign had ended: "It is a magnificent achievement, and . . . a tribute to the bravery, pluck, and endurance of our American soldiers. Now that their efforts have brought final and complete success, I believe their campaign will be recorded as one of the most glorious pages of our military history. Not more than 10,000 men were engaged when the serious fighting occurred, but they pushed forward and created a condition which has brought the surrender of 25,000 men."

The American troops had good reason to be thankful Santiago had capitulated, as detailed by correspondent James F. J. Archibald: "Between the lines, and . . . as we neared the city, the condition was terrible. All along the road were carcasses of horses . . . the saddle, bridle, and . . . saddlebags full of effects, [still] on the[m]. . . . This state . . . showed the hasty retreat under . . . fire the enemy experienced during the three days' battle. Shallow graves . . . had been scratched open by . . . vultures and the odor was horrible. . . . The first barricade we encountered was . . . [a] barbed wire entanglement that . . . compelled one entering to zigzag back and forth so that entrance under fire would have been . . . impossible. Then came barricades of sand-filled barrels covering trenches. Side streets were blocked with paving stones, leaving loopholes. . . . [T]hick-walled houses were . . . loopholed . . . [making] excellent fortifications. To have attempted [an] infantry assault would have meant the loss of thousands of our men."

American soldiers in Cuba celebrated in their own ways. Sherwood Anderson tells of the night celebration, in his *Memoirs*: "We tramped down into the city. The citizens were waiting for us. The Spanish soldiers were waiting. It was a wild night, a memorable night. It was like the first Armistice Day, in American cities, at the end of the World War.

"The Spanish soldiers were going home. Some of them had been in service, in Cuba, for years. They were half drunk with joy.

"There had been the long struggle, the hatred between the army and the citizens. Now all of that was at an end. They embraced us . . . brought us drinks. And more drinks. And more. . . .

"We marched arm in arm with them through the streets. We sang. We shouted. It must have been well on toward morning when Bert [a comrade] and I helped each . . . to our camp."

While there was exuberance in Santiago, the men of Carl Sandburg's company were bitterly disappointed upon arriving in Guantánamo Bay to the music of the band on the *Rita*— the first ship the Americans captured from the Spanish—and cheers from the battleships *Oregon*, *Indiana*, and *Iowa*. Col. Jack Foster and other officers went ashore and came back with the news that Santiago had been vanquished. "Why were we sent for?" wondered the soldiers. They lay at anchor. With no war, they battled mosquitoes, dysentery, contaminated food, hellish heat, and, worst of all, boredom and frustration.

But maybe not for long. Puerto Rico had been on the military minds for some time; now the landing was imminent. At a meeting at the War Department office, the map of Puerto Rico was carefully studied by Gen. Brooke, who would lead the army of invasion; Secretary Alger; Gen. Corbin; and Col. Hecker, chief of the Transportation Bureau.

To date the plan called for landing on the south coast of Ponce, then marching to San Juan on the north coast. The city would be assaulted from the rear, in combination with the bombardment of the fortifications and shelling of the city by the American fleet. San Juan was well defended and probably could survive bombardment for some time. Another potential landing site was Arecibo, but its winds were so strong that vessels could not rest in safety.

The regiments of Gen. Keifer in Miami were being equipped as rapidly as possible so that they could join the Puerto Rico campaign. Six of his regiments would be detached from the 7th Army Corps and join one of the commands under Gen. Miles.

It was a most fitting day for sermons, the Sunday of surrender. Themes of heroes and heroism filled the pulpit. The Rev. Horace Porter spoke at Plymouth Church in Brooklyn on "Heroes and Heroisms of Our Day." He said, in part: "The world's standard of heroism has probably never been so high as today. The spirit of the heroic . . . is with us in two forms: First in the high ideals and requirements of public opinion. . . . [O]ne of our naval commanders recently remarked that there can be no such thing as defeat for any American commander or army today; that the requirement of the American people is that they will have absolute victory or death. . . .

"In the second place, the heroic in our time lies more in human nature than ever before. Men are requiring more of themselves . . . the world . . . full of heroes . . . Hobson does his daring deed, and we discover that . . . thousands of men . . . pleaded to be permitted to do and dare as Hobson did. For every daring deed . . . there are hundreds of men eager to do and dare just as loyally."

What was the resolution of the Spanish arms issue? The Spaniards did not take their arms home. More important, militarily, were the heavy guns and vessels that fell into American hands. The armaments of the shore batteries consisted of five brass six-inch muzzle-loaders in the Morro Castle fortifications; two six-inch Hontorias from the cruiser *Reina Mercedes*, and three twenty-one-centimeter mortars in the Zocapa upper battery; two eight-centimeter muzzle-loaders, and four eight-centimeter fieldpieces in the Estrella battery; one 57-millimeter and one 25-millimeter Nordenfeldt, and one 37-millimeter Hotchkiss in the Zocapa lower battery, and two 6-inch Honotorias, two 9-centimeter Krupps, and two 15-centimeter mortars at Punta Gorda.

MONDAY, JULY 18: The Sampson-Schley rivalry came out into the open once more. In reviewing the armaments of the captured forts around Santiago, the military realized that the fortifications were weaker than had been thought. Regret was voiced that Schley was not allowed to force an entrance to Santiago Harbor and spare the presence of the army.

Commodore Schley himself made an inspection of the forts and saw they did not have guns that would be a menace to Sampson's fleet. Said one naval officer, "It is strange that when the Commodore came to Santiago with his squadron, the Admiral hastened to his assistance . . . as if [he] . . . did not want to be upstaged and have the Commodore rashly brave the barriers and penetrate the harbor in which the Spaniards had taken refuge."

"Schley had a contempt for Spanish marksmanship," said another naval officer, "and he had great faith in the unexpected rush. . . . The battle with Cervera's fleet has shown with what spirit the fleet would have been assailed in Santiago Harbor. We should not have lost a vessel.

"I confess to a degree of surprise that our naval officers did not learn accurately about the armament of the forts that have been found to be so feeble in power and so easy to overcome, if they had been assailed on the land side."

The strength of Toral's army was greater, numerically speaking, than perceived. Gen. Shafter sent a dispatch to the War Department that he had received a roster of prisoners totalling 22,780. In another dispatch, the General said he would send officers and troops on July 19 to receive the surrender of 2,000 men in the interior garrisons and would also dispatch officers to accept the surrender of coast garrisons at Guantánamo, Baracoa, and Sagua de Tanamo.

Confusion reigned among some Spanish troops, who had been away from home for three years and longer. Some of the soldiers camped around Santiago Harbor told American soldiers they had heard the United States would pay them arrears and return them to Spain. They were astounded to learn that Spain surrendered and simply did not believe it.

On his return Gen. Toral might have become the most surprised man in Spain. Madrid papers focused on the capitulation of Santiago and were stunned that Toral had agreed to include the whole military division of the province in the surrender. There was speculation that he could be court-martialed.

Another story of the army invasion was told to the *New York Times* by Lieut. George J. Godfrey of the 22nd infantry, formerly stationed at Fort Crook, Nebraska. Lieut. Godfrey, of 516 E. 121st Street, gained distinction as the first member of the invading army to arrive in Cuba. He came home on two months' sick leave, having been struck in the head by a Mauser bullet at El Caney.

He spoke of the landing on Daiquirí: "The men-of-war led the way to Daiquirí, and at sunrise on June 22 . . . gathered outside of the transports and began to shell the hills. The cannonade was . . . deafening, but it made a fitting landing for the troops, and the

Spaniards who had occupied the place . . . cleared out in a hurry after firing a few shots, which did little or no harm.

"The men of Company A, 22nd Infantry, of which I had command, were placed in a number of whaleboats, and Ensign Halligan was assigned to tow us ashore. As we started away from the transport, a number of launches with boats in tow cast off their lines and . . . began an exciting race for shore. Between the cheering of the men and the continual booming of the big guns, one's fighting blood was stirred to its highest pitch. . . .

"It was nip and tuck for several minutes. Then our boat began to forge ahead, and with a final spurt, we reached the old pier at Daiquirí a couple of boat lengths ahead of the 8th's. With the help of two sailors I scrambled up the side and onto the pier, and a moment later the 8th's men were landing. A mighty cheer followed the little incident, and as soon as Company A landed I formed a single line and we advanced up the steep hill fronting upon the harbor. We took up a position on the hill that would enable us to protect the troops' landing from the fire of any Spaniards on the hill."

TUESDAY, JULY 19: Gen. Miles expected to leave for Puerto Rico tonight and sent farewell messages to his family. At the moment Miles was aboard the *Yale*, with the 6th Massachusetts Volunteers, having reached Santiago just before the surrender. The men had never disembarked.

With the Santiago campaign over, the government was devoting much attention to the enemy yellow fever. Surgeon Gen. Sternberg announced the welcome news that no fear existed of a general epidemic among American troops at Santiago. As an insurance measure after the surrender, American soldiers were sent as rapidly as possible to the hills north of Santiago. As a point of comparison, the death rate among typhoid fever patients at Chickamauga was reported as higher than among troops suffering from yellow fever in Cuba.

More about the heroism of the black troops continued to be told. From Siboney, Sgt. Maj. Benjamin F. Sayre, Company C, 24th Infantry, told his friend: "The steady advance of the black troops under . . . fire nonplussed the enemy; they became panic-stricken and . . . fled shamefully. In a few minutes we were . . . firing down on them as they ran . . . among the trees and high grass. The hill-top, blockhouse, and trenches were literally filled with their dead and wounded. . . . [T]he name of the 24th Regiment is on everyone's lips. Soldiers and Cubans alike vie with each other in doing honor to any 24th man . . . they meet" (Washington 67).

After the battlefield, the black soldiers were ordered to Siboney for hospital service in the battle against yellow fever. They served with dedication and distinction.

Concludes Booker Washington in *A New Negro for a New Century*: "Thus, in the field, in the camp, and in the hospital, facing Mauser bullets, or what not, and yellow jack, the deadliest of foes, these black troopers, . . . without the incentive of ever being promoted beyond a non-commissioned officer's rank, acquitted themselves as heroes. . . . A few . . . were promoted to be second lieutenants and assigned to immune regiments, but all . . . have now been mustered out . . . turned out on the cold world in their old age . . . with their honors full upon them, . . . not good enough to be officers in the regular army of the Republic!" (Washington 70–71).

15

THE PUERTO RICAN CAMPAIGN

WEDNESDAY, JULY 20: As bands played and 30,000 cheered, an expedition—consisting of the 2nd and 3rd Wisconsin and 16th Pennsylvania Regiments, and two companies of the 6th Illinois under the command of Maj. Gen. J. H. Wilson—left Charleston, South Carolina, for Puerto Rico. For two days and nights, the loading of baggage and provisions had proceeded under rush orders. All Charleston stevedores had been assigned to the task, aided by details of men from the various regiments, and by government laborers who would be working on the roads and bridges in Cuba.

An angered General Miles was unable to leave for Puerto Rico because he lacked a naval convoy. Secretary Alger was quite surprised because earlier in the day he had received a cablegram from Miles saying he had 10 transports with him at Guantánamo; that the transports *Lampasas* and *Nuecces*, which left Key West on July 16 with ambulance, engineer and signal corps, and some cavalry, artillery, horses and supplies had reported to him; and that he was prepared to depart as soon as Admiral Sampson provided ships to protect the expedition. The only explanation Alger had was that Miles' delay was the fault of the navy, and specifically, Admiral Sampson, who had not provided the convoy.

Gen. Miles was assured "full complements of infantry, cavalry and artillery, with plenty of hospital aides, surgeons, signalmen, and engineers," by the War Department. "With laborers, lumber and wagons and mules, the expedition will be the most businesslike and complete movement that has yet been undertaken." The men would have no food problems either. The *Massachusetts* was scheduled to arrive at the landing place next week with 6 million pounds of rations and 300,000 pounds of fresh beef.

The expedition was designed to be so imposing that it would overwhelm the relatively small Spanish force in Puerto Rico and keep American casualties to a minimum. One weakness, however, was the small proportion of regulars. Three regiments of infantry, one of cavalry, and six batteries of artillery now totalled 6,000.

Military men wondered how well volunteers armed with Springfields would fare against Spanish regulars and volunteers with Mausers.

The War Department was forced to admit it erred when a dispatch listing states not meeting their quotas under the President's calls said Massachusetts had only provided 511 soldiers. Not so, said the Bay State's angered militia, and Sgt. Gen. Dalton retracted: "As a matter of fact, Massachusetts has placed . . . 1,200 more than [it was] . . . asked for in the two calls."

THURSDAY, JULY 21: President McKinley had assigned the Puerto Rican expedition his personal attention, so he was miffed over the delay in Miles' expedition, especially since Miles' troops had been sweltering for days, cooped up in their transports at Playa del Este. Naval officials were "exasperated by the deliberation" Sampson had exercised in getting Miles the warships. It was also feared that if Gen. Wilson's command arrived before Gen. Miles and the naval convoys, Wilson's ship would remain without protection. The President issued personal orders, through Secretary Long, that Admiral Sampson should go immediately to Puerto Rico with Gen. Miles.

So Gen. Miles finally left—that afternoon—for Puerto Rico, having received his convoy. He sent the War Department a three-page message, but all that was made public was the time of departure and the warships that would accompany him, which included the first-class battleship, the *Massachusetts*; an effective cruiser, the *Cincinnati*; a speedy, well-armed gunboat, the *Annapolis*; and four auxiliary naval vessels whose offensive power had already been proven in Cuban waters, the *Dixie*, *Gloucester*, *Wasp*, and *Leyden*. In addition, the War Department announced that orders to proceed to Puerto Rico were given to three potent monitors: the *Terror*, *Amphitrite*, and *Puritan*. They would help reduce the Spanish forces on the island.

Sandburg and his fellow soldiers finally learned they were leaving Guantánamo, as well. Writes Sandburg: "We . . . knew no more than the nakedest Zulu in the African jungles. Even the commander of . . . this expedition to Puerto Rico, Gen. Nelson A. Miles, who had commanded a brigade in Gen. Grant's army in 1864, didn't know where we were going" (Sandburg 412–13).

The logical reason for not making Miles' entire dispatch public was that it contained details about the number and personnel of the force accompanying him from Santiago. The best estimates were that 18 to 19 thousand men would land in Puerto Rico: 6,000 with Miles, 6,000 from Tampa, 3,500 from Charleston, and 4,500 from Chickamauga. They would be matched up against—at most—20,000 Spanish regulars and volunteers.

With most of the Spanish force at San Juan, Gen. Miles should have little trouble taking Ponce, on the south coast of the island, and fortifying a strong position there prior to the landing of all of the available soldiers and the advance on the capital from the rear. Ponce had very few effective troops, so the land force should be resisted as poorly as Shafter's men at Santiago.

The victory at San Juan Hill continued to elicit admiration for the American troops and, significantly, the black soldiers. Correspondent Stephen Bonsal "was not the only man who had come to recognize the justice of certain Constitutional amendments, in the light of the gallant behavior of the colored troops. . . . The fortune of war had, of course, present[ed] to the colored troops the opportunities for distinguished service, of which they . . . availed themselves to the fullest . . . ; but the confidence of the . . . officers in their superb gallantry, which . . . proved not to be displaced, added still more, and . . . the services of no four white regiments can be compared with those rendered by . . . the 9th and 10th Cavalry and the 24th and 25th Infantry."

FRIDAY, JULY 22: Gen. Miles had left, as officially noted in a cable received at the War Department this morning detailing the makeup of Miles' forces "en route to Puerto Rico." Sailing east along the north coast of Haiti, Miles was bound for the appointed rendezvous with Wilson and his men. A major surprise was that Miles' force was smaller than most naval officers had thought.

Assurances about the control of yellow fever were not so convincing. When death from illness struck, health authorities were quick to deny yellow fever as the cause. The Chesapeake and Ohio Railways were carrying 135 sick soldiers from Tampa to the hospital at Fort Thomas. When two previous trains had brought 225 wounded and sick, and two dead bodies were taken off, surgeons were reluctant to attribute cause, denying it was yellow fever. Many of the soldiers who came on this day were seriously sick.

Sgt. Howard H. Kiersted of Company H, 2nd New Jersey, was buried at the North Orange (New Jersey) Baptist Church, dressed in the uniform of the volunteers, with his casket wrapped in the flag. He died at Jacksonville on July 18. Health officials gave the cause as typhoid fever, but the family was not convinced.

The men of Gen. Shafter's 5th Corps at Santiago were anxious to return home, but they were on hold until every trace of yellow fever was eliminated from their area. No way would authorities risk "importing" yellow fever into America. A possible solution was to send the soldiers straight to a camp on the coast of Maine or in the mountains of North Carolina until all health problems were resolved. But transports would be needed to carry it out, and the official line of the War Department, given by Adjt. Gen. Corbin, was: "We can't fight [the fever] anywhere else as well as right there [in Santiago]. To undertake to bring them back . . . would infect every transport we have, and. . . . There is no city on the coast that would not rise up in arms at the very suggestion of landing a fever-infected army within its limits.

"Besides, there is no reason to believe that a removal at this time would be of advantage to the men themselves. . . .

"There is no concealing . . . that the authorities regard the situation seriously, though there is no disposition to panic. The wide dissemination . . . makes the problem difficult, but . . . the fever is . . . particular[ly] mild . . . the death rate being marvelously low." The President, Alger, and Corbin all stressed the importance of improving sanitary conditions at the camps.

Two officers returned home. Maj. James M. Bell of the 1st Cavalry, wounded in the battle of June 24, deplored the state of America's hospital facilities. After being wounded, he remained on board a transport for 16 days before leaving for New York. From the *Olivette* he was taken to Fort Wadsworth Hospital. As difficult as was the life of the soldier, he said, much more horrid was the life of the wounded: "[T]he details of our confinement . . . are revolting. . . . [W]e lived on hardtack and canned beef. . . . Nothing was hot except our coffee and . . . we didn't have sugar . . . [or] milk! The care . . . was a disgrace. No change of clothing or bed linen. . . . The boat was much too filled to permit looking after us. . . . [T]he medical officers . . . did remarkably well . . . considering the tools they had. . . . [But] Washington had no idea . . . the killed and wounded would reach anywhere near the number they actually did, and were consequently unprepared."

Captain Walter Joyce of Company H, who was sunstruck during the charge up San Juan Hill, was the first commander of the 71st regiment to return from the front. After passing out during the charge, he was unconscious for several days afterward. Upon returning to his post, he contracted malarial fever. Col. Downs ordered him home. Down from 250 pounds to 175, Joyce was not the man he was when he left home. Dr. C. E. Phillips, Joyce's doctor said, "He will soon be well. . . . But he never should have gone. . . . He was sunstruck . . . at the State camp and [having] suffered nearly every year from malaria . . . Cuba was no country for him."

To date, more than 250,000 men had been equipped and placed in the field, according to a statement prepared by Maj. John A. Johnson, Assistant Adjutant General. Foreign experts were amazed that 250,000 men could be recruited, mustered, and placed in the field in less than 90 days, with every man undergoing a strict medical examination. "Incredible" and "a wonderful achievement," said armed forces officers from various European nations.

Of the 275,000 men authorized by Congress, 254,479 had been mustered to date. Of the 23,021 needed to complete the authorized quota, 13,308 were regulars, 8,000 volunteers, 862 immunes, and 851 engineers. Minus recent casualties, the strength of the regular army was 47,692; the number of volunteers was 192,000.

"It is a gratifying achievement," said Johnson. "The men were recruited by a limited number of recruiting officers, for the most part strangers in the country canvased, and during a period of competition by state authorities for the same men."

SATURDAY, JULY 23: According to the War Department, the first landing of American troops in Puerto Rico was expected by Monday. The landing places remained Ponce and Guánica. The latter, 15 miles due west of Ponce, was the port of the City of Yauco, which would be the first stopping place of the force after debarkation. Considered the best harbor in Puerto Rico, Guánica was a mile and a half long and a quarter mile wide. The banks of the bay are steep and form so perfect a natural wharf that three large ships could lie alongside and unload by merely throwing planks ashore.

The media was relentless in its coverage of yellow fever. To an extent, it overshadowed war news. A dispatch from Gen. Shafter to Gen. Corbin, dateline Santiago, listed six men who died on this day of yellow fever at the Siboney hospital. Some 1,500 were sick with fever; 150 had yellow fever. The troops were moved to fresh ground and cavalry moved about three miles.

The Adjutant General was also kept busy with what was to be known as the "*Seneca* Affair." It was charged that the transport *Seneca*, which carried the sick and wounded from Shafter's army to New York, left Cuba with inadequate medical supplies and was otherwise unfit to deal with the medical problems. The only "explanation" was poor weather conditions, but that hardly seemed to answer the lack of supplies.

No complaints, however, emanated from the U.S. Hospital at Fort Monroe, Virginia, where 440 patients were being treated under the direction of Chief Surgeon Donald Maclean and Surgeon in Charge Maj. Calvin De Witt. Of especial cheer to the infirm had been the care of the volunteer nurses, including three who had been prominent in the social life of Old Point: Mrs. Marsh, wife of an officer on the *New York*; Miss Virginia Evans, daughter of Capt. Robley D. Evans; and Mrs. Marie Cushman, wife of Lieut. Cushman of the *Indiana*. The Cushmans had one of the war's storybook romances: The officer's ship was at Dry Tortugas when he received orders to go to the front. Desirous of tying the knot before the ship sailed, they married quickly at Dry Tortugas.

New York was well represented at the hospital by 40 members of the 71st regiment. One of the more talkative inmates, Trooper Albert C. McMillan of Troop B, Roosevelt's Rough Riders, whose father, Samuel McMillan, was a former City Park Commissioner and President of the New York Driving Club, suffered a shock from a shell exploding under his nose and then contracted malarial fever. Interestingly, he had a greater aversion to the Cubans than to the Spanish: "I had the opportunity to talk with some of the Spaniards. In my opinion, they are far more intelligent than the Cubans. I asked one of the Lieutenants . . . if they had any personal enmity toward the 'Americanos.' . . . 'Not a bit of it,' he replied. . . . Nine out of ten [American] men in this war have as their motto, 'Remember the *Maine*.' Were they to pause . . . and reflect that the Cubans were the people they were fighting for . . . [it] would be, 'What a fool I am.'"

The controversy over who deserves credit for sinking Cervera's fleet was now the topic among foreign naval officers. "I think . . . Admiral Sampson," asserted Lieut. S. Akijama of the Japanese Navy, who was visiting New York. "It is true that Commodore Schley commanded the attack, but it was Sampson's plan. . . . He had issued orders . . . of the course to be pursued in case Cervera tried to escape . . . and those orders were carried out."

The *London Spectator* focused on the achievements of the volunteers, wondering about the necessity of standing armies: "[T]he difference between a large supply of volunteers would not, as regards efficiency, be very great. After all, you can only get out of discipline perfect obedience, and readiness to incur suffering or death rather than disobey, and these two conditions were fulfilled by the American volunteers in the attack on Santiago. No regular soldiers would have obeyed their officers more perfectly than the regiment of volunteers from Michigan or the . . . 'rough riders' or have gone on with more . . . courage."

The Confederate Veterans Association adopted a resolution praising McKinley's conduct of the war. The President responded graciously to the association's President J. B. Gordon: "The present war has . . . completely obliterat[ed] the sectional lines drawn in the last one. The response to the Nation's call . . . equally spontaneous and patriotic in all parts of the country. Veterans of the gray as well as of the blue . . . fighting side by side, winning equal renown. . . . To have such a hearty commendation from yourself and your colleagues of the work of this Administration . . . and the pledge of whatever support may be needed to help bring [the war] to a successful completion is, indeed, gratifying."

SUNDAY, JULY 24: News about Gen. Miles' movements in Puerto Rico would not be available until July 25 at the earliest, according to the War Department. Whether or not he would make a landing in advance of the arrival of the entire expedition might depend on the size of the Spanish force on the coast. Troops en route from Tampa and Charleston might arrive later in the week. In any event, the land campaign would not start until week's end.

A plea for colored soldiers was made by the Twelfth Baptist Church in Boston, which adopted the following resolutions: "Resolved, That the President . . . institute a free military school . . . to educate colored soldiers for the position of commissioned officers, which was done [in 1864] for white soldiers . . . appointed to lead colored troops, and that the men chosen . . . be taken from those who have won distinction on the battlefield.

"Resolved, That the . . . assembled recognize with gratitude the courage and soldierly qualities of the blacks now in Cuba, who made the victory of Santiago a possibility. As the climate of Cuba . . . is adapted to promote the highest development of the black, it is our hope to see [Cuba] become to America what it has never been to Spain—the home of a thrifty and happy people.

"Resolved, That . . . the black man has been educated and trained to fulfill an important mission not only for Cuba, but for the Spanish possessions that are to come under our control. The Cubans. . . . when asked to do menial work, declined. . . . The Negro, [who was] faithful to his master before emancipation . . . [and as] a soldier as faithful in burden bearing as he was brave in battle, . . . occupies the proud position he holds in the eye of the world because . . . 'he that humbles himself shall be exalted.'"

Now a free man, Hobson went to Washington to meet with the Navy Department to pursue his plan of salvaging Spanish cruisers. While in New York he completed arrangements with Merritt and Chapman for saving the warships. The wreckers guaranteed putting together the pontoons, air bags, and compressed air apparatus necessary to lift and right the vessels, and expected to start this material on its way to Santiago, from New York, within three days on a speedy ship.

Secretary Long gave his assent to Hobson's plan for raising the *Cristobal Colón*. He called the plan "feasible." It involved methods and tools not usually employed in wrecking, including air appliances that perhaps had never been employed on vessels the size and weight of the *Colón*.

MONDAY, JULY 25: If Gen. Miles had arrived, no one knew about it because midnight passed without a cable. Adjt. Corbin was not surprised because no cable facilities existed at the point chosen for debarkation. The first report of the landing would have to be sent by dispatch boat to St. Thomas or Puerto Rico on the north coast of Haiti, and cable offices closed there about 9 p.m.

What surprised observers was a change of plans: Fajardo, a regular port of call for steamers between the United States and Puerto Rico, had been named as the place of landing instead of Ponce or Guánica. A fishing town of less than 9,000 people, Fajardo was on the east coast about five miles south of Cape San Juan, at the extreme north-easterly corner of Puerto Rico.

The expedition, when complete, would total some 30,000 men—among them 20,000 volunteer infantry, 3,500 regular infantry, 3,000 artillery, 3,000 cavalry. The 20,000 volunteers were expected to be armed with Krag-Jorgensen magazine rifles, like the regular army's, before fighting began. Moving the force would present no problem, according to a report of the Transportation Department of the Adjutant General's office. The ships now belonging to the department, by charter or purchase, had a capacity for 2,117 officers, 38,585 men, and 15,726 animals. The only problems were getting the ships to the right locations and loading them expeditiously.

The Adjutant General's office marked three months since the Congressional declaration of war. Gen. Corbin announced that 261,400 men had been recruited, mustered, equipped, and placed in the field. Of the 216,500 volunteers authorized by Congress, 212,000 had been placed, and in a few days the entire volunteer army would be thoroughly organized into regiments, brigades, divisions, and army corps. He called American soldiers "the finest soldiers in the world" and stressed that every man recruited, regulars and volunteers, "had undergone a careful physical examination by disinterested and competent officers."

However, the splendid work of the examining surgeons was evaded by a clever design of Company F of the 109th Regiment. Sgt. William Bodamer and Corp. Reidy had been rejected several times, but Company F's officers wanted them mustered in. Orders were given to a Private Betts and Private Louis Hahns to put on the uniforms of the rejected men and impersonate them before the Surgeon, and it worked. Betts and Hahns passed, the mustering officer at Peekskill totally unaware of the deceit, and the former rejects went to Chickamauga.

After getting information about the fraud, Maj. William Wolcott Marks, a former Captain of Company F who during the time of the fraud was home for business reasons, began to investigate and sent his findings to Col. Greene, in command of the regiment at Chickamauga. "Bringing in substitutes set at naught the splendidly conscientious work of the surgeons who worked day and night to see that the rules were carried out," said Marks. "Dr. L'Hommedieu, the Surgeon before whom the men appeared, was one of the most painstaking and faithful doctors to be found anywhere, and the trick by which his vigilance was evaded was unworthy of any officer in the 9th Regiment, where the standard of honor was so high. I have received no word as yet from Col. Greene, but I know that he is so strict a disciplinarian that full justice will be done in the matter."

Much more serious than impersonation at mustering in was the report from Camp Alger, where 16 patients with typhoid fever were taken to Fort Meyer Hospital, the largest number of cases in one day at the camp yet. The disease was also found in regiments previously uninfected.

TUESDAY, JULY 26: The War Department learned that Gen. Miles had not landed at Fajardo, but at the opposite end of the island at Guánica, as originally planned. Several days before, he had informed Captain Francis J. Higginson of the

Massachusetts, "As it is always advisable not to do what your enemy expects you to do, . . . after going around the northeast corner . . . [we shall] go immediately to Guánica and land this force and move on to Ponce." Although Higginson argued that the harbor was too shallow for the *Massachusetts*, *Columbia*, and *Dixie*, he yielded to Miles.

Miles' first reply to the War Department was, "Circumstances were such that I deemed it advisable to take the harbor Guánica first." He later elaborated to Secretary Alger that "marching across the country . . . will have . . . a desirable effect on the inhabitants of the country." Having an aversion to a large role for the navy, Miles opposed *any* plans to bombard San Juan.

The War Department also learned of the first American "encounter" during the morning of the 25th. The *Gloucester* was commanded inside the harbor by Higginson, and its tiny force scattered the few Spanish defenders. The ships entered Guánica without many shots from the foes, and after taking Guánica, the expedition came into the harbor and started the disembarkation of troops and supplies. The American flag was hoisted at 11 a.m.

The Spaniards had planned to defend Ponce by blowing up the railroad connecting it with Yauco, about five miles to its west, halfway to Guánica. Moving to seize Ponce, Miles ordered Brig. Gen. George A. Garretson to move on Yauco with six companies from the 6th Massachusetts and one from the 6th Illinois. The first engagement in Puerto Rico was on at dawn, but it was brief. The Spanish defenders withdrew, the force at Yauco having little desire for a skirmish. In fact, most fled to Ponce, leaving only a few to blow up the railroad, and they eschewed the assignment.

Carl Sandburg described the arrival of the 6th Illinois: "Ahead we saw gunfire from a ship and landing boats filled with bluepockets moving toward shore. We were ordered to . . . get into full marching outfits. We heard shooting, glanced toward shore . . . and saw white puffs of smoke while we stood waiting . . . to climb down . . . into long boats called lighters. Holding rifles over our heads, we waded ashore . . . in Guánica, a one-street town with palm and coconut trees [which were] new to us. We expected to be ordered into action . . . [but] were marched to a field . . . where we waited . . . ate our supper . . . and soon after were ordered to march. . . .

"A story arose that 6th Illinois troops that night did some wild firing . . . hitting the transport on which Gen. Miles was sleeping . . . [and] a ship carrying Red Cross nurses. I can merely testify that neither Company C nor the companies on our flanks did any firing that night."

A yellow flag flew from the transport *Hudson*, the sign of sickness on board, as the ship arrived in Hampton Roads. In addition to the sick, the remains of Capt. Capron and Sgt. Fish were on board, as were 11 wounded, primarily officers, among them Private Stanley Hollister of the Rough Riders—a star player with Harvard's football team, who sustained a shell wound in the left breast and a gunshot wound in the left hip joint—and Cadet E. E. Haskell, an Acting Lieutenant of the Rough Riders, who was shot through the intestines. Unconfirmed was a report that the vessel also carried Henry Sylvester Scovel, a New York journalist who was asked to leave Cuba because he insulted Gen. Shafter.

Peace talks were imminent, according to newspaper reports via the Associated Press. The *New York Evening World* blared on its front page: "Spain Cries Enough."

WEDNESDAY, JULY 27: Having received no information by midday, the War Department issued speculative information about the Miles expedition: It was expected that Brig. Gen. Oswald Ernst's brigade had reinforced Gen. Miles' advance guard, and they expected little difficulty in capturing Ponce since, according to reports received by the Bureau of Military Information, the only guns mounted there were howitzers and fieldpieces placed in the hills behind the city to command the road from Ponce to San Juan.

Detailed information was finally received late in the evening. The Navy Department got a wire from Henry Lee Higginson, with a St. Thomas July 26 dateline: "Arrived here with Gen. Miles and the U.S. troops today at 9:15 a.m. Landed them safely . . . no batteries outside. *Gloucester* entered the harbor and landed a company under the command of Lieut. Harry P. Huse, U.S. Navy, and Lieut. Wood. Dispersed a small company of Spanish soldiers. Hoisted flag. Commend Lieut. Commander Richard Wainright and officers for gallantry in capturing Guánica. Transports discharged without any opposition, assisted by the boats of the *Massachusetts*." The popular and dashing "Dick" Wainwright was the only officer in Sampson's fleet who had been *twice* commended since the outbreak of hostilities.

Today's events centered on *Dixie* Commander Charles H. Davis, who came ashore with a detachment of naval personnel at the Port of Ponce, two miles south of the main city. The city and port of Ponce *supposedly* surrendered to Davis, but correspondent Harding Davis set the record straight: "[Ponce] was possessed of the surrender habit in a most aggravating form. . . . [F]or anyone in uniform it was . . . unsafe to enter the town . . . unless he came prepared to accept its unconditional surrender. In the official count . . . the city of Ponce and the port surrendered to Commander Davis of the *Dixie*. . . . But, as a matter of fact, the town *first* surrendered to Ensign Curtin of the *Wasp*, *then* to three officers who strayed into it by mistake, *then* to Commander Davis, and *finally* to Gen. Miles."

Back home, mobilization continued. Upon telegraphing from Newport News, Gen. Brooke was told to leave directly for Fajardo with his force composed of artillery, cavalry, and infantry. Also ordered to join Miles was the 1st Regiment of Volunteer Engineers, with a rendezvous at Peekskill, New York. The commander of the regiment, Col. Eugene Griffin, received his orders at a War Department meeting; the 1st greeted the news with enthusiasm.

However, there was no joy among the 5th Illinois at Chickamauga. Along with the 3rd Kentucky and the 3rd Battalion of the 16th Pennsylvania, the 5th Illinois left the park under orders to head for Puerto Rico. However, Secretary Alger delivered an order for the Illinois regiment to return to camp, replaced by the 116th Indiana. As this was their second return-to-camp order, the men leveled all sorts of "unsavory" charges against their commanding officer, Col. Culver, and all semblance of order broke down. Nearly 100 members left camp, most without leave, and departed for the city. One of them broke his gun over a tree.

According to observers at Chickamauga, the men "claim that their regiment has been betrayed by Col. Culver, who represented to President McKinley that the regiment was not fit for field duty. Subordinates insisted they were in excellent condition."

As new men left for the front, many returned. Funeral services were held in St. Paul's Episcopal Church in Washington for Capt. Allyn Capron, one of Roosevelt's Rough Riders, who died at Siboney. The body was taken for burial in Arlington Cemetery, escorted by 100 men of the 15th Pennsylvania Regiment. Capt. Capron's mother and wife were present, but his father remained with his battery of artillery in Cuba.

Private Weichert of the 9th regulars was injured in the wrist and recuperated at Fort McPherson. He returned home to Newberry, South Carolina, to tell the *Observer* of combat at Santiago: "There are three forts . . . the Americans had to encounter. One was a blockhouse . . . guarding the pathway leading up to [a hill] . . . impenetrable by rifle bullets, thirty-two Spaniards . . . stationed [inside]. In the walls . . . were holes just large enough to shoot through, and . . . the Spanish soldiers fired . . . rapid[ly]. . . . Our boys dropped like tenpins. A colored sergeant scaled the wall and tore from its staff the Spanish flag. . . . [T]he Spaniards fired . . . and he dropped . . . dead. Three . . . Americans dropped in . . . from above. . . . [T]hey were riddled with bullets . . . [and] mutilated with bayonets. . . . [Fifteen] American privates appeared on the wall, I being among them. The sight of our . . . comrades was galling. . . . [E]ach of [us] . . . sprang into the pit. . . . I was shot in the wrist but killed the Spaniards who shot me. . . . [Most of us] were wounded but not one killed . . . 32 against our 15. . . . Upon the death of all the Spaniards, the door was forced open and . . . [we] regained the regiment."

Lieut. W. S. Wood, Adjutant of the 9th Cavalry, one of the colored regiments that fought so gallantly during the battle of Santiago, was disabled by a Mauser bullet that passed through his lower jaw and lodged in his shoulder while he was leading his forces. He was brought to Washington on one of the hospital ships and landed in a dentist's chair to fix his jaw so he could chew. He got good news from the Surgeon General when he visited the War Department. Yes, the government would pay for his dental surgery.

There were casualties, too, among the soldiers who never went to the front. Private William A. Wray of the 69th Regiment died of illness at Fort Thomas, Kentucky. His mother had no money to transport his body north, so Mrs. Jessie C. Lane, of 36 West Washington Square, stepped forward to comfort her and try to raise funds. A nurse during the Civil War, Mrs. Lane said she would speak to Pennsylvania Railroad officials to see if they could forward the body. If not, she would arrange for burial in her private plot in Newport, Kentucky. Formerly a porter with the Stock Exchange, Private Wray had sent his mother many letters and mementos from camp in Tampa, where he was before becoming ill.

Ten new cases of typhoid were sent from Camp Alger to Fort Meyer. There were also many cases of malarial intermittent fever and other ailments that could develop into typhoid. With a heavy incidence, Company G, 12th Pennsylvania, had to be isolated.

16

PREPARATIONS FOR PEACE NEGOTIATIONS BEGIN

THURSDAY, JULY 28: The citizens of Ponce welcomed General Miles after obligingly surrendering. He put them at ease with a proclamation that Americans were not enslavers but liberators and would respect their personal and property rights. Harding Davis observed that the General did not need to offer the townspeople any sign of goodwill; they were already happy: "Nothing could have been more enthusiastic . . . than [Ponce's] open-air reception [in tribute to the Americans]. The fire companies paraded in their honor and ran over three of their own men, which gave the local Red Cross . . . a grand chance to appear on the scene, each man wearing four red crosses, to carry away the wounded."

Meanwhile, Sandburg and his fellow soldiers settled into Puerto Rico, and the conditions were difficult. Yauco and Ponce had already surrendered, so they camped in a wooded ravine. "After the first two or three hours . . . sleeping in our underwear and barefoot, we put on our pants, wool shirts, and socks, for all of the moist heat. The . . . mosquitoes [were] of the type you say, 'One could kill a dog, two could kill a man' . . . large, ravenous, pitiless. . . . After an hour I would wake with an aching head from foul air, . . . [I would] throw the poncho off, beat away the mosquitoes, wrap the poncho around my head again, then sleep till awaking with a headache—and repeat."

The Navy Department released additional reports from commanders of vessels in the vicinity when Cervera's fleet was demolished on July 3: Capt. Francis A. Cook of the *Brooklyn*; Lieut. Nathaniel Usher, commanding the torpedo boat *Ericsson*; Capt. Charles S. Cotton of the *Harvard*; Lieut. Sharp, commanding the *Vixen*; and Commander Eaton of the *Resolute*. In his report, Captain Cook spoke of the intense battle leading to two casualties: Yeoman George H. Ellis, killed, and Fireman First Class J. Burns, wounded: "The ship was struck 20 times by whole shot and many times by pieces of bursting shell and from small shot from machine guns. No serious injury was done to the ship, and all repairs can be temporarily done by the ship's force."

According to Dr. Alexander W. Kent, the Red Cross Agent at Jacksonville, Florida, in a letter to Stephen E. Barton of the Red Cross: "I rode through the camp and investigated the conditions of the hospital. The 2nd Division was well provided for and the men had blessings for the Red Cross. Some of the regiment hospitals were not so comfortable. I am doing the best to supply all deficiencies.

"At the 3rd Division hospital, . . . which has already 50 patients, and will have more when it has accommodations, I found things in pretty bad shape. [And] I have . . . received word from Miami that affairs are in bad shape there."

As losses mounted for Spain, Madrid's desire for peace talks increased. While no terms had been firmly set, America had decided that Spain must abandon Cuba, and Puerto Rico had to be ceded to America. The future of the Philippines was uncertain. In any event, there would be no suspension of hostilities prior to an agreement to suspend military operations.

FRIDAY, JULY 29: Three days of the Puerto Rican campaign having ended, Gen. Miles reported gratifying results to the War Department: the capture of the town of Yauco, occupation of the city and port of Ponce, and raising of the flag over 50,000 former subjects of Spain. Washington observers felt that these feats were worthy of the praise engendered by the destruction of the Spanish fleets at Manila and Santiago and the capitulation at Santiago. However, the Cabinet was busy with what they felt were imminent discussions. The victories in Puerto Rico were especially welcome now— before peace negotiations could deprive the United States of gains in Puerto Rico.

Miles was overjoyed by his success. "This is a prosperous and beautiful country," he cabled Alger. "The army will be soon in a mountain region; weather delightful; troops in best of health and spirits; anticipate no insurmountable obstacles in future. Results thus far . . . without the loss of a single life. . . .

"The populace received [us] with wild enthusiasm. The navy has several prizes, also seventy fighters. . . . The Spanish retreat was precipitous, leaving rifles and ammunition in barracks and forty or fifty sick in the hospital. The people are enjoying a holiday in honor of our arrival."

Miles' detailed report of the capture of Ponce and Yauco referred to the force led by Brig. Gen. George A. Garretson, composed of the 6th Massachusetts and the 6th Illinois. He was aided by Brig. Gen. Guy V. Henry. Garretson gave Miles further information about his advance guard, which took not only Ponce but also Tallaboa, Sabana Grande, and Panuelas. The flag raiser was identified as Maj. Webb Hayes of 6th Ohio, son of the former President.

Miles' indication that the troops would soon be "in the mountain region" meant he intended to drive from Ponce to San Juan immediately. The retreat of the Spanish garrison and the general withdrawal of all the company's regulars into San Juan suggested that American troops would have little difficulty reaching the city. According to the Paris correspondent of *Temps* in San Juan, Spanish troops in Puerto Rico were poorly equipped and conditioned, so little resistance to the Americans was expected.

SATURDAY, JULY 30: Peace talks were advanced that afternoon at the White House at a meeting between the President, Secretary Day, and Ambassador Pierre Cambdon, France's Envoy Extraordinary and Plenipotentiary to Spain. America told the French diplomat of the U.S. position on Cuba, Puerto Rico, the Philippines, the Ladrones, indemnity, armistice, and other relevant issues.

The status of the Philippines took center stage with action in Puerto Rico negligible. At a White House meeting of the Cabinet, agreement was reached that America should retain Manila Bay, with the city and surrounding territory, until formulation of plans for a future government.

Strong sentiment was voiced to support insurgent chief Emilio Aguinaldo, until Admiral Dewey cabled that the chief was a defiant personality. In fact, said Dewey, it would take a large American force to repel the insurgents. A special cable to the *New York Evening Journal* from U.S. Consul General Rounsvelle Wildman reproduced a letter sent to the Consul by Aguinaldo: "I have read in the *Journal* that I am getting the 'big head' and not behaving as I promised you. In reply I ask, 'Why should America expect me to outline my policy, present and future, and fight blindly for her interests when America will not be frank with me?' Tell me this: Am I fighting for annexation, protection, or independence? It is for America to say, not me.

"I can take Manila as I have defeated the Spanish everywhere, but what would be the use? If America takes Manila, I can save my men and arms for what the future has in store for me. Now, good friend, believe me, I am not both fool and rogue. The interests of my people are as sacred to me as are the interests of your people to you."

In Santiago, the 24th Infantry lost its last Captain with the death of Captain Dodge, 44, who succumbed to yellow fever. Adjt. Gen. Corbin noted the high rate of mortality among officers of the American Army. He was more personally affected by this death because Dodge had been Lieutenant in the same company that formed the Adjutant General's first command when the Lieutenant became a Captain. Corbin considered Dodge a younger brother.

Gallant and meritorious service in battle was rewarded as six sergeants in two colored regiments were named Second Lieutenants. Both regiments were in the thick of the battles at El Caney and San Juan. The 9th Cavalry also took part at the battle of Las Guásimas with the Rough Riders.

The heroism of the 25th Infantry was detailed by First Sergeant M. W. Sadler of Company D, as he painted the capture of El Caney, for the *New York Age*: "The enemy began showering down on us . . . and numberless sharpshooters hid away in . . . places of concealment. Our men began to fall, many . . . to never rise again, but so steady was the advance and so effective was our fire that the Spaniards became unnerved. . . . When they saw we were 'colored soldiers,' they knew their doom was sealed . . . for every time a [Spanish] head was raised there was one Spaniard less. . . .

"If any one doubts the fitness of the colored soldier for active field service, . . . ask the regimental commanders of the 24th and 25th Infantries, and the 9th and 10th Cavalries; ask Generals Kent and Wheeler, of whose divisions these regiments formed a part. . . . All we need [now are] . . . leaders of our own race to make war records, so that their names may go down in history as a reward for the price of our precious blood."

With the destruction of Cervera's fleet and the surrender of Santiago, most Americans felt the war had ended. The seizing of Puerto Rico hardly seemed necessary. But the *Desert Weekly* said, "Puerto Rico must be taken . . . more [Spanish] lives . . . lost and . . . valuable property destroyed . . . [and] perhaps, Spain must be attacked and her coast cities devastated before the leading spirits of that country will sacrifice their 'honor' and their 'pride' for the benefit of their country."

SUNDAY, JULY 31: As the citizens cheered, America raised its flag over another Puerto Rican town. Juana Díaz, now occupied by Col. Hullings and ten companies of the 16th Pennsylvania, was about eight miles northeast of Ponce on the road to San Juan.

According to reports, Gen. Ortega was marching with a force of Spanish regulars, headed for Albonito, further northeast from Juana Díaz. Some Spanish volunteers who had deserted reported a small force of Spanish regulars at Coamo, midway between the two, also on the road between Ponce and San Juan. If the enemy were to enjoy any advantage, it would be the mountains.

Brig. Gen. Theodore Schwan arrived in Ponce from Tampa with close to 3,000 men. Gen. Brooke arrived at Arroyo, 45 miles east of Ponce, with about 5,000 troops. Seven companies of the 19th Regular Infantry arrived on the *Cherokee*.

Some of the troops might be sent to Guayama, 27 miles east of Ponce. Its citizens asked Gen. Miles for help after 200 Spanish regulars allegedly seized funds from the town under instructions from the Consul General.

The ebullient spirit of Gen. Miles came through in his cable to Secretary Alger, with a 3:35 Ponce dateline: "Volunteers are surrendering . . . with arms and ammunition. Four-fifths of the people are overjoyed at the arrival of the army. Two thousand . . . have volunteered to serve with it. They are bringing in transportation beef cattle, and other needed supplies. . . . As soon as the troops . . . disembark . . . , they will be in readiness to move."

The cable then asked "[for] National colors . . . to be given to the different municipalities . . . [and] that the question of the tariff rate . . . be submitted to the President for his action."

Spanish Gen. Manuel Macías y Casado was still talking tough, but it was merely words. San Juan's former U.S. Consul, P. C. Hanna, released the following text from an unnamed Spanish official in the northern part of Puerto Rico: "Resistance is impossible. The volunteers have refused to march, and we have no ammunition." Understandably, few thought Spain could continue fighting much longer. McKinley was so confident about hostilities ending, he accepted an invitation to leave next week for a vacation of a month or more to Seabright. A five-man commission was being organized to commence peace negotiations. The three Americans to be appointed were thought to be Gen. Stewart L. Woodford, Minister to Spain; former Secretary of State Richard Olney; and former Vermont U.S. Senator George F. Edmunds.

The most difficult question for negotiations would concern the Philippines. Did America want coaling stations and naval stations? Did they want annexations? Spain was bent on retaining the island. The Madrid correspondent of the *London Times* wrote: "I am confident that the more [the question of the Philippines] is considered the less will America be inclined to annexation. Spain has . . . maintained sovereignty there by the aid of the religious orders. . . . Even the least clerical of the Captains General have admitted . . . that, without the friars, who are mostly able men and ardent Spanish patriots, an army corps . . . would be permanently required to maintain order. Any other powers seizing the Philippines would be obliged to abolish this medieval administration and introduce a much costlier system."

Meanwhile, another hero was emerging, destined for fame in the Philippines. Arthur MacArthur, appointed Brigadier General, arrived with command of the 2nd Brigade of the 1st Division. He would later be promoted to Major General of Volunteers, assigned to command the 2nd Division of the 8th Army Corps, an appointment that would greatly affect his son, Douglas, who at 18, seriously considered passing up his cadetship to enlist in the conflict. However, "Wise counsel prevailed," the now legendary Douglas MacArthur would write in his *Reminiscences*, telling of his father's advice and brilliant prediction: "My son, there will be plenty of fighting in coming years and of a magnitude far beyond this. Prepare yourself" (MacArthur 19).

MONDAY, AUGUST 1: Gen. John J. Coppinger, headquartered in Tampa, received orders to proceed to Puerto Rico immediately and attach himself to the Miles expedition. He was scheduled to sail on August 2 on the transport *Arkansas*.

In order to meet the volunteers' demand to serve at the front, Maj. Gen. James F. Wade was ordered to lead a provisional division of 15 infantry regiments from Chickamauga to bolster Miles' army. The telegram ordered Wade "to give . . . several States in the Union representation in the field." Secretary Alger readily admitted America already had more than enough troops there for offense, defense, and occupation purposes. The highest total of Spanish regulars came only to 8,000—with loyal volunteers 14,000—arrayed against an American force of 25,000, equipped with smokeless powder magazine rifles and a full complement of cavalry and artillery.

A story from the Madrid correspondent of the *London Times* placed the Spanish force a little higher: "Macías has decided to entrench in San Juan. A majority of his *18,000* men . . . spread over the island . . . have been ordered to defend themselves as long as possible and as a last resort to retire to the capital. It is feared . . . Americans will easily secure San Juan . . . the natives are not likely to resist. It is believed that the garrison . . . will fight with Spanish heroism . . . unhampered, as was the garrison at Santiago . . . by lack of food and ammunition."

Col. Hullings advanced to Coamo and was enthusiastically greeted by a delegation of townspeople, who told him the Spaniards had looted all funds that had not been hidden and that the enemy had retreated to Aibonito to make a stand. Gen. Roy Stone left with a small force for Adjuntas, where Spanish outrages were reported, then pushed across to Arecibo on the north coast. The brigade of Gen. George Garretson, consisting of the 6th Massachusetts, 6th Illinois, four batteries of the regular artillery, and a battalion of regulars, was loudly cheered by the citizens when they arrived at Ponce, from Yauco. Military men said that with peace talks near and no loyalty from the natives, Madrid had told Spanish soldiers not to lay down their lives uselessly when faced with superior force.

Meanwhile, the situation in the Philippines was far more dangerous than on any other front. Gen. Merritt not only had to fight the Spanish, he had to protect the citizens from the savagery of the insurgents who were numerous, well armed, and arrogant because of their victories over their Spanish enemies. The General said he and Dewey would jointly ask Manila's surrender, thereby heading off the insurgents. The American force totalled 12,000, with an additional 8,000 planned.

At home, health was again in the news. Surgeon Gen. Sternberg said the campsites in the South had to be changed because "the business of soldiering leads to accumulated filth." In particular, he asked that Camp Alger, which might have been healthy at first, be moved from its location because it had now become foul due to careless sanitation and a disregard of other health regulations.

Dr. Olin F. Harvey, the examining physician of regulars in Wilkes-Barre and Scranton, Pennsylvania, issued a lengthy statement on the need for sounder health practices among *would-be* soldiers. He had examined 500 men in Wilkes-Barre; only 151 were fit. In Scranton, he'd examined 400 and accepted only 175. The rejection rate was originally up to four out of five, but after word spread, many probable rejects did not bother to show up.

Dr. Harvey's reasons for rejection? "A good stomach makes a good soldier, and good teeth . . . keep the stomach healthy. Lots of hearty boys . . . could not be recommended because of bad teeth. . . .

"I . . . reject[ed] a large number for insufficient chest expansion. . . . [N]early all were young farmers. Brought up to run a plow or hoe and scrape the ground with long-handed tools, they had . . . strong arms and back, but were muscle bound and bent over. . . . [F]ew . . . could expand on inhalation the requisite two inches. . . .

"I found . . . many . . . cases of hypertrophied heart . . . [with] careless and reckless bicycle riding . . . largely responsible. . . .

"[Thirty] percent of the boys . . . had . . . myopia and[/or] astigmatism. It is not comfortable to think that with our modern school buildings and . . . improved methods of lighting . . . one-third of our young men are wearing their eyes out."

What did the doctor recommend? "1. Look out for the eyes of the young . . . that they are not allowed to overwork or strain them; 2. Let the young farmer boys . . . try sitting-up exercise as a regular routine; 3. Bicycle riders ought to beware of scorching and racing and . . . long and tedious rides across country; and 4. Take care of the teeth and look after them earnestly."

The day's hero in the news was the ever-popular Lieut. Richmond Pearson Hobson, who was cheered wildly by Southern admirers in Lithia Springs, near Atlanta. His mother waited for him at the train station, with a large crowd of guests from the Sweetwater Park Hotel. Reported the *New York Times*: "[F]or several moments the naval hero was a busy man . . . shaking hands until each individual had been saluted. Mr. Hobson received the attention shown him with the coolness which marked his deed for daring on the *Merrimac*."

Politics, but not as usual: With a Governor's race a few months away, New York Secretary of State Palmer dispatched Maj. Hobbes to Peekskill to deliver registration papers to the State members of the engineer regiment. His upcoming itinerary: Santiago de Cuba and Puerto Rico. Other agents would be sent for registration purposes to the Southern camps. The 1st Regiment would get their papers by mail in Honolulu.

The press usually devoted several columns comparing Sampson and Schley, but today the *Index* (of Williamsport, Pennsylvania) compared Capt. John Philip of the *Texas* to Capt. Robley D. Evans of the *Iowa*, a comparison that was *not* a military one. Philip was praised for "after-action prayer" for having thanked the Lord after a naval encounter at Santiago, while Evans was castigated for "frequently published profanity." Evans responded, defending himself: "I am sure . . . a great majority of officers . . . do not consider it necessary, to announce . . . that 'they believe in the Almighty God' [echoing the words of Philip]. I think that goes without saying. . . . Capt. Philip had a perfect right to [do] . . . as he did; it was . . . a matter of taste.

"Shortly after the . . . *Vizcaya* had struck . . . and my crew had secured the guns, the Chaplain . . . said, '[S]hall I say a few words of thanks to Almighty God . . . ?' [and] I said, 'By all means. . . . I will have the men sent aft for that purpose' and was . . . [about to do] so when . . . a Spanish battleship was standing toward us. . . . My first duty . . . to God and my country was to sink this . . . battleship. . . . When it was discovered . . . this ship was . . . Austrian, . . . carrying dying and wounded prisoners. . . . To leave these men to suffer for want of food and clothing while I called my men aft to offer prayers was not my idea of either Christianity or religion. . . . I do not know whether I will stand with Captain Philip . . . in the hereafter, but . . . every drop of [my] blood . . . on the afternoon of the 3rd . . . was singing thanks and praise."

TUESDAY, AUGUST 2: Washington made its peace terms public today. They were contained in a note for transmittal to Spain by Ambassador Cambon that said: "The President does not now put forward any claim for pecuniary indemnity, but requires the relinquishment of all claim of sovereignty over or title to the Island of Cuba . . . the immediate evacuation of Puerto Rico and other islands under Spanish Sovereignty in the West Indies and . . . cession of an island in the Ladrones. The United States will occupy and hold the city, bay, and harbor of Manila pending the conclusion of a treaty of peace."

The Philippines promised to be a major problem that would only grow worse. America had assumed a moral obligation to protect not only the foreign residents of Manila, but also the women, children, priests, and nuns of its Spanish community. Americans received reports that the insurgents were threatening the lives of monks, so American commanders were ordered to act appropriately in the name of humanity.

On an economic level, America assumed a commitment to pay the indebted claims by its citizens against Spain for injury to their personal property in Cuba. Part of this liability might later be placed against the government of Cuba once one was duly recognized. Estimates showed the claims exceeding $20 million.

Two thousand volunteers surrendered to Americans in Puerto Rico, according to a private dispatch from San Juan. Augustus Peabody Gardner, a staff officer of Gen. Wilson's, spoke for many when he wrote his wife, "The rumors of peace are thick, and everyone is more disgusted than ever. I am not bloodthirsty; but I should like to see a little real fighting after all the farce."

Never to see fighting again were those on the newest list of yellow fever victims reported from Santiago by Gen. Shafter. One, August Grahn, Company L, 71st Regiment, had immigrated to New York several years ago with his older sister,

Johanna; their parents remained in Germany. When war broke out he sought to enlist with the Rough Riders, but there were no openings. Instead, he enlisted with the 71st, lying that he was 21. He was only 18 when he died.

The Rough Riders were in the news, at Governors Island. An unidentified source maintained that Col. Roosevelt was among the wounded being treated at the facility. The source also maintained that a Spanish shell had exploded above the leader of the Rough Riders and a group of five other officers. Furthermore, a scrap had grazed the back of the Colonel's right hand. Further inquiry could not locate the source or confirm the Colonel's injury. Commenting on the report, one of Roosevelt's political opponents said sarcastically, "[He] would have to be wounded before he would be a dangerous candidate for Governor."

Over the objections of summer residents, sick soldiers would be transferred from Santiago to a planned military hospital at Montauk, with 500 beds to be sent there shortly. William F. Forward, Chief Surgeon of the Soldiers' Home in the District of Columbia, selected the hospital site, and since tracks would be needed to get the troops from the terminal to Fort Pond Bay, the Long Island Railroad had to bring in six carloads of ties and three of steel rails, plus 200 section laborers.

WEDNESDAY, AUGUST 3: Firing was exchanged in Ponce between the Spaniards and the pickets of Capt. Austin, who comprised Miles' advance guard. American troops in Ponce numbered about 9,000—equal to the entire Spanish force on the island. A prominent marine insurance man, who insisted he remain anonymous, claimed he had a letter from a merchant in Ponce saying the Spaniards would surrender Puerto Rico, including San Juan, within two days.

If the report were true, Gen. Wade needed to hurry his "personally conducted excursion" of Puerto Rico. Being organized into six brigades were 18 regiments from 14 states: three presently at Jacksonville; six each at Chickamauga and Alger; one each at Fort Slocum, Middletown, and Fort Monroe. The plan was to give a taste of war to those states not yet represented. However, Mississippi and South Carolina were still excluded; Tennessee, Iowa, New York, and Maryland were already represented in Cuba, and Texas had an immune regiment at Santiago.

Even with the war winding down, America had time to unveil a new hero: Boatswain Mate Nevis. Accompanied by the converted yacht *Eagle*, which had been covering the blockading station near the Isle of Pines near Key West, the gunboat *Bancroft* spotted a Spanish schooner in Siguanea Bay. Within minutes the *Nito* was captured—a paltry prize with hardly any cargo. In fact, the Captain was American, with a Cuban wife and seven children, all pledging loyalty to Cuba. He pleaded to keep the schooner, which was his livelihood, and *Bancroft*'s Captain Glover agreed to return it at a later time. For now, he told Nevis to anchor the prize near the wrecked transatlantic liner *Santo Domingo*. The *Bancroft* and *Eagle* then sailed off to keep in touch with the insurgent camp.

In anchoring the schooner, Nevis noticed two other small Spanish boats near the wreck. Quickly, he took the Spanish colors of the schooner, ran them up, and sailed on. The six men on the Spanish boats rushed out to greet their fellow countrymen— only to discover they had been duped. They immediately surrendered when Nevis and another navyman whipped out their rifles. Aside from the prize and capture of the Spaniards, Nevis secured important information about the town of Cortez Province of Pinar del Rio, two miles from the wreck.

In Boston for a short stay with the Jesuit Fathers of St. Mary's Church, the Most Reverend Sebastian Martinelli, Papal Delegate in the United States, stated, "I . . . do not know enough about [Puerto Rico] to tell whether it will . . . benefit [the United States] . . . to own it or not [but] . . . there is no doubt . . . [the Puerto Ricans] will profit by the change." Their Catholicism, he felt, would prosper under the rule of the United States.

THURSDAY, AUGUST 4: Americans took peaceful possession of the eastern portion of Puerto Rico, landing off San Juan to the greetings of its citizens. Spanish Captain Gen. Macías y Casado defiantly issued a proclamation: "Spain has not sued for peace, and I can drive off . . . American boats now as I did Sampson's attempt before." Four warships, the *Montgomery*, *Annapolis*, *Puritan*, and *Amphitrite* were all in the area. The *New Orleans* was the only vessel maintaining the blockade off San Juan.

On land, the 16th Pennsylvania of Gen. Oswald's Brigade advanced six miles beyond Juana Díaz on the road to San Juan and seized the bridge over the river, ensuring control of the road to Coamo. They would be joined by the 2nd and 3rd Wisconsin on August 5. While no sign of the enemy was observed, the Spaniards numbered about 400 between this point and Coamo.

Plans for Wade's "junketing party" proceeded. Ordered to report to the Major, for duty with his troops in Puerto Rico, were Gens. George W. Davis and George M. Randall, 2nd Army Corps; Gens. R. H. Hall and W. W. Gordon, 4th Army Corps; Gen. H. C. Hasbrouck, 7th Army Corps; and Gen. John A. Wiley, 1st Army Corps. Seven regiments at Chickamauga and the 1st New Jersey Regiment at Sea Girt rejoiced when they heard they would be going to Puerto Rico. The 2nd New Jersey Regiment of Volunteers would probably join them under the command of Gen. Fitzhugh Lee.

Not so jubilant was Secretary Alger. Nearly every regiment not named was disappointed. Those who believed there were good reasons for their selection were outraged. There was no real military reason for the tour. Nobody ever said that those chosen were the most capable. Brigades were chopped up, demoralizing the men who would go. To add to the "irregularities," no orders had been issued to the named regiments. Maj. Gen. Matthew Butler stormed into Alger's office to protest the detailing of four regiments for Wade's "pleasure party."

On top of this, Alger was involved in another controversy, this one with Col. Roosevelt. He cabled his reply today to a July 23 letter from Santiago in which Roosevelt had said, "We . . . hope that you will send most of the regulars, and at any rate the cavalry division including the Rough Riders, who are as good as any regulars, and three times as good as any State troops, to Puerto Rico. There are 1,800 effective men in this division; if those . . . left behind were joined to them, we could land . . . in this cavalry division, close to 4,000 men . . . worth, easily, any 10,000 National Guards, armed with . . . Springfields or other archaic weapons." Alger's reply angrily states: "The regular army, the volunteer army, and the Rough Riders have done well, but I suggest that unless you want to spoil the effects and glory of your victory, you make no invidious comparisons. The Rough Riders are no better than other volunteers. They had an advantage in their arms, for which they ought to be grateful."

To aggravate the situation, Alger also had to contend with one more hospital ship horror. The *Santiago* arrived from Egmont Key, Florida, with sick and wounded on board in wretched conditions comparable to those on the *Seneca* and the *Concho*. The *Santiago* had been used to transport the horses of Brig. Gen. W. F. Randolph's artillery brigade to Santiago. The *New York Journal* referred to the prisoners on board as "ill and dying in floating stable."

Once more the spotlight shone on Lieut. Richmond Pearson Hobson. Thousands filled the Metropolitan Opera House to display their patriotism and give homage to America's favorite Navy Constructor. The evening was sponsored by the New York Soldiers' and Sailors' Families Protective Association, who gave monetary and emotional aid to relatives of those who served their country. The *New York Times* report left no doubt that the star of the evening was Hobson: "The men, women, and youngsters who looked up . . . into Hobson's quiet, earnest face or craned their necks . . . to catch his words, saw . . . a brave man . . . of brains and force."

The House was appropriately decorated: large stairways draped in the national colors; huge American flags filling the stage; and the Stars and Stripes as well as an American flag and shield adorning Box 7, where the Hobsons sat. All stopped when, in the middle of the singing of the National Anthem, Association President Maj. John Byrne entered the stage, accompanied by Hobson. Reported the *Times*, "It was Hobson they had come to see, and they sprang from their chairs to greet him with a wild enthusiasm born of admiration for his valor and the love of their common country." Hobson accepted the ovation "with quiet self-possession."

America's Minister to Spain, Gen. Stewart L. Woodford, was one of the first to shake Hobson's hand, after which the Southern-born hero was introduced by Maj. Byrne to deafening applause and the playing of "Dixie." Not at a lack for humor, Hobson hollered to the band, "Don't you know that we want a 'Yankee Doodle'?" The band obliged.

While retracing the heroics of the *Merrimac* incident, he talked of his training days: "I was at the Naval Academy when . . . I saw an incident of the American sailors' pluck. Our ship was about 500 yards from shore when a man unable to swim fell overboard. . . . [A] sailor immediately sprang after him. Another man followed . . . and [then] one after another . . . until the officer . . . gave a stern command, 'No more men overboard.' This was my introduction to the . . . Jackies—the sailors."

Hobson also spoke of Admiral Cervera, the "gallant, manly chief of the Spanish forces," which elicited great applause, and of his compatriots, "these . . . samples of the knights of our navy . . . willing to die under any condition . . . [give] an accurate idea, more or less of the American sailor." At the end of the meeting, a unanimous resolution thanked Admiral Cervera for his courtesy to Lieut. Hobson.

An official dispatch from San Juan related that Col. San Martín, in command of the Spanish garrison at Ponce, was court-martialed and shot for ceding the garrison without resistance. His second in command, Lt. Col. Puiz, committed suicide.

FRIDAY, AUGUST 5: There were many red faces in the War Department when a *New York Times* headline announced, "Wade's Picnic Abandoned." Explanations varied. The most "acceptable" was that it was a "paper" division, drawn up to satisfy friends and supporters of those state troops "assigned" to it, so the soldiers could at least say they were ordered to the front. By including every state (although several states *were* omitted) no state could say it was slighted. But this was a lame explanation, especially since no regiment ever even received a formal order. The "official" explanation was that Shafter's soldiers were returning to America, so no transports were available.

The 6th Illinois had now been in Ponce two days. Once again, they had discovered on arrival that their target had surrendered. "The August heat was on," said Carl Sandburg. "We carried cartridge belt, rifle, bayonet, blanket . . . tent, haversack . . . a coat. We still wore . . . blue-wool pants . . . and thick canvas leggings laced from ankles to knees. . . . Men fell out, worn out, and there were sunstroke cases . . . on the ground raving about the heat."

Was a battle on? "[A]ll was quiet about midnight. Suddenly came a shriek. Then . . . yells and shrieks and seven companies . . . rushing headlong down the slope to the road. Men . . . were trampled and bruised. . . . [O]ne of the bullocks had got loose . . . trampled on a sleeper who gave the first . . . shriek. . . . We went up the slope and back to our sleep calling it the 'First Battle of Bull Run.'"

Miles told his troops he would conduct the war regardless of peace negotiations, unless he was told to stop. He reported that Col. Hullings captured 5,000 pounds of rice, without hindrance. Maj. Gen. Brooke finally arrived at Arroyo, 40 miles east of Ponce, with troops from the *Roumanian*: four batteries of the 27th Indiana; the 1st Missouri; and 5th Illinois. The Morgan troop of the 5th Cavalry and the Missouri Commissaries also arrived.

On another front, Miles informed Massachusetts Gov. Wolcott of the resignation of the Colonel, Lieutenant Colonel, three Majors, and three Captains of the 6th Massachusetts Regiment, all charged with incompetency and lack of discipline, partly due to their refusal to return the salutes of their colored companies. Miles recommended as Colonel, Lieut. Col. Edmund Rice, who had a highly respected regiment in the Army of the Potomac.

How close were America and Spain to peace? According to the Madrid correspondent of the *London Daily Mail*: "The [Spanish] Government has not yet answered the American note, nor received President McKinley's reply to the explanations asked by Señor Sagasta. The Premier said today that the Government would reply to the American demands early next week. In consulting the party leaders, Sagasta is following the precedent of Castelar when the Virginius affair threatened war with the United States."

SATURDAY, AUGUST 6: Guayama was captured by Hain's brigade—the 4th Ohio and 3rd Illinois—said Gen. Miles in a dispatch to the War Department. Three Americans were wounded, none seriously, in the slight skirmish with a small enemy force of about 500.

It was obviously just bravado when Spanish authorities said they were resolved to fight to the end. U.S. Consul Hanna said foreign Consuls at San Juan advised them to surrender, but Spain refused. The Consuls then advised Capt. Macías they would establish a neutral zone between Bayamon and Rio Piedras, where foreign residents and their movable property could assemble to ensure their safety in case of American bombardment.

Back home, the debate over the future of the Philippines heated up. Ohio U.S. Senator Foraker argued: "I think it would be . . . a crime to return them to . . . the tyranny Spain has practiced over [them] . . . for years. . . . It is . . . a corrupt and tax-ridden country . . . [and] I feel that the United States has a mission . . . by Divine Providence . . . and that we shall fail to manifest its purposes if we allow the Philippines to remain under [Spain's] yoke and . . . darkness."

Hero Hobson was in New York consulting with Merritt and Chapman about plans for raising the *Cristobal Colón*. "It will probably take another 10 days before all is readiness," he said, "but when the work is started there will be no . . . lack of wrecking material." With the war nearly over, what were his plans? "I have as yet no idea what my future plans may be. I . . . talk[ed] with the Secretary of the Navy, and have requested . . . duty with the Eastern Squadron if it moves on Spain . . . but the chances for a naval force going to Spain seem to be rather slim."

A delightful vignette appeared in the *New York Journal*, datelined Long Beach, New York. The story, titled "How Hero Hobson Kisses [as] Told by Pretty Miss Emma Arnold, Who Knows from Experience," took place at a Long Beach hotel, where a large crowd hoped for a glimpse—or more—of their hero. The men got handshakes; children got kisses and autographs. As Miss Arnold watched, she became jealous, so when she was introduced to Hobson, the St. Louis lass said impulsively, "I almost wish I were a child again." The gallant Hobson responded, "Then, let me treat you as one," and kissed her. Miss Arnold elaborated: "Lieut. Hobson . . . treated [the children] . . . so tenderly . . . I also desired that treatment. . . . That's all there is to it. I am very proud to have been kissed by such a man."

As the war neared its end in Puerto Rico, James Miller, a black soldier who took part in the invasion of the island, related his experiences and impressions to the *Savannah Tribune*: "The troops got here in time to save the natives. . . . The Spaniards had . . . laid the law down that any man or woman who rebelled . . . would be punished: Corset jackets with nails in them for women and children and gloves the same for men. This was to have been put into effect July 29, but we arrived July 28, and the executors flew to the mountains in the inland."

What really impressed Miller was that "This is the first place in my life . . . I have . . . found no distinction in color. . . . What suits me best of all, the island is covered with beautiful women and girls and they fairly worship an American."

SUNDAY, AUGUST 7: American troops advanced in different directions. Gen. Ernst's brigade, constituting the advance center, was supported by two batteries. Part of the 7th Infantry of Gen. Guy V. Henry started to the left toward Adjuntas. Gen. Theodore Schwan moved with the 11th Regular Infantry and two batteries, through Yauco toward Mayaguez, to get back into the interior and reach Arecibo by way of Lares. He was told by Miles, "[D]rive out or capture all Spanish troops in the western portion . . . take all the necessary precautions . . . against being surprised . . . by the enemy, and make the movement as rapidly as possible . . . exercising your best judgment . . . to accomplish the object of your expedition."

Gen. James H. Wilson moved the headquarters of his division from Ponce to Juana Díaz. Gen. Brooke was moving north from Guayama with 10,000 men—Troop A of New York, the Philadelphia City Troop, and Troop II of the 6th Regulars—convoying his transportation column along the coast road through Salinas, 36 miles from San Juan.

Worn out but thrilled to be going home, Col. Roosevelt, who contrary to earlier rumors was *not* in already in New York recuperating, led his Rough Riders down the Alameda, ready to board the *Miami*. It was a motley crew: Some wore new khaki uniforms; others, heavy blue flannel shirts with their old equipment. While happy to leave Santiago, they were sorry to leave five sick comrades behind. They would savor their time at home but were quite willing to go back for a campaign in Havana.

Peace negotiations continued with Spain responding to Washington's peace note. The French Ambassador, presenting Spain's response, met with the Cabinet at the White House. The prolonged discussion seemed to say the Spanish answer was not fully satisfactory, the best guess being that Madrid had attached certain conditions to accepting Washington's terms.

MONDAY, AUGUST 8: With peace talks nearing and cessation of arms a possibility, Gen. Miles was seemingly racing against time to gain territory. He swept on toward San Juan by roads from the east, west, and center. Brig. Gen. Guy V. Henry was advancing on Arecibo. The artillery was heading to Yauco, most likely to threaten Mayaguez. Gen. Brooke was ordered to seize Cayey to isolate the Spanish position at Aibonito. Brooke had to move quickly but carefully. "Envelop or outflank the enemy rather than attack in front," Miles told him, "and [don't] . . . assault entrenched lines. Take every precaution against ambuscade and mined roads." Brooke had the advantage of troop superiority.

In Santiago, Gen. Shafter contended with problems of the sick and wounded. In a report to the War Department, he denied responsibility for their inadequate provisions on the *Seneca* and *Concho*: "There is no excuse for lack of food, as there has at all times been plenty. . . . [I'm sure] many more were put on the ship than should have been because of the great desire to get home . . . fear of yellow fever, and . . . [the lack of] hospital accommodation.

"The sick and wounded had only the clothing that they wore into battle . . . ragged and worn out by the time they reached home. There was none to issue to them at the time they left and their own . . . they could not get at. There has never been . . . suffering here that could be remedied by the means at hand. . . . The Surgeons have worked as well as any men . . . [considering the] lack of means and facilities. I do not complain . . . for no one would have foreseen all that would be required, but I will not quietly submit to having the onus laid on me." His latest sanitary report listed 3,445 sick, including 412 new cases.

Col. Roosevelt pledged that he would seek a court-martial against Shafter for allowing these awful conditions. Roosevelt's critics contended that he was gearing up for politics, perhaps a race for New York State Governor or even President.

On the other side, Shafter was defended by Gen. Corbin, who said that in light of the need of pressing the war effort, Shafter could not have done more. "It was a question of getting [to Santiago] . . . at once," he said, "and of taking the city with utmost speed. Gen. Shafter knew that disease was to be feared and that the longer his men stood still, the greater would be the danger that . . . the campaign would be defeated and the men . . . used up by the climate and the ailments."

The problems of the wounded and sick were graphic as 600 members of the 6th U.S. Cavalry, the advance guard of returning troops, arrived at Montauk Point from Fernandina, Florida. They arrived separately, in two battalions. Their condition was described by the *New York Times*: "The privates . . . were in shabby condition. Their uniforms . . . well worn . . . some of them . . . nearly barefooted. The men said they had but two meals a day since their departure from Florida . . . [and] had been unable . . . to get enough good water. Many of them . . . had malaria and chills and fever which left them weak and without ambition." But Montauk promised to revive them. Officials said the general hospital there would be one of the most complete camp hospitals ever built.

Perhaps arising from his rivalry with Schley, Sampson was attacked in letters to Secretary Long criticizing him for not moving to attack Puerto Rico, not sending his ships into the harbor, and being obsessed with personal glory. Long answered one of the critics in a long letter released to the press. The navy did not move on Puerto Rico, he said, because "at that time the Spanish fleet was strong." As for sending the fleet into the harbor, "Admiral Sampson was acting under . . . explicit orders . . . not to expose his armored ships to the risk of . . . mines. . . . He waited, as he should have . . . for the cooperation of the army."

On the issue of personal glory, Long insisted the Admiral "never pushes himself forward, and when you accuse him . . . you do most cruel injustice to a man who has never sought favor . . . in any other way than by the simple discharge of his duty. . . . I can think of nothing more cruel than a deprecation of . . . the faithful, devoted, patriotic Commander-in-Chief, physically frail, worn with sleepless vigil, weighed with measureless responsibilities and details, letting no duty go undone."

Another who let no duty go undone was Naval Constructor Hobson, who received unhappy news from Merritt and Chapman that they found the *Cristobal Colón* in a very bad condition that would most likely preclude saving her. However, the day was still memorable for the *Merrimac* hero, who was brought together with Admiral Cervera. Hobson took a Washington train to Annapolis, where the Spaniard was being held. The reunion, wrote a correspondent, "was like that of father and son. The grey-bearded Admiral first laid his hands on the shoulders of the young hero and then embraced him with Spanish fervor. . . . The meeting ended with an invitation by the Spaniard that Hobson visit him at his home in Spain."

Secretary of State Day confirmed reports that once the peace treaty was completed, he would return to private life. He would soon leave his post to sit in Paris with the peace commission being set up to complete the negotiations.

TUESDAY, AUGUST 9: In what military officers described as the first major combat of the Puerto Rican campaign, the command of Gen. Wilson, under the immediate command of Brig. Gen. Oswald, advanced from Ponce toward Aibonito. Led by Lieut. Col. John Biddle, the 16th Pennsylvania traveled through the night over a mountain trail, emerging on the road to San Juan, north of the Spaniards' position. Ernst then followed. In the consequent battle, the enemy lost its Commander and Second-in-Command, 40 others were killed or wounded, and 167 were captured. The Americans had succeeded in opening the road to Aibonito.

Malata, on Manila Bay, had seen fierce encounters between the insurgents and the Spaniards, but now the Americans and Spaniards skirmished. One of those killed was Sgt. Maurice Justa, 24, a former employee of a local wholesale clothing store who was the first California volunteer accepted by the examining surgeon and the only Californian killed at Malate. Among the wounded was another Californian, Capt. Reinhold Richter, 48, a native of Australia, who first joined the regular army in 1880 and went to Manila as Captain of Company I, 1st Infantry.

In Cuba, where fighting had ended weeks before, the morning saw action between Spaniards in Morro Castle and the converted yacht *Silvia*. According to a later report in the *New York Journal American*, *Silvia* lay near the flagship *San Francisco* and was assigned to bring papers to the blockaded city of Havana. Manned by the 2nd Battalion of the 1st Division of the Brooklyn Naval Reserve, the *Silvia* bore the fire of the castle and steamed into Havana with the dispatches. Her crewmen were described as young men who "dance and dine at the fashionable houses on Prospect Heights." When they enlisted for the war, "it was pleasantly predicted that if they ever met the Spaniards, it would probably be at a ball at the Governor General's Palace."

The front page of the *New York Times* screamed: "Awful Suffering at Camp Thomas," as told by Captain William F. Morris of Company K, 9th New York Volunteers, a highly respected officer, Superintendent of Station D of the Brooklyn Post Office and President of the Delinquency Court of the 9th Regiment.

Morris returned from camp after he resigned a week earlier, the last line officer to go. He was incensed at the treatment of the troops, calling the camp at Chickamauga "a modern Andersonville" (referring to the dreaded site of the Confederate prison) and blaming the head of the 9th, Col. Greene. "I could not remain longer," he said, "realizing my inability to alleviate the sufferings of the men."

He recalled his days at Camp Thomas, which were "like an awful dream." The hospital "seems like a door of despair" to the men. "They look upon it as the house of doom." One of the men of the 9th was dying of typhoid fever. "When I reached his cot," said Morris, "I nearly staggered with horror. The man's face was . . . black with flies. His mouth . . . open— . . . [he] was too weak to close it—was filled with flies. . . . The person in charge nonchalantly remarked . . . there were not enough nurses . . . [and] I told him . . . emphatically . . . his duty was to let the men of the company know, and they would gladly have acted as volunteer nurses."

After several hours, Morris arranged some ice for the dying soldier: "A pound exactly. With this . . . [the volunteer nurse] was expected to lower the temperature of a man dying with fever. Several days later the man was dead."

"In another case," continued Morris, "a man who died in the . . . hospital was found to be literally alive with maggots under his armpits . . . his dying agonies . . . intensified by the[ir] movements." The hospital was treating 280 soldiers, but only two thermometers could be found.

Greene was accused of not consulting with regimental officers, and his approach was cruel, alleged Morris: "[He] compelled the man on guard . . . to stand unprotected in the driving rain for hours," he said. "Not the slightest . . . shelter . . . , and many cases of [serious] illness . . . are traceable to this neglect."

"Once," cried Morris, "our company after a hard tour . . . early in the morning was ordered to march off about 10 a.m. for outpost duty . . . miles from camp. The thermometer marked 95 in the shade. I suggested . . . it would be wise to have the wagons to carry the shelter tents. 'They'll find it a blanked sight hotter yet before they get back!' was [Colonel Greene's] reply. So, loaded with . . . clothing and . . . tents, they had to march miles under the blazing sun. I also asked for a wagon to haul water . . . [and again] the Colonel refused."

Camp Black also had its trouble, but not of the magnitude at Camp Thomas. When Lieut. Hare of the 202nd Regiment, in command of one of the companies of the 71st New York Volunteers, and Officer of the Day, ordered Gus Cedargreen, the 71st's bugler, to sound retreat, he refused because Lieut. Capt. Stoddard told him not to. Angered, Hare placed the bugler under arrest. Twenty minutes later, Stoddard shouted to Hare, "Why did you reverse my orders?" and ordered the bugler released. Contrary to rules, the men cheered the bugler and Stoddard, then put together an effigy of Hare, affixed his name on it, made the rounds of the camp, and set it on fire. That won't be the end of it, vowed Gen. Gillespie in calling for a court of inquiry.

WEDNESDAY, AUGUST 10: A correspondent of the *London Times* in Cavite visited Camp Dewey and recorded his impressions of conditions in the Manila trenches: "Artillery were . . . throwing up advance earthworks . . . under protection of the Nebraska volunteers. From the upper floor of a European house . . . I was observing the Spanish positions, when a Nebraska sharpshooter beside me fired a first shot . . . upon the Spaniards. . . . I was impressed by the nonchalant demeanor of the Americans in the fighting line . . . like high-spirited youths out on a picnic, while . . . in the second line [they] were playing cards. Had the Spaniards . . . dropped shrapnel from Malate first, they would have wrought terrific havoc."

In Puerto Rico it was three cheers for Troop C of New York, who on August 9 pursued Spanish troops after the capture of Coamo, four miles along the road to Aibonito. They were checked at the Guyon River, where the enemy had blown up the bridge, and were shelled from a Spanish battery on Asoniante Mountain. Troop C returned the fire and held its position until fortified by the 3rd Wisconsin Volunteers. Gen. Wilson's column spent the rest of the day repairing the bridge and scouting the enemy's position.

The battle was begun at 8 a.m. by Captain Avlerson's battery of the 4th Regular Artillery. The battery unlimbered in an open field 1,500 yards from a blockhouse that commanded the road into Coamo and began firing with four guns, silencing the Mausers the Spaniards responded with. They then moved to the hill commanding the town. Troop C flanked the town on the right, the 2nd Wisconsin on the left of the main road, and the 3rd on the right advanced with the skirmishers. The Coamo River was forded, the bridge having been burned. Throughout Brooklyn, home of Troop C, beaming faces greeted one another on the street. The troop was one of the youngest organizations in the field.

As the Brooklyn soldiers got their recognition, so did Private MacNeale, belatedly, for his heroism in the battle with Cervera's fleet. Captain Paul St. C. Murphy, commander of the marine guard on the flagship *Brooklyn*, filed his report which cited the unknown private: "[A] projectile . . . had become jammed in the bore of the starboard six-pounder . . . [and] Corporal Robert Gray . . . and Quartermaster W. H. Smith each had made a[n] . . . unsuccessful attempt to drive [it]. . . . There seemed to be nothing left to do but dismount the gun, when MacNeale volunteered to make a final effort. . . . The gun was hot, and it was necessary to cling to the Jacob's ladder . . . while . . . manipulat[ing] . . . [the] rammer. He . . . eject[ed] the . . . shell while blasts nearly shook him overboard."

The latest report from the General Hospital at Fort McPherson showed 618 patients in the hospital, 400 with typhoid fever, and 5 dead from the fever. One of the dead was Rough Rider Troop K's Gerard M. Ives, 23, who came home to 338 West 71st Street, Manhattan, on August 7, and died three days later. At the war's start, Ives left his business position to join Squadron A. When he found out the squadron was not going to the front, he opted for the Rough Riders, but he tragically became one of the few who did not procure full equipment and had to stay in Tampa.

He had been sick since June 10 and became so ill that he wanted to die at home. He boarded a train—alone—and was so weak he could not ask for food or assistance. His family never got his telegram that he was arriving, so he dragged himself home. Upon arrival, he became unconscious. The medics were outraged that he was left to travel such a great distance alone.

Born in Rome and a Yale graduate, Ives came from a distinguished family, his father, Chauncey Ives, a renowned sculptor. A detail from Squadron A planned to attend the funeral.

Camp Montauk Point, New York, was hoping to welcome yellow fever patients and other sick returnees from Santiago. However, 200 workmen at the station were demanding shelter and daily pay and 47 went on strike, threatening those who did not. Gen. Young threatened to call out the troops, but order was restored when he promised the men regular pay. However, the next day, the "agreement" broke down, and when some 200 carpenters went on strike, work on all government buildings stopped. On top of that, provisions were in short supply; only one quart of milk could be found in the camp, where there were close to 50 patients.

Among naval personalities in the news was Naval Constructor Richmond Hobson. While in the Metropolitan New York region the previous week, in Newark, he descended from the railroad station at Market Street and tried to catch an Orange car. Realizing he needed the car at another point, he changed direction. Walking near him was Patrick Halloran, a cripple on crutches, who turned to catch a car and found himself directly in front of a quickly approaching trolley. Alerted by the outcries of the crowd, Hobson whizzed around, jumped on the track, lifted Halloran and together they sprang back from danger, as the trolley whirled through. Hobson shook hands with

Halloran, bid him farewell, and hopped on the next Orange car. The incident came to light only because of witnesses at the scene.

Georgia Congressman L. F. Livingston introduced a House resolution extending Congressional thanks to Dewey for the victory at Manila Bay. Dewey told Congress, in a letter released on this date, "It is a source of additional pleasure to me, a Vermonter, that the mover of the resolution was . . . from the South . . . the good signs of the times. In the hour of danger there is . . . but one united Country. May we never hear of sectionalism again!"

Admiral Sampson was lashed, this time by Chaplain J. P. McIntyre of the battleship *Oregon*, addressing the Young Men's Christian Association in Denver: "I looked back [and saw] . . . a faint smudge of smoke . . . where Sampson, the *Texas*, the *Indiana*, and . . . [Captain Evans] were lying, 10 miles away. . . . Sampson . . . reported himself within four miles of the *Cristobal Colón* when she hauled down her flag . . . for the ship must be within four miles to share in the prize money. So Sampson will get $10,000 . . . and Capt. Charles E. Clark, who fought . . . as never man fought ship before, will get only $500, and . . . every one of you . . . who had as much to do with the battle as Sampson did, will not get a cent." The chaplain later claimed he was misquoted. However, S. W. DeWitt, U.S. District Attorney of Washington, D.C., attended the lecture and said, "I read the account . . . [and] every word of it is true. . . . I went to hear something about the battle [of Santiago] and I left the church in disgust."

Leonard Woolsey Bacon of Norwich, Connecticut, also attacked Capt. Evans, in an open letter concerned about Evans' boasting and immorality, especially when compared to the pious Capt. Philip: "You justly say that the approval of Capt. Philip's brief word of faith and thanksgiving to God is 'a matter of taste,' implying that in your opinion it was in bad taste. . . . On this question of taste, I think you will find the mind of the American public . . . to be distinctly made up. . . . [T]he simple, spontaneous act of a sincere believer in God, uttered at that thrilling moment . . . seems to us full of a noble and beautiful dignity; it gives him a place in our hearts. . . . We believe you to be brave in battle and generous in victory . . . notwithstanding your talking so much about it. The utmost that can be claimed . . . is that you are as good as the rest, but even this remains to be proved."

THURSDAY, AUGUST 11: Miles' men continued their triumphant march across Puerto Rico. Schwan drove on toward Arecibo and chased the Spaniards toward Lares, with the intent of grabbing it. Garretson's column advanced along a mountain trail north of Adjuntas. The trail had been discovered earlier by the engineers of Gen. Roy Stone, who improved it to the point of usability.

It was one of the busiest diplomatic days in Madrid since the outbreak of hostilities. Aside from a number of diplomatic conferences, the cabinet held two councils. According to all indications, American terms had not been changed.

Another key that the end of the war was imminent was the attitude of the Cubans under Gen. Gómez in the northern part of Santiago Province. Spanish garrisons in Holguín, and smaller towns on the north coast and interior, were in great need for food and war supplies. The epidemic of fever had forestalled Shafter's soldiers from forcing a surrender of these scattered detachments of Spanish troops, but now Gómez and his men were taking the towns and approaching Holguín. The question arises: Does America recognize the government set up by Gómez in his march or challenge the insurgents and forbid them for conducting further operations, except under American direction?

A human side of the war—one that would not end with the peace treaty—was in full view under bright skies in Central Park in Manhattan. Some 6,000 people, women and children, and most notably their husbands and fathers—invalid soldiers and sailors who had returned from the front—enjoyed a lawn party under the auspices of the Women's Patriotic Relief Association.

The wounded men limping on the lawn—most on crutches and others more sadly crippled—were the center of attraction. Each one gave his autograph for those in attendance. They delighted themselves with ice cream, cake, and cigars.

Mrs. Howard Carroll, President of the Association, traveled 200 miles from Fultonville to be with those heroes. Constructor Hobson was the desired speaker, but he sent his regrets in a letter read on the occasion: "I beg to express my thanks and appreciation for the kind invitation . . . and regret very much that duty interferes and will prevent my being present for your noble cause, which appeals to my deepest sympathies. Wishing success."

Loud cheers followed the reading, and Mrs. Samuel Miller, in charge of the souvenir department, promised that each soldier and sailor would receive a facsimile lithographed copy as a souvenir.

17

HOSTILITIES SUSPENDED . . . PROTOCOL SIGNED

FRIDAY, AUGUST 12: Racing toward the end, much planning and activity filled the day's record. Colonel Roosevelt began his two-day mustering out of the Rough Riders. In bidding farewell he paid special tribute to the black troops of the 9th and 10th Cavalries in saving the Rough Riders from a Spanish ambush. He never "expected to have . . . could not ask to have, better men beside him in a hard fight."

Gen. Wilson wanted to pass the troops near Aibonito while calling on the town's defenders to surrender. Toward that end, Col. Tasker H. Bliss brought a flag of truce to Aibonito and met with the Spanish second in command. While there, Bliss surveyed the position, his report passed on by Wilson to Miles: "[A]fter it passes beyond our sight it is swept by rifle trenches as completely as it is on this side of the ridge."

Wilson then sent Gen. Ernst from Barranquitas on a march south over the Honduras River to attack the main road some two miles east of Aibonito, still beyond the Spaniards' range. All was on hold until the Governor General responded to the American call for surrender; his answer, relayed by Bliss to Wilson, firm and negative: "If any further flags of truce are sent by us upon any condition whatever they will not be received and . . . if we wish to avoid further effusion of blood we should not move from the camps which we occupy." It mattered little, however. "Suspend all hostilities," came a message at 4:23 p.m. from Gen. Corbin to Gen. Miles. An armistice had been declared between the United States and Spain, and peace negotiations had begun.

The message from Madrid was a long one, transmitted to the French Embassy in Washington starting at 12:30 and received in full at 2:43. Embassy Secretary Thiebaut came to the State Department to tell Secretary Day that he was empowered to sign the protocol for Spain. The President received the French diplomat at 4 p.m. for a signing ceremony attended also by the Assistant Secretaries of State. The exact signing took place at 4:23; those affixed were U.S. Secretary Day and Ambassador Extraordinary and Plenipotentiary of France Jules Cambon. The protocol called, in brief, for Spain's yielding of Cuba and Puerto Rico to the United States and U.S. occupation of Manila.

The day was one that "will always linger in my memory," Isidore Weill told the *Jewish Veteran* of May 1938. He was with the infantry at Aibonito: "Just as the light artillery batteries were ready to open fire across the valley, and the infantry ready to charge, Lieut. William C. McLoughlin of the Signal Corps rushed up to the commanding officer and handed him the telegram from Gen. Miles' headquarters announcing the signing of the armistice."

Destined for fame as a writer, Carl Sandburg noted in his pocket journal from Puerto Rico, "Washed. The camp was one slippery mudhole. Mounted guard at 6 p.m. A farce." The 6th Illinois received news of the protocol while camped at Utuado. As tropical rain pelted them, the men shouted, "Hurrah for the Protocol!" Noted Sandburg, "It was a new funny word we liked. Instead of 'Good morning,' we said, 'How's your old protocol?' We slept . . . in a building used for drying coffee. Each man fitted nicely into a dry bin . . . rich with a coffee smell" (Sandburg 416). When he left Puerto Rico, Sandburg fully realized and rejoiced that he was now out of "hobo jungles."

Secretary Day released the following official statement to the press of the terms of the protocol: "1. Spain will relinquish all claims of sovereignty over and title to Cuba.

2. Puerto Rico and other Spanish islands in the West Indies and an island in the Ladrones to be selected by the United States shall be ceded to the latter.

3. The United States will occupy and hold the city, bay, and harbor of Manila, pending the conclusion of the treaty of peace, which shall determine the control, disposition, and government of the Philippines.

4. Cuba, Puerto Rico, and other Spanish islands in the West Indies shall be immediately evacuated and Commissioners, to be appointed within ten days, shall, within thirty days from the signing of the protocol, meet at Havana and San Juan, respectively, to arrange and execute the details of evacuation.

5. The United States and Spain will each appoint not more than five Commissioners to negotiate and conclude a treaty of peace. The Commissioners are to meet at Paris not later than the 1st of October.

6. On the signing of the protocol hostilities will be suspended and notice to that effect will be given as soon as possible by each Government to the commanders of its military and naval forces."

The United States went to war not to acquire but to free Cuba. No one knew for certain what would happen to Cuba except that Spain was leaving. The Cubans were confident that Cuba would be given to them. Gen. Tomas Estrada Palma, Delegate at Large of the Cuban Republic, issued a statement at the office of the Cuban Junta in New York and said in part: "As far as the present Government of Cuba is concerned, the leading men of that Government, from President Maso down, have implicit confidence in the declaration that the United States Government went to war not for the acquisition of Cuba but to free the island for the Cubans. It may be that in years to come the Cubans may of their own volition request this country to annex Cuba, but that is not for the present. Whether the present Government of Cuba will be recognized or not is no matter now. The Cubans do not wish to embarrass the Washington authorities and have no doubt what is done will be for the best."

It was the press, the jingoist newspapers, that helped flame the spirit of nationalism, to avenge the *Maine* and take America into war. They rejoiced in the coming peace: Spain had been punished, the *Maine* was avenged, Cuba was free. Two of the leading players had been William Randolph Hearst of the *New York Journal* and Joseph Pulitzer of the *New York World*. The former celebrated "peace" in an editorial by that title: "A glorious war has ended in a peace still more glorious. Victorious at every point, America is calmly considering the terms she will grant to her beaten adversary. Under . . . her own conscience, she . . . [will] determine how much generosity to the humbled enemy is compatible with her duty to the oppressed people . . . and . . . for her own interests.

"The Cubans are to be free . . . the clear object of the war on our part, has been conceded by Spain. . . . Twenty-four sunk or captured Spanish warships have avenged the *Maine*. Puerto Rico is ours and its inhabitants . . . lifted from the sixteenth century into the nineteenth. We hold Manila and with our flag once hoisted there no Blount in America will venture to haul it down."

The protocol ensured "Peace With Freedom," in the words of the title of an editorial in the *World*: "It is peace with honor because it secures . . . freedom for the oppressed. For weeks before the war . . . Spain knew that this country was for 'peace with—a But.' . . . Cuba should be free. . . . By forcing and prolonging the war, Spain also loses the rich island of Puerto Rico . . . her other possessions in this hemisphere . . . an island in the Ladrones [and] . . . occupation . . . of Manila, pending the conclusion of a treaty. . . .

"These terms express the inescapable logic of events . . . the will of this Nation. They are necessary to execute justice and to insure permanent peace and tranquility. Spain will ultimately be better off. She loses colonies . . . the holding of which sapped her strength and drained her resources."

President McKinley was the focus for the *New York Times* editorial, also titled "Peace": "The fruits of the war and the great distinction President McKinley has won in beginning and conducting it are to be looked for in the pages of history. . . . A work of imperative necessity . . . it has been evident that it would one day be a work of obligation for us. That day fell within the Administration of William McKinley. . . . It fell to him to accomplish a work of destiny by driving Spain out of the hemisphere and to paralyze on both sides of the world that power of colonial control that she has abused for centuries."

Spanish and American Commissioners met in October 1898 in Paris to negotiate a peace treaty. In addition to surrendering all claim to Cuba, Spain ceded to the United States Puerto Rico, the Pacific island of Guam, and the Philippines, for which the United States paid $20 million to Spain. America had landed on Wake Island on July 4, 1898, and acquired Wake as a result of the war.

American forces were withdrawn from Cuba in 1902. The Philippines were granted full independence on July 4, 1946. The annexationists won out regarding Hawaii, which became the fiftieth state in 1959.

WORKS CITED

Diary of a Dirty Little War has made use of news reports and articles from the *New York Times*, Associated Press, *New York Sun, New York Tribune, New York World, Chicago Tribune, Annals of Knox County* (Illinois), *New York World, London Times, American Hebrew, American Israelite*. In the interest of readability, textnotes have been provided for secondary sources. Only historical periodicals are given citations.

Anderson, Sherwood. *Memoirs*. New York: Harcourt, Brace & Co., 1942.
——. *A Story Teller's Story*. New York: Grove Press, 1924.
Brown, Charles H. *The Correspondents' War*. New York: Charles Scribner's Sons, 1967.
Day, Robert B. *They Made Mormon History*. Salt Lake City: Desert Book Co., 1973.
Friedman, J. George. "The Jews in the Spanish-American War." *The Jewish Veteran* 30 (April 1938), 8+.
Friedman, J. George, and Louise A. Falk. *Jews in the American Wars*. Washington, D.C.: Jewish War Veterans of the U.S., 1954.
Gatewood, Willard B. *Smoked Yankees and the Struggle for Empire: Letters from Negro Soldiers, 1898–1902*. Urbana: University of Illinois Press, 1977.
Hobson, Richmond Pearson. *The Sinking of the Merrimac*. Annapolis, MD: Naval Institute Press, 1987.
Linderman, Gerald F. *The Mirror of War: American Society and the Spanish-American War*. Ann Arbor: University of Michigan Press, 1974.
Mabey, Charles R. *The Utah Batteries: A History*. Salt Lake City: Daily Reporter, 1900.
MacArthur, Douglas. *Reminiscences*. New York: McGraw Hill, 1964.
Melzer, Richard, and Phyllis Ann Mingus. "Wild to Fight: The New Mexico Rough Riders in the Spanish-American War." *New Mexico Historical Review* 59 (April 1984), 109–36.
Natsky, Martin G., and Edward L. Beach. "The Trouble with Admiral Sampson." *Naval History* 9 (December 1995), 8–16.
Prentiss, A., ed. *The History of the Utah Volunteers in the Spanish-American War and in the Philippine Islands*. Salt Lake City: Tribune Publishing, 1900.
Sandburg, Carl. *Always the Young Strangers*. New York: Harcourt, Brace & Co., 1952.

Steward, Theophilus. *The Colored Regulars in the U.S. Army*. Philadelphia: A. M. E. Book Concern, 1904.

Walker, Dale. "New Mexico's Last Rough Rider." *New Mexico* 18 (June 1949), 33+.

Washington, Booker T. *A New Negro for a New Century: An Up-to-Date Account of the Upward Struggles of the Negro Race*. Miami: Mnemosyne Publishers, 1969.

Weill, Isidore. "The War with Spain: A Jewish Volunteer Reminisces." *The Jewish Veteran* 30 (February 1938), 5+.

The following are valuable for further reference:

Beer, Thomas. *Stephen Crane: A Study in American Letters*. New York: Alfred A. Knopf, 1929.

Carter, Henry Rose. *Yellow Fever: An Epidemiological and Historical Study of Its Place of Origin*. Baltimore: The Williams & Wilkins Co., 1931.

Davis, Richard Harding. *The Cuban and Porto Rico Campaigns*. New York: Charles Scribner's Sons, 1898.

Feuer, A. B., ed. *The Spanish-American War at Sea: Naval Action in the Atlantic*. Westport, CT: Praeger, 1995.

Healy, David F. *The United States in Cuba, 1898–1902: Generals, Politicians, and the Search for Policy*. Madison: The University of Wisconsin Press, 1963.

Hobson, Richmond Pearson. *The Sinking of the Merrimac*. New York: The Century Co., 1899.

Hofstadter, Richard. *The Paranoid Style in American Politics and Other Essays*. New York: Alfred A. Knopf, 1966.

Langley, Wright. *Key West and the Spanish-American War*. Key West, FL: Langley Press, Inc., 1997.

Millet, Frank D. *The Expedition to the Philippines*. New York: Harper & Brother, 1899.

Morgan H. Wayne. *William McKinley and His America*. Syracuse: Syracuse University Press, 1963.

Musicant, Ivan. *Empire by Default: The Spanish-American War and the Dawn of the American Century*. New York: Henry Holt and Company, 1998.

Renehan, Edward. *The Lion's Pride*. New York: Oxford University Press, 1998.

Roosevelt, Theodore. *The Rough Riders*. New York: Charles Scribner's Sons, 1902.

Ross, Isabel. *Angel of the Battlefield: The Life of Clara Barton*. New York: Harper & Brothers, 1956.

Samuels, Peggy, and Harold Samuels. *Remembering the Maine*. Washington, D.C.: Smithsonian, 1995.

——. *Teddy Roosevelt at San Juan*. College Station: Texas A & M Press, 1997.

Trask, David. *The War with Spain in 1898*. New York: Macmillan, 1981.

Walker, Dale L. *Rough Rider*. Lincoln: University of Nebraska Press, 1997.

Weems, Edward. *The Fate of the Maine*. New York: Macmillan and Co., 1967.

Westermeier, Clifford Peters. *Who Rush to Glory: The Cowboy Volunteers of 1898*. Caldwell, ID: The Caxton Printer, Ltd., 1958.

INDEX

About the Author

HARVEY ROSENFELD teaches English at St. John's University and Pace University and is the editor of *Martyrdom and Resistance*, a Holocaust bimonthly of the International Society for Yad Vashem. He is the author of *Raoul Wallenberg: Angel of Rescue* (1995), as well as biographies of Roger Maris and Cal Ripken, Jr.

ISBN 0-275-96673-9

9 780275 966737

HARDCOVER BAR CODE